Scottish Hill and Mountain Names

The origin and meaning of the names of Scotland's hills and mountains

PETER DRUMMOND

with assistance from
DONALD WILLIAM STEWART

and drawings by
JOHN MITCHELL

SCOTTISH MOUNTAINEERING TRUST

First published in Great Britain in 1991 by the Scottish Mountaineering Trust

Copyright © by Peter Drummond

British Library Cataloguing in Publication Data
Drummond, Peter
  Scottish hill and mountain names.
  1. Scotland. Place names
  I. Title II. Scottish Mountaineering Trust
  914.110014

ISBN 0-907521-30-4

Cover Illustrations:
Front: Sgurr na Ciche, peak of the breast *D. Rubens*
Back: Na Coireachan Leithe, the grey corries *K.M. Andrew*

Typeset by Newtext Composition Ltd, Glasgow.
Printed and bound by Billings, Worcester

Distributed by Cordee, 3a De Montfort Street, Leicester LE1 7HD.

Scottish Hill

and

Mountain Names

Contents

Dedication

To my parents, Jeanne and John Drummond

Acknowledgements

My thanks especially are due to Donald William Stewart, whose thorough and scholarly review of the manuscript was instrumental in clarifying many meanings and who was responsible for the Gaelic pronunciation guide. Any errors of fact, spelling or interpretation remaining are entirely my own responsibility.

Thanks also to Iseabail Macleod for her editorial advice; to Angus MacKenzie of Inverness who took the trouble and considerable time to read through an earlier draft and make several suggestions as to Gaelic name meanings; to Ian Fraser of the School of Scottish Studies' Place-name Survey who advised on some names; to Sheila Gear of Foula who sent me her translations of the island's Norse hill-names; to Donald Bennet who read the manuscript from a hill-walking and topographical perspective; and last but not least to my wife Wendy for her forbearance for winter sitting-rooms littered with books, maps and papers.

Reader's Guide

Virtually all the hill- and mountain-names in the text of this book are typeset in **bold,** to help you locate them when using the index. At the foot of most pages is a pronunciation guide for Gaelic mountain-names, and if a bold-printed name in the text has a small asterisk* beside it, this tells you that at the foot of that page you will find its pronunciation key. More detailed advice on how to use these pronunciation guides follows below.

Some of the bold-printed names in the text also have a small dagger† sign beside them, and this indicates that this is the correct Gaelic spelling and differs slightly from the usual map or book spelling, usually only by the addition of a 'h' or an 'i'. If the correct Gaelic spelling is substantially different from the usual map version, I have placed the common version first, and then bracketed the correct spelling with the words ("properly . . .").

The pronunciation guides appear as footnotes and give a phonetic guide to the pronunciation, by English-speakers, of Gaelic names. The phonetic script used is based on English spelling and it is therefore impossible to give more than a very rough approximation of the Gaelic sounds, which are quite different from those of English. But it should enable users to pronounce the names in such a way that they would at least be understood by a Gaelic speaker.

Gaelic pronunciation differs from area to area and it is not possible to cover regional variations here. Therefore you may hear quite different pronunciations in some places as well as anglicized versions, hence the book's occasional use of the bracketed phrase "(locally pronounced . . .)".

Note that the key is based on standard Scottish pronunciation and not on standard Southern English. For example, 'day' and 'road' have simple vowels and not diphthongs. Note also that 'r' is always pronounced.

Bold type indicates the stressed syllable. Where there might be confusion a hyphen has been used to separate syllables, while a colon indicates the lengthening of a preceding vowel.

Vowels

a   as in lesser
a   as in tap
aa as in father
ay as in day
e   as in red
ee as in deed, weak
i   as in tip
Y   as in by
o   as in top
u   as in but
oa as in road
aw as in bawl
oo as in pool
ow as in owl
oi as in boil
oe approximately the sound in French oeuf or German Österreich.

Consonants

Most of the consonants represent *approximately* the same sounds in English. Note the following:

g   as in get
s   as in sit
y   as in yet

ch as in loch; this is pronounced by putting the tip of your tongue on the back of your lower teeth, narrowing the gap at the back of your throat using your tongue and exhaling through this gap to make a sound without using your vocal chords.

gh has no equivalent in English; it is a voiced ch (i.e. it is pronounced like 'ch', but using the vocal chords).

d and t are pronounced with the tip of the tongue touching the back of the lower teeth (and not the teeth ridge as in English).

b is often transcribed as p although the sound is actually somewhere between these two sounds in English, but somewhat closer to p: similarly d is often transcribed as t and g as k.

A small y (eg – neet[y]) indicates a nasal y as in the word million.

Chapter One

Introduction

This book is about the origin and meaning of the names of Scotland's hills and mountains.

Scotland's hill-names are more than just names. They are part of our heritage. For they allow us to see how Gaelic and Scottish culture "saw" the hills – their colours, their shape, their legends and their practical functions – through eyes that have been blinded now for most of us by our urban and industrial culture.

In most European nations the names of the hills present no difficulty for they are in the living language of the local people. In Scotland, however, most of the hill-names are in one of four languages other than the English which most of us speak. Of these four, two (Brittonic and Norse) are dead, one (Scots) is in a critical condition, and the other (Gaelic) is a living language for only a relatively small number of people, mainly in the Western Isles.

Of these four languages, Brittonic (or Old Welsh) is the oldest, and was used in the Scottish Lowlands by 'the Britons' until south-east Scotland was taken over by the Angles, and the south-west absorbed into the Gaelic-speaking Kingdom of the Scots (from Ireland), although the language lived on in pockets until the 12th century. Dumbarton Rock remains named as it was, the 'fort of the Britons', and they left behind a few ancient hill-names like Ochils and Pentlands.

Old Norse, the language of the Viking invaders, was widely spoken in the islands – Orkney and Shetland, the Hebrides – from the 9th to the 13th centuries, and its impact on names is largely confined to these islands and to a few northern coastal areas. On the Scottish mainland, only amongst the hills of Caithness and Sutherland are there many direct traces of their tongue, although later Gaelic hill-words like *sgùrr* may well have a Norse origin. In northern England the Lake District hills contain a lot of Norse names reflecting their settlement there, and some of their hill-words like rigg, dodd and fell migrated north of the Border where they were adopted by Scots speakers.

Scots is related to English, and is spoken over most of the Borders and the Lowlands of Scotland. It has many distinctive hill-words like law, fell and bin, derived from Anglo-Saxon, from Norse, and from Gaelic. This language was at its peak in the 15th and 16th centuries, and since then has been on the decline among the Scottish people, especially under an anglicised education system and media.

Gaelic is by far the most important language in hill-words: virtually every hill in the Highlands has a Gaelic name, and many in the Lowlands too; only the south-eastern Borders are untouched by it. Some of these Gaelic names were, however, changed or corrupted by the passage of time, which makes it difficult to pin down the original meanings. Gaelic culture was passed on by word of mouth, not in writing. And although this oral link may have been perfectly accurate while Gaelic was strong, and the local dialect unchanged, many centuries may have elapsed between the names being given by the local people and their being written down (often inaccurately) by the mainly English-speaking Ordnance Survey mapmakers in the mid-19th century, so that the original form of the name may have changed. This is especially true in the east and south of the Highlands, as well in the south-west of Scotland, where the dying out of Gaelic by the time of the O.S. mapping added further difficulty to correct transcription. This whole process is illustrated by the several possible interpretations of the names of higher peaks like Ben Nevis, Ben Alder and Ben Macdhui: naturally they, being highest, were named earliest and the long time exposure since then has blurred the picture we now have of their meanings. By contrast lower and less significant peaks, which would have been named later (in a process of 'filling in the gaps' between bigger hills), are often easy to decipher from a Gaelic dictionary, provided the Ordnance Survey maps have recorded the correct spelling. In some cases they recorded the approximate pronunciation rather than the correct spelling, as with Ben Attow rather than Beinn Fhada.

The O.S. carried out their first mapping in the mid-19th century. They were therefore in time to record many of the local Gaelic names of the hills, but sadly many of the memories and tales behind the names left the glens during the 19th century. For the cruel winds of the Highland Clearances and poverty-driven emigration swept many of the people out like so many autumn leaves, and their memories of hill-names, passed on through generations in the glens, would moulder and die with them in city tenements or New World plains. In spite of this loss, much of this book is able to state or suggest *why* hills were given certain names.

The reader might object that for some hill-names with several possible meanings I have too often used words like 'perhaps', 'possibly' or 'probably' to indicate that we cannot be absolutely sure. This is unavoidable given the historical factors just mentioned, and the alternative explanations that are on offer for many names from earlier authorities like Professor W. J. Watson, the Reverend J. B. Johnston, and others appearing in Scottish Mountaineering Club (SMC) guidebooks. I have tried to lay out these various alternatives, seeing how well they fit the evidence, and as far as possible I have gone for the alternative that fits best in the context – the context of neighbouring hills, or of the normal distribution of the names (eg – that Norse names are confined to the northern and western isles and the north-west), or of similar instances elsewhere. For instance I reject one suggestion for the Cuillin mountains, namely that it is from the Gaelic *cuilionn* meaning holly (because of their jagged shape), and prefer instead the alternative of the Norse *kiolen* meaning high rocky mountain: this is because most of the names of Skye's high peaks are Norse, not Gaelic; because Gaelic tree hill-names are *not* named from the hill's shape; and because there are Norwegian mountains with the name Kiolen, overlooking the fiords from where the Vikings sailed to conquer Skye.

Many Gaelic names are, however, quite clear in their meaning. They reveal an astonishing variety, without European parallel. In addition to a very large selection of names for the different shapes and sizes of hills, Gaelic hill-names contain scores of different colours, of body parts, of people and creatures and plants of nature. It is exploring this huge and fascinating variety that makes up the bulk of this book.

Chapter Two

The Top Twenty

This section covers the twenty highest separate Scottish mountains, as defined by the Munro's Tables, in order of height. The first eight are four-thousand-footers, the rest not far behind.

1. **Ben Nevis** (4406 feet, 1344m) (Beinn Nibheis*)
This is known to climbers simply as 'The Ben'. This is so because it is the highest in the land, the Queen of Scotland's mountains, *beinn* being a feminine Gaelic noun. As if in deference to its unique status, none of the high peaks beside it is a *beinn*, being instead càrns or aonachs, mullachs or stobs, sgùrrs or binneins. Although it is only one amongst over 1,000 Scottish beinns or bens, this one alone could bear the definite article "the" without need of further explanation. The Gaels, however, did *not* call it A'Bheinn (The Ben), in the way that other hills like An Tòrr and An Stùc were named. Instead they left us a puzzle in the word Nevis.

The earliest versions of the name appear as Neevush (1532) and Nevess (1552). Timothy Pont's map of 1595 gives Bin Novesh, while Gordon in 1640 renders it as Bin Nevis, the first appearance of the modern anglicised form. A century later the great mapmaker William Roy, who completed the first very accurate map of Scotland for the government, concurred with Ben Nevis, so Thomas Pennant who toured the Highlands some years later must have done so without the aid of Roy's map, for he writes:

> ". . . Fort William is surrounded by vast mountains, which occasion almost perpetual rain: the loftiest are on the south side – Benevish soars above the rest and ends, as I was told, in a point . . . whose height is said to be 1450 yards."

But what does Nevis mean? Unlike other nations' highest peaks, like Mont Blanc, Chomolungma (Everest), or Snowdon, whose meanings are quite clear to their local peoples, the origin of the name Nevis is misted over by time as much as its top often is by cloud.

The commonest explanation is that it means evil or venomous mountain, from *nimheil* or *nibheis*. When the yearly toll of death and injury, to tourists,

---

Ben Nevis – Gaelic: Beinn Nibheis – bYn **neev**ash

walkers and serious climbers, is added up, this name seems ominously appropriate. But the name was given long before 20th-century travellers came from afar to dice with death on its cliffs. The doyen of Gaelic place-name study, Professor W.J. Watson, who wrote in the era before mass tourism, argued in his *History of the Celtic Place-names of Scotland* that the 'venomous' name came from the River and Glen Nevis at its foot. This was by repute a barren glen, described by one Gaelic poet as ". . . A glen on which God has turned his back: the slop-pail of the great world." Another rhyme tells of:

> "Gleann Nibheis, gleann na gcloch,
> Gleann am bi an gart anmoch;
> Gleann fada fiadhaich, fas,
> Sluagh bradach an mhioghnais."

> ("Glen Nevis, glen of stones,
> A glen where corn ripens late;
> A long wild waste glen,
> With thievish folk of evil habit.")

Professor Watson says the name Nevis is an anglicisation of an old Gaelic form *neimheas* (latterly *nimheas*, or *nimheis*) from *neimh* meaning poison or venom, derived from an Old Irish root *nem*, venom. Now it is true that names of rivers are often the oldest, being major natural obstacles to early peoples. And the 'evil' name certainly fits upper Glen Nevis, today deserted by all inhabitants bar a few campers braving its marshy pitches. And elsewhere in the world there are 'wicked' peaks such as Mont Maudit, a shoulder of Mont Blanc. (Coincidentally there is a genuinely "evil" hill in lower Glen Nevis, the **Cnocan Mi-chomhairle**[*] (knoll of the evil counsel) where a gathering of Mackintoshes plotted an attack on the MacSorlies.) And the pronunciation of *nimheis* (nee-vash) certainly fits the earliest, 1532, spelling. Loch Nevis, 40 kilometres away, derived from the same root, also has an evil reputation in Gaelic folklore.

However, Professor Watson's explanation doesn't provide a cut-and-dried 'solution' to our mystery, for there are clues pointing in a different direction. The mountain's huge cliffs and corrie face *away* from the river; and how likely is it that the highest mountain in Scotland, outstretching even its nearest neighbours by 400 feet (120m), and rising literally from sea-level, should be named after a not-very-large river, when few other Scots mountains are?

Watson himself dismissed the suggestion by the Gaelic scholar Alexander MacBain that Nevis comes from an old European root-word *neb* meaning cloud or water, as found in the Spanish river name Nebis or Nebya. Yet Ben Nevis stands in a prime position to tear open the underbelly of every grey Atlantic cloudwave, thus giving its footfort town the highest rainfall total of any in Scotland. (This watery meaning might also suit Loch Nevis.) And since

---

Cnocan Mi-chomhairle – crochk*a*n **mee**cho-*a*rly*a*

Ben Nevis was probably one of the first mountains to be named, being so high, it may well have had a pre-Gaelic name (perhaps from this European root-word *neb*) to which the Gaels then applied their most similar-sounding adjective (*nimheis*).

Other plausible Gaelic heirs claimant to the Nevis estate include *nèamh* meaning the sky – or indeed Heaven – and its adjective *nèamhaidh* (pronounced **nye:vee**) meaning heavenly or divine: in similar vein, the book *Companion to Scottish Culture* has proposed *neimhidh*, sacred, as the name's origin. More profane is the suggestion in some books of *beinn-nimh-bhathais*, the mountain with its head in the clouds, or the mountain with a cold brow. Both of these possible meanings are good descriptions of a summit completely clear on only a handful of days each year, and with snow lying for over half the year on top, and almost permanently in the gloomy heart of its northern corries. Other less plausible suggestions for the name have included derivations of Gaelic words *uamhais*, dread, or *ni-mhaise*, literally no-beauty, and *neamh*, supposedly meaning a raw biting wind. Further the word *neimh*, besides meaning venom, can also refer to the sting of a cold frost.

Earlier, mention was made of the mountain's familiar name, 'The Ben'. (Or as the Scottish Tourist Board puts it ". . . the *Real* Big Ben . . ."!) In one sense this simple name, The Ben, avoids the agony of choice involved in selecting from the many possible meanings. Perhaps, however, the ambiguity of the name itself is apt, for the mountain herself is enigmatic: her reputation attracts not only the hardest of climbers but also the most soft-soled of casual tourists; presenting on the one side the largest cliff face in Britain, and round the back a heavily eroded tourist path which zigzags up a slope with all the charm of an elephant's flank; and offering on both sides and in all seasons superb days or foul, and great mountain days or sudden death with little predictability.

2. Ben Macdhui* (4296 feet, 1309m) (Beinn Macduibh)

Although second to Nevis in the land, this mountain is number one in the Cairngorms. For many years this was thought – by the locals at least – to be the highest Scottish mountain, although Gordon of Straloch's 1662 map made no mention of it, noting instead nearby Ben Bhrotain and Cairn Gorm. It was not until 1810 that it was removed from its presumed pole position by the survey of Dr George Keith (who, incidentally, spelled it Ben Macdouie). The Ordnance Survey of 1847 fixed this downgrading to second place (by 100 feet, 30m) in the concrete of its trig points, and in spite of the appeals of old Macdhui sentimentalists. Such was the sense of outrage that there was even a plan mooted by the landowner Earl of Fife to build himself a burial pyramid

Ben Macdhui – ben m*a*c **dooee**

of stones on the summit over 30 metres high, to carry Macdhui back to the commanding height as well, presumably, as his own soul to even higher places. (His family name may well have played a part in the mountain's name, as we will see.)

One feature Macdhui does share with Ben Nevis is the ambiguity of its name. One popular interpretation derives the name from *beinn na muic duibh*, mountain of the black pig. Set amidst Gaelic names which translated include a blue hill, a middle hill, a rounded peak and grey heights, this meaning certainly has the asset of dramatic contrast. The local Forestry Commission Guide puts this porcine meaning down to "its shape". However, it is unlikely, for the domestic pig was never the universal animal of the Highlands in the way that cattle, which gave their name to many hills, were. Its forerunner the wild boar rummaged in oak woods, not found here in the heart of the Cairngorms and by the 15th century when mountains were being named, their domesticated descendants were confined to the far west. In any case the Gaelic word for boar is *torc*, as in Càrn an Tuirc above Glen Clunie. There is a suggestion that the name was first used not by knowledgeable locals but by a minister of Crathie and Braemar parish, writing of 'Binn-na-muick-duibh' in the first Statistical Account, and that this colourful porcine explanation then took wings in subsequent years in the oft-used form of Ben Muick Dhui.

A more prosaic (and probably more accurate) interpretation of the name says that it is from *beinn mhic dhuibhe* or *mhac dhuibhe*, hill of the son of *dubh* (the black one), or hill of the sons of Duff. The Duff (or Fife) family owned much of the Aberdeenshire part of the mountain until they sold out to a Swiss owner in the 1960s. 'Duff' is a common anglicisation of *dubh* – witness the several Torduff Hills in southern Scotland – and the common Gaelic prefix *mac* means son of. Indeed one of Timothy Pont's maps in 1608 shows it as Ben Macduff. This suggestion is the most plausible, and accords well with General Roy's 1750 map name of Beinn Mac Dui, and there are other Highland mountain names taken from personal names, like Sgòrr Dhonuill or Beinn Fhionnlaidh.

A third suggestion for the name given by one authority, Diack, was for an original form of 'Binnmach Duibh', with *mach* (he says) being an obsolete Gaelic suffix, leaving the rest as the simple 'dark hills'. If true this is certainly an apt description since this the highest mountain in the area will be the first to catch the clouds and collect their shadows. (**Clashmach Hill** near Huntly seems to have this suffix *mach* added to *clach*, a stone.)

In Gaelic the word *muc* meaning pig or sow can sometimes suggest a heap, and while 'mountain of the dark heap' is not very noble, it shares the merit of Diack's suggestion, focussing on the dark shades chasing over its sides. And it is certainly a mountain of colour contrasts. Famous for its legendary spectre Am Fear Mòr Liath (the Grey Man), it is also known for its subsidiary

8

features **Sròn Riach*** (speckled nose), **Fèith Bhuidhe*** (yellow bog), **Sputan Dearg*** (red spout), and its Lochan Uaine (green loch). Appropriate then that the man after whose family it is probably named, MacDuff, had himself a 'colour' name!

3. **Braeriach** (4248 feet, 1296m) (Am Bràigh Riabhach*)
This mountain giant has a rather unexciting name in translation, as the grey, drab or brindled upland. The original Gaelic was **Am Bràigh Riabhach**, literally the brindled upland – many local people still refer to it, correctly, as **The** Braeriach. *Bràigh*, upland or upper part, has of course passed into Scots as brae; while the usual translation of *riabhach* is 'grizzled' or 'brindled', words which have become obsolete in English and mean (in modern parlance) streaked, mottled or dappled. This description of a 'mottled grey height' may well come from the patchy pattern of the hardy dwarf arctic vegetation that struggles to survive in the harsh conditions amongst the granite gravel spreads on its plateau.

Of more dramatic note, in the midst of this plateau lies the true source of the River Dee, the highest spring in Britain (at 3,900 feet, 1190m), a trickle that spills over Braeriach's cliffs into the An Garbh Choire. It is this, 'the rough corrie', and the mountain's other corries, that distinguish Braeriach. An Garbh Choire, known to many climbers as the Garracorrie, is a deep boulder-bottomed bowl in the hillside. Off it runs Coire Bhrochain, literally porridge corrie (for the broken boulders on its floor), where mists may bubble up to the very summit, while on the northern slopes are Coire an Lochain (corrie with the little loch), Coire Beannaidh (peaked), Coire Ruadh (russet-red, from the weathered granite) and Coire Gorm (blue).

4. **Cairn Toul** (4241 feet, 1293m) (Càrn an t-Sabhail*)
On the southern edge of An Garbh Choire of Braeriach stands Cairn Toul, an anglicised version of the Gaelic Càrn an t-Sabhail, peak of the barn. (After the definite article t-, the following consonant, in this case the s, falls silent. And the same word, and the same 'ool' sound in anglicised speech, can be found in Màm Sodhail, pronounced 'mam **sool**' above Glen Affric)

Now a 'barn' can either be the farm building for cattle or crop storage, or it can refer to the wartlike granite tors that outcrop on other Cairngorm hills like Beinn Mheadhoin, Ben Avon, and indeed on the Barns of Bynack near the top of Bynack More. However although Cairn Toul is part of the same mass of granite rock, there are no tors or barns near its summit. So the description

---

Sròn Riach – (properly, Sròn Riabhach) – strawn **ree**avoch
Fèith Bhuidhe – fay **vooy**a
Sputan Dearg – spoohtan **dyer**ak
Braeriach (properly, Am Bràigh Riabhach) – am brY **ree**avoch
Cairn Toul – (Gaelic: Càrn an t-Sabhail – kaarn an **toa**-al)

must refer to its barn-like shape, for when seen from the east, from Ben Macdhui, or the south-west, its summit and corrie have the shape of a ridged roof, with a flat top framed by two angled spurs dropping away from it. This explanation is the more credible because the corrie thus framed, the smallest of the mountain's trio on the north-east slope, is the Coire an t-Sabhail.

Cairn Toul

Indeed the mountain as a whole is sometimes known locally as Sabhal Beinn Macdhui, the barn of Ben Macdhui. Other Highland peaks have similar names comparing them with buildings: **Sgùrr a'Mhuilinn**[*] (peak of the mill), **Meall a' Phùbuill**[*] (hill of the tent), **Am Bàthach**[*] (the cowhouse or byre) and **Tigh Mòr na Seilge**[*] (big house of the hunt).

A suggestion has been made that the name comes from Càrn an t-Seallaidh, meaning mountain of the prospect or view (as in Balquhidder's **Meall an t-Seallaidh**)[*], but the pronunciation does not fit this.

A subsidiary top of the mountain, the shapely cone on the ridge running out to the north-west, is known as **The Angel's Peak**: it was named by a Victorian gentleman Mr Copland as a genteel counterweight to the Devil's Point on the south side of the mountain. But while the Devil's Point is a polite translation of the Gaelic *Bod an Deamhain*, the demon's penis, the 'Angel' name is really bogus, for this top's original name is **Sgòr an Lochain Uaine**[*], pinnacle of the green lochan (which lies in the corrie below).

Sgùrr a'Mhuilinn – skoor *a* **vooleen**[y]
Meall a'Phùbuill – myowl *a* **foo:beel**[y]
Am Bàthach – *a*m **ba:hoch**
Tigh Mòr na Seilge – tY moa:r n*a* **shay**l*aga*
Meall an t-Seallaidh – myowl *a*n **tyalee**
Sgòr an Lochain Uaine – skor *a*n lochan-y **oo-any***a*

5. Cairn Gorm (4084 feet, 1245m), (Càrn Gorm*)

Although the smallest of the four Cairngorm four-thousand footers, this is probably the best known because it has given its name to the whole mountain group. In Gaelic the range is known as Am Monadh Ruadh, the red mountain-land, from the pink colour of the granite that composes them. It became known universally in English as the Cairngorms in the last century, taking the name from this one rounded swell of a mountain that is prominent in the view from Speyside. The mountain's name comes from the Gaelic *Càrn Gorm*, blue mountain, called this because like many hills seen from a distance it appears blue because the atmosphere has filtered out the red wavelengths from the spectrum. The change from *càrn* to cairn, a process that affected many a Carn in the north-east, began early in writing, for MacFarlane's 1670 manuscripts speak of 'Kairne Gorum'.

6. Aonach Beag* (4060 feet, 1234m)

Aonach means a ridge-shaped mountain. In the case of Aonach Beag (wee ridged mountain) and Aonach Mòr (big ridged mountain), the word *aonach* precisely describes their shape. Together – for they are a pair – they form one magnificent long high ridge running from Glen Lundy near Fort William, with the outlying shoulder called **Aonach an Nid*** (ridge of the nest), south to a vantage point above Glen Nevis.

However while the *aonach* is exactly right, the adjectives *mòr* and *beag* are inexact, for the "wee" Aonach Beag is the higher of the two by some 60 feet (20 metres). The whole ridge is more easily seen from the north, rather than from the narrow mouth of Glen Nevis in the south; and from the north the Aonach Mòr, being nearest to the glen and therefore foreshortened, would appear to the local people to be the higher. The coming of the Ordnance Survey and their precise height measurements could hardly be expected to upset an old traditional name. Besides, the local name has some modern backers who claim that the Mòr is of larger mass, and *mòr* in Gaelic *does* tend to refer to size rather than height. The Mòr, too, has a longer *ridge*, the Beag being more hump-shaped.

7. Càrn Mòr Dearg* (4012 feet, 1223m)

Càrn Mor Dearg is the junior partner of Ben Nevis, facing across to its huge northern cliffs. It is joined to it by a narrow swooping ridge, of Alpine difficulty in winter, and known appropriately as the Càrn Mòr Dearg arête. It means big red cairn, and all three terms in its name are relative to the surrounding hills. *Càrn* emphasises the conical shape of this hill, compared to

---

Cairn Gorm – (Gaelic: Càrn Gorm – kaarn **gorom**)
Aonach Beag – oe:noch **bayk**
Aonach an Nid – oe:noch *an* **nyeet**ʸ
Càrn Mòr Dearg – kaarn moa:r **dyer**ak

the broad-shouldered Ben of Nevis and the long ridge of Aonach Mor. *Dearg*, red, picks out the pinkish hue of its granite rock screes in contrast to the grey andesite cliffs of The Ben across Coire Leis. And while the *Mòr* might be thought to refer to its absolute height as Scotland's number 7 peak, it is of course outstretched by both its neighbours on either side. In fact its 'bigness' is in relation to the two other summits on the long north-running ridge which it heads, known as the middle and little red cairns – **Càrn Dearg Meadhonach***** and **Càrn Beag Dearg***.** Indeed there are two other **Càrn Dearg** hills across on the western side of the Ben Nevis massif, one of them above Fort William reaching not far short of the 'Mòr' itself.

8. Aonach Mòr* (3999 feet, 1221m)
(See Aonach Beag above)

9. Ben Lawers (3984 feet, 1214m)
Ben Lawers is a single peak that has given its name to the range of six Munros, standing high above Loch Tay, often referred to collectively simply as Ben Lawers. There are two suggested origins: the Gaelic word *labhar* (pronounced **lavar**) meaning loud or noisy in the manner of a stream; and the Gaelic *ladhar* (pronounced **lu-ar**) for a hoof or claw.

The 'hoof' or 'claw' explanation might seem to fit better both by its pronunciation compared to the modern name Lawers, and because of the overall shape of the massif, with great ridges and spurs sweeping round like talons to enclose corries. And other names on the massif hint at this hooked shape: **Meall Corranaich***** has several possible interpretations, but among them is hill of the sickle (*corran*); a top just beyond the main peak is **Creag an Fhithich*,** cliff of the raven; while on the far side lies Gleann Dà-ghob, glen of two beaks or two forks. There's another 'hoof mountain' in **Ladhar Bheinn** in Knoydart in the west. And there might seem to be a connection between Ben Lawers' apparent 'claw' name and Lochan nan Cat, lochan of the wild cats, lying in the deepest of these corries.

However the word *ladhar* often refers to paws rather than claws, albeit paws with claws! And there are some other awkward facts confronting a 'claw' meaning, such as the name's English plural ending in '-s' (the Gaelic plural would end in - an); and the absence of the proper form (if it *is* mountain of the claw) as *beinn a' ladhair*.

And there are strong arguments for *labhar*, loud. This same Lochan nan Cat feeds the Lawers Burn, a substantial stream running down to Loch Tay; it is loud certainly, especially when fed by spring snowmelt or summer storm, its

---

Càrn Dearg Meadhonach – kaarn dye**r**ak **mee**anach
Càrn Beag Dearg – kaarn bayk **dye**rak Meall Corranaich – myowl **kor**aneech
Aonach Mòr – oe:noch **moa:r** Creag an Fhithich – krayk *an* **ee**-eech

background clatter throwing the rest of the great silence into relief. Beinn Labhair was the spelling and local pronunciation recorded by Professor W.J. Watson, by folk-song collectors, and by dictionary-maker Edward Dwelly at the start of the 20th century. The loud stream in question was called Labhar by Alasdair MacMhaighstir Alasdair, the great 18th-century poet and scholar. The three local land divisions of the resulting name of Labhar district, based on the stream name, became Lawers as their English plural form, and this would also explain the '-s' of Lawers. 'Loud' or 'noisy' mountains are not unusual in the Highlands, as names like Gleouraich (roaring) or Lochnagar (loch of laughter) indicate, and indeed there's another stream called Uisge Labhair flowing west from Ben Alder. And *beinn labhair*, the loud mountain, would be a correct Gaelic form. All these details shout a 'loud' meaning from the hill-tops!

Lawers' other peaks include **Beinn Ghlas***(grey-green mountain), **Meall Garbh*** (rough hill), **An Stùc*** (the rocky cone) and **Meall Greigh*** (usually interpreted as the hill of the horse stud or cattle herd from *greigh;* but one older version has it as Meall Gruaidh, meaning the cheek, or profile).

10. Beinn a'Bhùird* (3924 feet, 1196m)

This is Scotland's answer to South Africa's **Table Mountain,** in name at least. At the risk of stating the obvious, it is almost certainly called this because of its two-mile-long, flat summit plateau, bounded by steep ciffs on the east – although whimsy might favour the granite tor near the north top as origin of the 'table' idea. The Gaelic word *bòrd* is related to the Scots or English 'board' for a table, and *bùird* is the genitive form. In the 17th century, mapmaker Blaeu recorded it as Bini Bourd.

A patch of snow lingers in summer high up in the corrie, and is the subject of a legend that if it disappears, the Farquharsons would lose their Invercauld estate. In fact it does disappear most summers, but the lairds' stock answer was that it may be very dirty but it was still there under the grime!

11. Càrn Eige* (3877 feet, 1183m)

Càrn Eige and its close neighbour Màm Sodhail are the two highest mountains west of the Great Glen, forming the high points of one of the great east-west ridges that run above the remote lochs of this area. The most usual interpretation of the name is as notch or file cairn, from the Gaelic *eag,* genitive form *eige;* the word can also refer to a peat-cutting tool, which perhaps lies more happily with the agricultural name of neighbour Màm Sodhail (originally *mam sabhail*), barn peak. The approach to Càrn Eige from the east is along a pinnacled, narrow ridge, sometimes described as gendarmed, and at one point a stalkers' path almost becomes a flight of stone steps on a steep bit. The corrie to the north is Coire Dhomhain, deep corrie,

Beinn Ghlas – bYn **ghlas**	Meall Greigh – myowl **gray**
Meall Garbh – myowl **garav**	Beinn a'Bhùird – bYn *a* **voo:rsht**
An Stùc – *an* **stoo:chk**	Càrn Eige – kaarn **ayg***a*

indicating that the sides fall away steeply into it. So the idea of the narrowness of a file nicely represents the ridge's shape.

Within sight of Càrn Eige's summit is Torridonian giant *Beinn Eighe*, another 'file' mountain with its long narrow crest. There is another, less likely possibility; *eigh* in Gaelic can also mean ice. But it would be unusual if this hill were to be the only Scottish mountain to carry the word ice on its name, for although it is obviously high enough to tempt lingering snow, it is far enough west to receive the douce blessings of the milder Atlantic weather.

12. Beinn Mheadhoin* (3883 feet, 1182m)

This means middle mountain. While this translation is straightforward, the pronunciation is more difficult for the English language speaker and early mapmakers struggled with Binnamain, Biny Main and Ben Mean: 'mh' is pronounced 'v' in Gaelic, so the second word is pronounced 'vane'. There are two other, better known Ben Vanes, one in the Trossachs and the other in the Arrochar Alps where it is piggy-in-the-middle between Beinn Ìme and Ben Vorlich: their nearness to the cities probably ensures they are more climbed than this Beinn Mheadhoin in the Cairngorms, where it lies at least six or seven walking miles from the nearest roads. And this is probably the clue to its name. For it does indeed lie in the middle of this mountain range.

The designation 'middle' sounds like a put-down – but it's in good international company, for La Meije, one of the jewels of the Dauphiné Alps, means just that. The Gaelic word *meadhon* can also have the connotation of 'the centre, the heart', and perhaps this is a fairer translation of its position in the Cairngorm range. From it streams flow north to join the River Avon and south to join the Dee. Certainly the mountain need fear no comparison with its higher neighbours when the character of the actual summits are compared, for Beinn Mheadhoin has a magnificent tor, about 40 feet (12 metres) high, of weathered granite. Lying on a plateau surface spread with the granite crumbles of this semi-arctic desert with tufts of short grass clinging to it, it looks like a butte from the American West.

13. Màm Sodhail* (3862 feet, 1180m)

Pronounced in English 'Mam Sool', the original Gaelic was Mam Sabhail. A *màm* is a rounded, breast-shaped hill, while *sabhal* is a barn. Cairn Toul (above) is also based on the concept of a barn, in its case probably from the shape of the summit. However there would be a contradiction here between a rounded breast shape and the flat-topped ridge shape of a barn. Nevertheless there is surely a connection between the name of one of the long south-eastern ridges dropping from Màm Sodhail towards Loch Affric, which is called **An Tudair*** (properly *An Tughadair*). This means 'the thatcher', and since the mountains were named long before the Americans got the dubious habit of

---

Beinn Mheadhoin – bYn **vee**-oin^y Màm Sodhail – maam **soa**-al (or maam **sool**)
An Tudair – (properly, An Tughadair) – *a*n **too**-*a*dar^y

naming peaks after national leaders, we can assume it refers to a roofing craftsman, who would thatch barns frequently. (A Gaelic poem refers to it as 'Màm Sodhail of the grass', *Màm Sabhail an fheòir*.)

14. Stob Choire Claurigh* (3858 feet, 1177m)
Perhaps the most modest of the top twenty, for its name refers to the corrie beneath it, identifying itself only as the Stob, or stubby top, above it. It is the highest point in the Grey Corries, a ridge whose slopes of quartzite grey screes give little quarter to vegetation. It has been suggested that the word *claurigh* derives from the Gaelic *clamhras* meaning brawling or clamouring – generally disturbing the peace! Peaks elsewhere in the Highlands have such meanings, among them **Gleouraich*** above Loch Quoich, meaning roaring or bellowing; autumn hillwalkers will know the heartfelt bellowing of stags at rut echoing in dark evening corries. A bare stony corrie such as this mountain's has a powerful amplifying effect on noises!

15. Ben More (3853 feet, 1174m)
Originally **Beinn Mhòr*** (and still thus in Gaelic), this translates simply as big mountain. There are two Munros with this plain name, the other being on the island of Mull. On the mainland there is another Beinn Mhòr in Kintail in the north-west, but it is better known as the Five Sisters of Kintail, whilst in the further north-west beyond Ullapool **Ben More Assynt** and **Ben Mòr Coigach** have incorporated the district name to distinguish them. (Assynt is from the Norse *àss* for a rocky ridge, while *còigeach* is Gaelic for a fifth share, a land division). Offshore again, a plain Beinn Mhòr is the second highest hill in Lewis, being at 1874 feet (570m) less than half the height of the Perthshire Ben More, the term *mòr* being, of course, relative rather than absolute, indicating its large size relative to its neighbours. This Ben More is the highest peak in the Crianlarich area. From a wide area of the southern Highlands the mountain and its twin Stob Binnein (or Stobinian) are unmistakeable, their fine cones drawing the eye to them, and many photographic panoramas are centred around their symmetry.

16. Ben Avon* (3843 feet, 1171m)
The northern foothills of this mountain are washed by the River Avon on its journey to the Moray Firth, and the river and mountain probably share the name. The name Avon is the archetypal British word for a river, there being at least three in Scotland, and five major ones in England, all deriving from an ancient Indo-European root word for water, with descendants in the Latin *abona* and Welsh *afon*. But this north-east name is *not* exactly the same word,

---

Stob Choire Claurigh – stop chor*a* **klowree**   Beinn Mhòr – bYn **voa:**r

Gleouraich – **glaw**reech   Ben Avon – Gaelic: Beinn Athfhinn – bYn a-*an*ʸ

and the identical spelling is the result of O.S. surveyors, familiar with the many River Avons down south, writing down the nearest equivalent to the Gaelic word *abhainn*, (pronounced roughly aving or awing) also meaning a river. A 1600 spelling of the name, by traveller John Taylor, as 'Benawne' is closer both to the original Gaelic, and to the modern hill-walkers' pronunciation as 'Ben Aan'.

Other suggestions on the watery note have included *àth fionn* or *abhainn fhionn*, white or very bright ford or stream, and a legend that it comes from Ath nam Fionn (the 'th' is silent in speech), meaning the ford of the Fingalians, referring to the Fords of Avon on the river below. The legend tells of Fionn's wife being swept away and drowned while crossing here. Fionn and the Fingalians exist in Celtic legend if not in historical reality, and several other hills elsewhere may well refer to them. The local Gaelic pronunciation for the strath *is* indeed *athfhinn*, but this pronunciation is apparently only two centuries old; and its 12th-century written spelling Strathouen suggests *strath abhann*, an archaic genitive form of *abhainn*, a river.

The sound of the name in speech as 'ben aan' recalls the hill in the Trossachs called Ben A'n. This latter name is probably a mistake by Sir Walter Scott for the original name *binnean*, a small peak. It might be thought that the tors on Ben Avon's summit ridge could be classed as *binnean*, but this Gaelic word is largely confined to southern parts of the Highlands, and the pronunciation would not really fit the name.

However Ben Avon does have a distinctive skyline because of these granite tors. As Olive Fraser's poem observed:

> "Yon's nae wife's hoose ayont A'an
> In the green lift ava,
> Yon's the cauld lums o' Ben A'an
> Wha's smeek is snaw."

These tors – known also as the Bads o' Ben A'an, or literally tufts – have their individual names, the summit rock itself being **Leabaidh an Daimh Bhuidhe,**[*] bed of the yellow stag. Other tops include **Clach Choutsaich**[*] (possibly stone of the chase, from *cluthaich*, or Coutts' stone), **Mullach Lochan nan Gabhar**[*] (summit of the goats' lochan), **Gorm Craig**[*] (blue crag) and **Stob Bac an Fhuarain**[*†] (top of the bank of the spring).

Another large tor, **Clach Bhan**[*] on the slopes above the River Avon, means the stone of the women. Legend has it that it was visited by Fingal's wife, and documented history attests that it was visited by pregnant women, as late as the 19th century, who bathed in its hollowed-out rock pools in the hope of easing their impending labour.

Leabaidh an Daimh Bhuidhe – lyepay *an* dev **voo**ye
Clach Choutsaich – klach **choot**seech
Mullach Lochan nan Gabhar – moolach lochan n*an* **gow**ar
Gorm Craig – **go**rom krayk   Clach Bhan – klach **van**
Stob Bac an Fhuarain – stob bachk *an* **oo**areen

Stob Binnein and Ben More

17. Stobinian* (3827 feet, 1165m)

Variously known as Stobinian, **Stob Binnein,** or **Am Binnein***, this mountain forms a pair with Ben More. It has a beautiful and distinctive summit, a long cone sliced off at an angle just below its apex; this shape has led to suggestions that its name comes from the Gaelic *innean* meaning anvil, a comparison it would be easy to agree with especially when seen from the Crianlarich area. It would be in respectable company. The Cobbler and An Teallach (the forge) are other instances of craftsmen and their tools in Highland hill-names, while furth of the Highlands, some tops in the Cleish Hills of Fife are known as **The Inneans** from Gaelic; and in Ireland the hill Mullagahoney means peak of the anvils. Half way round the world on the San Fernandez islands in the Pacific is a flat-topped hill called El Yunque, the anvil; it too has a Scots connection, for on its top for four years sat Alexander Selkirk, model for Robinson Crusoe, scanning the horizon for ships. Not so far away, high up in Glen Coe a projecting rock known as **The Study** is a corruption of the Scots *stiddie,* an anvil; and near it is **Inneoin a'Cheathaich*** (properly *innean*), anvil of the mist.

More prosaically it may simply be *stob,* meaning a peak, and *binnein,* meaning a pinnacle or conical peak, come together. However the most usual use of *stob* in peak-names refers to features *below* the top. In this part of Perthshire, Stob Coire an Lochain, Stob Invercarnaig and Stob Garbh, all

Stobinian – stob **bin**y*a*n
Inneoin a'Cheathaich – eenyan *a* **che**heech
Am Binnein – *a*m **bee**ny*a*n

refer to the corries, farms or ground beneath them, which would make Stob Innean or Stob Binnein the 'odd man out', since the 'anvil' here – or the *binnean* – refer to the summit itself. Alternatively the older name of **Am Binnein** (the peak) may have been the original version; the Stob, the actual summit alone, may have 'taken over' ownership of the name from the previous landlord of the whole mountain, Am Binnein.

However, these possible meanings fade away if you view the mountain from west of Crianlarich, perhaps from a bridge over the Fillan, for you'll be left in little doubt that the Gaels saw what you see in its summit outline . . . a smith's anvil.

18. Beinn Bhrotain* (3795 feet, 1157m)

The old mapmakers got their pronounciation of 'bh' correct when they spelt this hill as Binwrodin, Binny-vroten and Beinn-na-Vrotan. Lying in the eastern Cairngorms above Coire Cath nam Fionn, the corrie of the battle of the Fingalians, it is fitting that this name too comes from ancient legend, from Brodan the fabled hound or mastiff. By repute a jet black hound, it chased the white fairy deer; and while it was probably owned by one of the Fingalians, like many aggressive dogs the specific owner preferred not to be identified.

19. Lochnagar* (3791 feet, 1155m)

On this hill we can observe the strange sight of a loch "running uphill", for the name of a corrie lochan has displaced the summit's original name. For the Gaelic name of this mountain was **Beinn nan Cìochan***, the mountain of the breasts referring to the granite tors on its corrie rim which today are known by the Scots names of the **Meikle Pap** and **Little Pap,** the big and little breast. In the corrie far below its plunging cliffs lay Loch-na-Garr (on Roy's 1750 map), which is the loch of noise or laughter (*gàire*). The sound 'garr' in a mountain-name might seem to point at the adjective *garbh* (pronounced garav), and certainly the granite cliffs spill a rough scree down into the loch – and *garbh* is a frequently used Gaelic mountain adjective. But the form of the name loch-na-gar indicates a noun, not the adjectival *garbh*: and besides the case for 'noisy' can draw on hill-names like Gairich and Gleouraich, both 'roaring' peaks.

Gradually, over the decades, the name of the 'noisy' loch below began to be used for the peak itself: initially in 1721, then in 1761, 1806 and with gathering pace in the 19th century, it was referred to as the Top of (ie-above), or Hill of, Lochan-y-gar. Englishman Thomas Pennant wrote in August 1769:

> ". . . I saw the great mountain Laghin y Gair, which is always covered with snow"

Beinn Bhrotain – bYn **vroh**tYn^y
Lochnagar – Gaelic: Loch na Gàire – loch n*a* **gaar***a*
Beinn nan Cìochan – bYn n*a*n **kee:**chan

The transformation was surely completed by the Romantic Lord Byron's famous poem on 'Dark Lochnagar' (quoted and discussed in the chapter on Gaelic colours) and Queen Victoria's adoption of the Balmoral estate at its foot would stamp the name-change with a *By Appointment* seal. She wrote in 1848 of the 'beautiful surrounding hills of Loch-na-gar'. A map of 1867 using the name Lochnagar for the lochan only, and the individual tops by their own names, was a last defiant fling for the old ways.

In addition to the two Paps, the summits of the massif include the highest points **Cac Càrn Beag*** and **Cac Càrn Mòr***, which are mistaken names on two counts. The Beag (wee cairn) is in fact 20 feet (6m) higher than the Mòr (big cairn). More seriously, the Cac is a corruption of *cadha*, meaning slope, or path up a slope: *cac* in Gaelic is connected with the Scots word keech, known to the English as faeces. Hardly the sort of name, however mistaken, to set before a Queen, especially Victoria, which is perhaps why the Balmoral royals were keen to encourage the name Lochnagar! **The Stuic,** the summit at the end of the north-western corrie, is from the Gaelic *stùc*, a projecting hill or round promontory, while **Cuidhe Crom*** (properly *cuithe chrom*) is crooked snow wreath, which often lies on its shaded north-east slope into summer. The hill above the shallow scoop on the southern slopes of the plateau is **Càrn a'Choire Bhòidhich***†, cairn of the beautiful corrie, a name that could apply equally to the granite-girt corrie harbouring the upstart Lochan na Gàire.

20. Derry Cairngorm (3788 feet, 1155m) (An Càrn Gorm)

Although there are several hills called Càrn Gorm (blue cairn) throughout Scotland, this one suffered from its close proximity to the famous Cairn Gorm, fifth highest in the land and namer of the Cairngorms range. Originally **An Càrn Gorm,*** the blue hill, from its blue appearance when seen from Linn of Dee several miles distant, it became known as Càrn Gorm an Doire to distinguish it from its big neighbour, (and even ignominiously as the Lesser or Eastern Cairngorm), before the Doire became anglicised to Derry. This suffix turned prefix originally meant oakwood, or more generally, wooded (*doireach*). The woods for which Glen Derry is still rightly famous are not oaks but the beautiful Scots pines. These relics of the ancient extensive wood of Caledon are living sculptures formed of soft russet-brown bark and dark green needles, contrasting their soft forest carpet of bilberry and juniper with their brittle twisted limbs. If this mountain had to be pushed into second place by the other Cairngorm, its consolation lies in taking its newly-added forename from a beautiful glen.

Cac Càrn Beag – (properly, Cadha Càrn Beag) – ka kaarn **bayk**
Cac Càrn Mòr – (properly, Cadha Càrn Mòr) – ka kaarn **moa:r**
Cuidhe Crom – kooy*a* **krowm**
Càrn a'Choire Bhòidhich – kaarn *a* chor*a* **vawyeech**
An Càrn Gorm – *a*n kaarn **gorom**

Chapter Three

Beinns and Sgùrrs – generic Gaelic mountain names

For most Lowland Scots a Highland mountain is simply a 'ben'. For a Gaelic speaker in the Highlands the word would be *beinn*, and he would be spoiled for choice among the many other words in the language for mountain, with *sgùrr* and *càrn* and *meall* outstanding among a collection of over seventy. As an 1897 poem in the *Scottish Mountaineering Club Journal*, by L.W.H., put it:

> "A mountain's a mountain in England, but when
> The climber's in Scotland, it may be a Beinn,
> A Creag or a Meall, a Spidean, a Sgor,
> A Carn or a Monadh, a Stac, or a Torr."

Of course many languages have several words for mountain. French gives us for instance *Mont* Blanc, the *Aiguille* Verte and the *Dent* Blanche, and Spanish offers *Monte* Perdido and the *Picos* d'Europa. German has more mountain-words including *Berg* (mountain), *Hügel* (hill), *Kopf* (head) and *Dom* (dome), and the most expressive – *horn* as in the Matterhorn. But Gaelic outdoes all these major languages with the range of generic words for describing hills.

Some European mountain-words are found all across the continent: German *spitze* is the Italian *pizzo*, French *pic*, Spanish *pico* and English pike and peak, but there's no Gaelic cousin. Indeed the only Gaelic mountain-names with close links with the main European languages are *ceap* (a head, paralleling *Kopf*, *kop* and cap), and *monadh* (with *mont*, *monte* and mountain): but neither of these names found much favour in the Highlands. Instead the Gaels here developed their own mountain-words, partly from their parent language of Irish Gaelic, partly from Norse, to create a choice that seems to be unique in Europe for variety and descriptiveness. In addition to the seventy or so in this chapter, other chapters cover the many body parts that anatomise the hills, like the Gaelic for nose, heel and so on. Further, by adding the diminutive suffix "-an" to many of the mountain-words small versions can be created, as in *meallan* and *cruachan* (little lump and little heap), and the grand total approaches 100.

Turning to statistics for a moment, we find that nearly 30% of the mountains in the Munro tables (those over 3000 feet, 914m) are either Beinns or Sgùrrs, as are nearly 50% of the Corbetts (mountains between 2500 and 3000 feet). A further 30% plus of the former and 25% of the latter are made up by four other common mountain-words – *càrn, meall, creag* and *stob*.

àirde*

Meaning simply a height, this is a very common element in village names from Ardentinny to Ardvourlie, but curiously it is rarely found in hill-names. It might best be translated as a block of higher ground or promontory jutting out into the sea, or above a settlement, like The Aird by Inverness or Àrd Mòr (160 feet, 49m) beside Waternish on Skye. Overlooking Kylesku is **Àird dà Loch***, height of the two lochs, a block of rugged land splitting the sea-loch. The word is often found in adjectival form as *àird*, as in **Cruach Àrdrain*** near Crianlarich and Sutherland's **Meall Àrd*** and **Fireach Àrd*** on Loch Duich, high hill.

aoineadh*

A steep rocky brae or promontory, this rare word is largely confined to Mull and Iona.

aonach*

An *aonach* is a mountain whose summit has the form of a ridge, generally with steepish sides. For example the long narrow plateau ridge which forms the central spine of the Blackmount (considered a classic traverse by ski-mountaineers) is **Aonach Mòr***, a 'big ridge'. Another better-known Aonach Mòr is near Ben Nevis with its summit at the fulcrum of a two-mile long north-south mountain axis running from Aonach an Nid to Aonach Beag, slinging the high contours between them like a trapeze wire. Glen Coe's north wall is formed by the **Aonach Eagach***, the notched ridge, a classic scramble along airy rock spires; from the north, against the light, it has the appearance of a fence of palings, like a Dolomite ridge. Beyond it, on the Glen's south side, Bidean nam Bian throws out three flat-topped spurs, the famous "**Three**

àirde – aard*a*	aoineadh – **oe:n***a*gh
Àird dà Loch – aard daa **loch**	aonach – **oe:**noch
Cruach Àrdrain – kroo*a*ch aardr*a*n	Aonach Mòr – **oe:**noch **moa:r**
Meall Àrd – myowl **aard**	Aonach Eagach – oe:noch **egoch**
Fireach Àrd – feeroch **aard**	

Aonach Eagach

Sisters of Glencoe" (named and painted by the Romantic Scottish artist MacCulloch). Two of the 'sisters' are **Aonach Dubh*** (dark ridge) and its stunted sibling **Geàrr Aonach*** (short ridge). As these examples show *aonach* hills as a group are high peaks, and are generally found in Lochaber, although there are some in the Glen Cluanie area. There are very few in the eastern Grampians, but then there are few long narrow ridges among their broad plateaux. (The similar-looking word in Meall an Aonaich in the far north-west is in fact the hill of the gathering, not a 'ridged' *aonach*.)

bac*
Bac an Eich is bank of the horses, while Skye's **Baca Ruadh** is red bank. Found mainly in the Hebrides and the west, it probably derives from Old Norse *bakkr*.

bad
Although in most placenames this means a thicket or simply a spot, it can also mean a tuft and is sometimes applied to hill granite tors like the **Bads of Ben Avon.**

Aonach Dubh – oe:noch **doo**
Geàrr Aonach – **gyaar** oe:noch
bac – bachk

22

bàrr

Bàrr is found mainly in the south-west of Scotland. It means a top or crest (and can imply in modern Gaelic the cream of the milk) rather than the whole body of a hill. One author on Argyll placenames wrote that it had more the nuance of an arable upland rather than a geographic feature, but in the south-west there are proper hills like **Barnean*** (*bàrr nan eun*, top of the birds) and **Barskeog** (thorn crest). One of the highest is is **Meall a'Bhàrr*** in Perthshire, hill of the top or summit, at 3295 feet (1004 metres), but the word usually applies to low hills and, as a result, it has often been swallowed up in village names, like Barrhead.

beinn*, ben

The commonest Gaelic hill-word, with over a thousand specimens on O.S maps, this means a mountain of any shape or size, although away from coastal areas it tends to indicate a higher, bulkier mountain than others. It is no coincidence that the highest mountain, Nevis, is a *beinn*, as are nine in the top thirty, and almost thirty in the top hundred. It is of Old Irish origin as *ben*, and in Scottish Gaelic is correctly *beinn*, although on maps it has often been anglicised (or scotticised!) back to *ben*. But there are relatively few *ben* mountains in Ireland, and it was in the Scottish Highlands that the word came into its own, like a child prospering once free of the bounds of home.

Although it is found almost all over the Highlands, it is commonest in the southern Hebrides and the western seaboard (especially on and within sight of Mull), and in the south-west Highlands between Clyde and Rannoch, where there is the greatest concentration: in the hills round Arrochar, for instance, almost every mountain in view is a *beinn*. Further east and north-east of these areas, the name *beinn* is confined mainly to the *highest* hills within an area (like Ben Alder, Ben MacDhui or Ben Avon), and thus it is significant that Ben Nevis is neighboured by hills with names with *càrn*, *mullach*, *binnein*, *aonach* and *stob*, but not *beinn*. In the far north-east they are almost unknown, while in the north-west Highlands, away from the seaboard, *sgùrr* tends to predominate in the highest hills, leaving *beinn* with lower peaks.

This pattern of distribution suggests that the name is very old, being brought from Ireland by the first Scottish settlers and their immediate descendants. Indeed the number of hill-names where *beinn* is the second element (Fionn Bheinn, Creach Bheinn, Ladhar Bheinn, and Morven, etc) also indicate antiquity. Possibly then it was supplanted by later names in some areas: we know that Beinn nan Cìochan became Lochnagar, Beinn Artair became The Cobbler, and Beinn Mhòr became the separate *sgùrr* peaks of the Five Sisters of Kintail; perhaps other *beinns* were elbowed aside by brash newcomers like *càrn*, *meall*, *sgùrr* and *stob!*

Barnean – Gaelic: Bàrr nan Eun – baar n*a*n **ay:n**
Meall a'Bhàrr – myowl *a* **vaar**   beinn – bYn

Beinn or *ben* however is a truly Scottish word, whose dominance in the whole country is shown by the fact that the anglicised version ben does not need translation. Indeed Scottish emigrants have taken it overseas to English-speaking places where it needs no explanation – a Ben Lomond mountain in Australia and a whole range in Tasmania, Ben Nevises in New Zealand and Hong Kong, and a Ben Macdhui in South Africa's Drakensbergs.

Ironically for a word that has fathered these emigrants, there are few bens in southern Scotland, with a very few in Galloway (where the element *fell* is commoner) and a sprinkling in the Ochils, but this reflects the vitality of the Scots language's own hill-words like *law* and *knowe* (see Scots names chapter). Ironic too that although the word *ben* has an Irish Gaelic origin, the best-known example there, the Twelve Bens (a group in south-west Ireland that Atlantic sailors watch for as first landfall), is a name applied by English speakers on the basis of a Scots word.

The diminutive *beannan* is found in names like Eigg's **Beannan Breaca*** (speckled), which can muster barely 1000 feet (300 metres), or **Am Beannan** above Loch Rannoch, a 386m shoulder.

bidean, bidein

Ths suffix *-an* is normally the Gaelic diminutive, in the way that a lochan is a small loch: and *bidean* is the diminutive of *biod* (see below). Yet there are *bideans* amongst the highest Munros, among them the mighty **Bidean nam Bian***, 3775 feet (1150 metres) above the sea at the mouth of Glen Coe. A Gaelic dictionary gives the meaning of *bidean* as a sharp point, pinnacle or top, so perhaps the implied smallness relates to the actual summit rather than to the whole bulk of the hill. As W.H. Murray wrote of Bidean nam Bian:

> ". (it) is the highest peak in Argyll and dominates Glencoe and Appin. But how small a summit for so large a mountain!"

And many of the *bidean* names refer to a corrie or hollow beneath them – like **Bidean a'Ghlas Thuill*** (top of the grey hollow) – this confirming the idea of a small point above some more striking feature.

Bidean nam Bian (the name that appears on the O.S. map) is often translated as the peak of the hides or pelts. But Seton Gordon says that Canon MacInnes of Glencoe, scholar and native Gaelic speaker, had said that it was in Gaelic originally Bidean nam Beann, the peak of the mountains or the 'chief of the hills'. This is the most likely name, for it is a large sprawling mountain with many subsidiary tops.

Beannan Breaca – ben*an* **brechk***a*
Bidean nam Bian – (properly, Bidean nam Beann) – beedyan n*a*m **byown**
Bidean a'Ghlas Thuill – beedy*an a* **ghlas** hil[y]

The other spelling *bidein*, with the same meaning of a small point, is found in places like Eigg, with **Bidein Bòidheach*** (beautiful) and **Bidein an Tighearna*** (of the landlord). In the Monar area, sharply-pointed peaks like **Bidein a'Choire Sheasgaich*** and **Bidean an Eòin Dearg*** show that there, the word suggests a definite shape.

binnein

Binnein, sometimes spelt *binnean*, like *bidean* ends apparently in the diminutive suffix *-an*, and it may be derived from *beinn* which originally meant simply the top of the hill; *binnein* itself usually means a pinnacle or conical top. Certainly the best-known *binnein* hills are not small hills: **Binnein Mòr*** dominates the eastern end of the Mamores with its roof-ridged outline. There are however few of the species around – about twenty, including Mòr's neighbour Beag, others near the Laggan valley, and some in the south-western seaboard area.

biod

An unusual word, meaning a pointed top, *biod* is found mainly in the far west. There are a dozen of this endangered species on Skye, like Biod Mòr and Biod Buidhe (big and yellow) but few on the mainland – there's a **Biod an Fhithich*** (raven) high on the Saddle. (The similar-sounding but unconnected word in **Am Bioran*** above St. Fillans means simply 'the stick'.)

bràigh*

This Gaelic word has passed into Scots as in the literary Braes o' Balwearie or the musical Braes o' Bonny Doon. Sometimes it means simply a steep slope, or in town a steep street such as Edinburgh's Liberton Brae. However it has come downhill from its origins, for in Gaelic it means the upper part, or the height above, as in Braeriach, the speckled high part. **Seana Bhràighe†** (old upland) in Ross-shire is one of the remotest Munros, while Breadalbane in north Perthshire is **Bràghaid Albann,*** the upper part of Scotland. Brae is very much an eastern and southern corruption, and *bràigh* names in the original are mainly to be found on the islands of the west, although there are some in the Cairngorms. The **Braes of Carse** above Perth are literally the heights above the flood plain (of the Tay).

Bidein Bòidheach – beedyin **baw**yoch

Bidein an Tighearna – beedyin *an* **tyee**-*a*rna

Bidein 'a Choire Sheasgaich – beedy*an a* kora **hays**geech

Bidean an Eòin Dearg – beedy*an an* **yaween**[y] **dyer**ak

Binnein Mòr – beeny*an* **moa:r**

Biod an Fhithich – bid *an* **ee**-eech

Am Bioran – *am* **biran**

bràigh – brY:

Bràghaid Alban – bra-id **alapYn**[y]

Caisteal Abhail

In the west there are several hills called **Braebeg, Breabeg** and **Briobaig** – these may well be *bràigh beag*, little height, for the best-known Breabag is a hill lying in the shadow of Ben More Assynt. Professor W.J. Watson speculated that it could be from *breab beag*, little kick, signifying that the hill was split from its neighbours as if by a little kick!

bruach
Bruach is a bank or a slope. **Bruach na Frìthe*** in the Cuillins (one of the few there not to be a *sgùrr!*) is the slope of the deer forest or wilderness.

caisteal
Literally castle, this word has been poetically rather than historically applied to several tops of squat, fortified appearance, while genuine historic hill-forts are normally identified by the word *dùn* rather than *caisteal*. **Creag Chaisteal*** (crag of castles) near Loch Pityoulish is an exception, being the site of an old Pictish fort.

There are some two dozen *caisteals*, mainly in the south-west and on the islands. On Arran **Caisteal Abhail*** is one of several castellated granite tors, although the Munro **An Caisteal*** (the castle) above Crianlarich is probably better-known if less clearly-shaped.

Bruach na Frìthe – broo-uch n*a* **free**:h*a*
Creag Chaisteal – krayk **chas**tyal

Caisteal Abhail – kashtyal av*al*^{y}
An Caisteal – *an* **kash**tyal

A rocky outcrop above Glen Lyon is **Caisteal Samhraidh,**[*] the 'summer castle' of long ago for some idling idylling cowherd!

càrn

Most of us probably have a mental picture of a *càrn* (or its anglicised version cairn) in which the hill resembles a larger version of the conical pile of stones that marks most summits. It is no surprise therefore that one leading Gaelic dictionary (MacLennan's) defines it as 'a heap of stones, or a rocky hill'. But nature does not imitate the idea, for just as real summit cairns are often weather-flattened assortments of rubble – or indeed the remains of a crashed aircraft's nose cone on **Càrn an t-Sagairt Mòr**[*] – similarly the Càrn mountains' shape usually belies the image of a rocky cone.

Although some of the western *càrn* hills like **Càrn Mòr Dearg** *are* conical, the majority of the higher Càrns are in the Monadh Liath and in the eastern Grampians, which means that they are often rounded grassy hills of little distinction, on which the summit cairn itself may be the only eye-catching feature in a landscape swelling gently with monotony. Doric poet Charles Murray, praising the virtues of his local hill Bennachie, rather dismissed them:

> ". . . an' mony a Carn I trow,
> That's smored in mist ayont Braemar . . ."

For hillwalkers the rounded grassy **Geal Chàrn**[*] hills, around the upper Spey (there are 19 of these white, or fair, *Càrns*) are proof positive that the Gaelic dictionary has got it wrong on the rocky bit. Could the name come from summit cairns? Unlikely, since many of these were built by walkers in recent times. The Geal Chàrn lying above the Drumochter Pass, has several old pillar-like cairns (deceiving motorists on the A9 far below that climbers are permanently aloft), but this hill is an exception.

Upright and soundly built cairns like this, or in some cases upended flagstones, are known in Gaelic as *fir bhrèige* or false men. Sometimes they are natural pinnacles left by erosion, as in Torridon's **Sgùrr nan Fear Duibhe**[†], the peak of the dark men on the Beinn Eighe massif, known in translation as **The Black Carls**; and sometimes they are man-made cairns said to have been erected to divert invading armies' attention from the enemy in hand. There are several **Firbriggs Hills** named after these 'false men' stones, and near Tyndrum is **Càrn Buachaille Brèig**, the hill of the false shepherd. **Finbracks Hill** in Angus may well be a corruption of *fir bhrèige*, too.

Caisteal Samhraidh – kashtyal **sow**ree
Càrn an t-Sagairt Mòr – kaarn *a*n tag*a*rsht **moa:r**
Geal Chàrn – **gyal** chaarn

However it was living men whom the Roman geographers described – based on the maps of the Greek Ptolemy – when they located the tribe Carnonacae in the north-west Highlands: this can translate either as the trumpet people (literally 'people of the horns') – for which there's no historical evidence – or as 'the people of the rocky hills', an apparent reference to Càrn hills. However these Latin names were given centuries before Gaelic – or indeed Norse – had arrived here. So there are two possibilities. One, that there is a mere coincidence between the name the Romans themselves chose to give the northern tribe, and the later Gaelic word *càrn* (that is certainly commoner in the Monadh Liath and Cairngorms areas than it is in the north-west). The other, that the Roman name was derived from the tribe's own name, perhaps based on the hills, in which case the later Norse or Gaelic speakers may have adopted this much older Pictish word. The possibility is strengthened by the rarity of the word in the traditional Gaelic source areas of south-western Scotland. Also there are several chambered cairns in Ross and Inverness called **Càrn Glas** or **Càrn Liath** (both grey cairns) and this may indicate the 'Carnonacae' tribe's burial practices. (Alternatively there's an origin in the Celtic word *corn*, a horn of pointed shape).

Cairns in the man-made sense take on a significance not just on the summits. Within living memory cairns were erected outside houses to mark a death, and these are often identified by the diminutive name *càrnan:* for instance **Càrnan Ghrulin** on Eigg, beside now-abandoned crofts. High above the River Dee at Monaltrie is a rocky hill called **Càrn na Cuimhne***, the cairn of remembrance. Clansmen marching past it on the way to a Chief's war had to deposit a stone here, and pick it up upon return, thus ensuring a 'body count' of those who did not return. (Its alternative name is **Càrn na Coinnimh,** meeting place, where the Farquharsons assembled for battle.) **Càrn nam Marbh,** cairn of the dead in Glen Lyon, was where bodies of plague victims were piled and buried. It is crowned by Clach a'Phlàigh, stone of the plague, and was the site of a great bonfire of whin at the time of Samhain or Hallowe'en, round which the local people danced sun-wise. In the Borders near Greenlaw, **Twin Law** hill has twin cairns on it, said to commemorate where two brothers slew each other.

ceann
Ceann, the head, is often anglicised to kin, and it can also mean 'end of', as in village names like Kingussie and Kinlochleven. Among the very few hill-names found are **Ceann Garbh***, rough head, and **Ceann na Beinne***, literally the end of the mountain, because it is a mere foothill rounding off the Cuillins. **Tom nan Ceann*** near Glentromie, the knoll of the heads, has a

---

Càrn na Cuimhne – kaarn na **kY**na   Tom nan Ceann – towm nan **kyown**
Ceann Garbh – kyown **gar**av
Ceann na Beinne – kyown na **bYn**-ya

more sinister significance, for here were heaped the heads of the decapitated Donalds after a bloody battle.

ceap

This means a lump, cap or a top of a hill, and appears in **Meall nan Ceapraichean***, hill of the stubby hillocks.

cìoch*

A breast. (See the chapter on the Body of the land).

cnagan*

A little knob, found mainly on Deeside.

cnap

Pronounced krahp as in the hill **Crappich** above Comrie, it means literally a lump or knob and is usually applied to hillocks. Knapdale in Argyll is a landscape of rugged little hills. It can also indicate hillocks on a big mountain's ridge, as in **Cnap a'Chlèirich*** (cleric's hillock) of Beinn a'Bhùird (most of the cnaps are here in the Cairngorms) or the **Cnap Coire na Sprèidhe** (hillock above the cattle corrie). The word may be distantly related to the Old Norse word *gnìpa*, a peak, found in the Northern Isles and in names like **Kneep** on Lewis: or more likely to the Norse *knappr*, a knob, as in Orkney's **Knap of Trowieglen** (hillock of the troll's glen).

cnoc*

Of Irish origin in *cnocc* it indicates a knoll or eminence (of no great height) and applies to rounded hillocks. Due to this height limitation it is confined to the peripheral hills all around the central Highland mass, where there are seven hundred hill-names with *cnoc*. There is a wide use made too of the anglicised (or Scotticised) version knock – there are for instance over two hundred knocks in Galloway alone. (See chapter on Scots names). The diminutive *Cnocans*, little knolls, were said to conceal fairy pleasure-domes where baccanalian enjoyment was continuous, perhaps in confusion with *sìthean* (see below).

corr

Corr means pointed, and the Gaelic dictionary says that a *corra-bheinn* is a pointed hill; although thus a *beinn*, it is not necessarily very high, for **Corra-**

Meall nan Ceapraichean – myowl nan kehpreechan
cìoch – kee:ch   cnagan – kragan
Cnap a'Chléirich – krahp *a* chlay:reech

bheinn*, and **An Corrach*** on Eigg are jagged fragments of the broken moorland overshadowed by An Sgùrr, and are barely above 300 metres (1000 feet). *Corrag* is 'the pointed one' as the rocky finger **Corrag Bhuidhe*** of An Teallach indicates. The **Core Hills** in the south-east, **Meall Corranaich*** of Ben Lawers, and **Little** and **Meikle Corum** in the Ochils, are all of this family. In the south-west the lovely hill-name **Curleywee** is from *cor na gaoith*, point of the wind. In Angus, **Corwharn Hill** is probably *corr fhuaran*, point of springs.

creachann

A *creachann* is a bare wind-swept summit, in which category many Scottish summits could be placed. However the name is relatively rare, with one or two instances in Argyll; Munro **Beinn a'Chreachain*** standing at 3540 feet (1077m) above Glen Lyon, suffers the indignity for a landlocked peak of the oft-used "translation" of its name as the shell mountain. But as *The Munros* guidebook says, it has a 'stony dome-shaped summit'. And Duncan Ban MacIntyre, in his poem in praise of Ben Dorain (very close to Beinn a'Chreachainn) says of a deer:

> "Gasganach, speireach,
> Feadh *chreachann* na beinne . . ."
> (Pert and slender-limbed,
> She keeps the *stony mountain summits* ...) (my emphases)

The word *creachann* initially meant a clamshell, and the analogy with a bare flattish top led to the word being used for hills too. The hill and seaside meanings are curiously combined in **Creachainn nan Sgadan,** near Alness, hill of the herring, for it is said that a cloudburst over the summit one day rained fish from the heavens – a meteorologically plausible fishy story!

creag

A cliff or precipice, *creag* has given us the Scots word craig. More unusually it is one of the few Celtic words that Old English (as spoken by the invading Anglo-Saxons) consented to adopt – Britain after all, was far more mountainous than the German plains! The word has a common root with other Celtic tongues in the Welsh word *craig* and the Irish *croag*, but at least one major English dictionary gives the Gaelic word the honour of parentage. *Creag* is not found among the names of many hill-tops, for such cliffs tend to be found lower down the slopes. However nine of the Munros, including the rocky amphitheatre of **Creag Meagaidh*,** bear the word, and it is commoner among the lower tops, especially where rounded hill-shoulders break off to fall

---

Corra-bheinn – korr*a* vYn

Corrag Bhuidhe – korak **vooy***a*

Creag Meagaidh – krayk **megee**

An Corrach – *a*n koroch

Meall Corranaich – myowl **koraneech**

Beinn a'Chreachain – bYn a **chre**chYn^Y

steeply down in cliffs, like classical statues with their long-shorn marble arms. Often these hills are named from features beneath them, as in **Creag an Dubh Loch*** (cliff of the dark loch – a severe test for cragsmen in the Mounth), the seventy-plus hills called **Creag Dubh***, and the several instances of **Creag a'Chaoruinn***, named after the hardy rowan-trees that sprout defiantly from the steepest and smoothest-shaven faces.

creapall*
A lump, as in the **Knowe of Crippley** in Angus. The word is possibly related to *cnap*, which is pronounced krahp.

croit
Croit often means a croft, the Highlander's farm and farmland, but can also mean a hump, as in **Croit Bheinn***, the humped mountain, in the west.

cruach
Not a flattering name for a hill, for it means heap or stack, applied to anything from hills to peatstacks. Indeed there is a **Tom na Cruaich**†* hill above Blair Atholl, said to have been the cutting-ground for the local peat supply. *Cruach* as a generic name is found mainly in the south-west Highlands, most famously in Munro **Cruach Àrdrain**, the high-stacked heap. There are other lesser examples, including at least four hills called **A' Chruach*** in Argyll alone. The mountain **Cruachan** comes from the diminutive form of the word, which has come to take on its own meaning as a conical hill – which is exactly how it is shaped. In south-west Scotland, the local anglicised form is *crochan*. A hill near Sanquhar called **Cruereach** might be a clumsy version of this, or may derive from crue, Scots for a sheep-pen.

crùlaist
A rare name meaning a rocky hill. **Beinn a'Chrùlaiste*** above Kingshouse on the edge of Rannoch Moor is the best-known, if overshadowed by much rockier hills to the west.

dronnag
Beinn Dronaig* near Strathcarron is an example of this species. Meaning humped, or (the mountain of) the little height, it's a modest name for this Corbett of nearly 2625 feet (800m); whereas the 'hump' name is just right for **Dron Hill** in Berwickshire.

Creag an Dubh Loch – krayk *an* **doo** loch
Creag Dubh – krayk **doo**
Creag a'Chaoruinn – krayk *a* **choe:r**Yn^y
creapall – **krehpal**
Croit Bheinn – **kroht**^y vYn

Tom na Cruaich – towm n*a* **kroo**-Ych
A 'Chruach – *a* **chroo**-*a*ch
Beinn a'Chrùlaiste – bYn *a* **chroo**:lasht*ya*
Beinn Dronaig – bYn **dron***a*k

druim

Druim is a ridge, of spinal form. The word originally applied to the human back, and was transferred by bodily analogy to hill-ground as were many other parts of the anatomy. (See the chapter on The Body of the Land) Naturally, it is a very common word with over 700 occurences in its various manifestations as *druim*, *drum* and *drim*, and even a plural in **Na Drommanan*** in the northwest. It is commonest in the southern fringes of the Highlands, and the Perthshire area's *dromannan* gave their name to the clan Drummond via **Drummond Hill** on Tayside. There are few high examples of the genus – an exception being **Druim Shionnach*** (foxes' ridge) above Loch Cluanie – and the lower hills were often swallowed up by man's domain. Thus many settlements from Glasgow's Drumchapel to Edinburgh's Drum Brae bear the name.

dùn*

Dùn means a fortress or castle. The word used on a hill signifies the site of an old hill-fort of Iron Age times. It is believed there may have been nearly 1,500 such forts scattered up and down the southern and western coasts (the east coast plains didn't offer such good defensive positions.) So the apparently singular An Dùn near Oban (*the* fort) was hardly unique, except in the sense that almost all of them were, to the locals, An Dùn (as English speakers might say 'the hill' without using the specific name). There's another **An Dùn*** in the Grampians, with no record of a hill-fort on it, but which must rank as one of the finest natural defensive positions in the country. It's a 2700 feet (825m) top, dropping steeply on all sides by at least 1000 feet (300m), and stands apparently in the middle of one of the wide north-south Mounth passes, the land having been etched away on all sides by three streams and a loch. Perhaps all traces of a fort have gone, bar the name. But on many others the builders' rocks remain.

Often the *dùns* were vitrified forts where, it is believed, the rock rubble was fused together by great licking bonfires. A hill is a good point for both defence and observation, but you don't need to go all the way up to the highest contours to get these advantages. For instance, although the highest *dùn* is **Dùn Dà Gaoithe*** (fort of the two winds) on Mull, the summit lies some distance above the recognised site of its fort; and most *dùns* are lower, like nearby Iona's **Dùn Ì*** at 332 feet (101m).

Curiously the highest-known definite hill-fort site is not a *dùn*, but a hill in Sutherland called **Ben Griam Beg*** (1903 feet, 580m), little lichen-covered mountain; perhaps the local folk-memory had let it slip through to be caught

---

Druim Shionnach – drim **hinoch**

dùn – doo:n   An Dùn – *an* **doo:n**

Ben Griam Beg – b*Y*n gree*a*m **bayk**

Na Drommanan – n*a* **droman***a*n

Dùn Ì – doon **ee:**

Dùn dà Gaoithe – doon **daa** goe-eeh*a*

only by later archaeologists. Also in Sutherland **Druim Chuibhe***, site of an ancient defensive broch, is not a *dùn* but a *druim* (ridge, of the stronghold).

Dùn is found all over Scotland, in Norse areas like Raasay's **Dùn Cana*** (**Dùn Caan** on the O.S. map), and throughout the Gaelic west, as well as the Pictish east where are Dunedin (Dùn-Èideann, now Edinburgh's Castle Rock) and Dundee. In the South the word *dùn* often became *dum* before the letters 'b', 'm' or 'p' (because the 'm' made it easier to say), as in Dumbarton Rock (fort of the Britons) and **Dumyat*** above Stirling (*dùn miathi*, fort of the Miathi tribe, old enemies of the Romans). At the western edge of the Campsies are

Dumgoyne.

Dumgoyne (arrow fort) and **Dumgoyach**; while on the southern slopes of the range lies **Meikle Rieve***, Scots for big ancient fortress. Unlike the *dùns* it is not on a hilltop, but is protected from above by steep screes and treacherous cliffs. Even at the very south-east limits of Gaelic we find the word appearing in the Lammermuirs in **Doon Hill,** for on top are the faint remains of a 7th-century palisaded palace of Angle kings. Some of the *dùn* names hark back to distant legends. Near Loch Ness are **Dunchea Hill,** from Cè, a legendary Pictish figure, and **Dùn Dearduill***, maybe from Deirdre, whose love affair with Naoise led to them being chased across the Highlands – there's another **Dùn Deardail** fort near Ben Nevis. Kintyre is an area rich in legended ridges,

---

Druim Chuibhe – drim **ch**Y*ve*	Dùn Cana – doon kan*a*
Dumyat – doom**Y**at	
Meikle Rieve – **meekil ree:**v	Dùn Dearduill – doo:n **dyerdeel**[y]

like **Dùn a'Chaisteil***, fortress castle and **Dùn a'Bhuilg***, quiver fort. And **Dùn a'Choin Dhuibhe***, fort of the black dog, is where a chief's huge black wolfhound gamely held attackers at bay while help was sent for.

gailbhinn*

A great rough hill. This word is the root of **Gelvin** hill near Crook of Devon in Fife, and possibly the western Munro **Gulvain***, which certainly fits the description better than the alternative name of **Gaor Bheinn**, filth mountain. However the apparently similar **Ben Gulabin** in Glenshee, formerly known as Ben Gulvin (in an ancient poem it was ". . . great Ben Gulbin's grassy height") is altogether different. It has been suggested that it may come from *gulban*, a beak, or the derivative *guilbneach*, a curlew (the 'beaked bird'). However, this name **Ben Gulbin** appears in several localities and signifies an association with the legendary Fingalian heroes: Ben Gulbin is the old name of Beinn Tianavaig in Skye, there's a **Ben Gullipen** near Callander, a **Beinn a'Ghuilbein** near Garve, and a **Beinn Chuilbin** near Aviemore. All these hills are reputed to be places where Fingalian hunter Diarmaid, his lover Grainne, and their two hounds lie buried on the slopes. And since they hunted the boar (*torc* in Gaelic), there's often a boar name nearby, for instance Brig o'Turk near Callander, **Càrn an Tuirc** at Glenshee, and a **Loch an Tuirc** on the very shoulder of the Garve hill.

grianan

This means a sunny hillock, a name found in several Highland spots. One example, **An Grianan*** high above Glen Lyon, sits on a sunny south-facing shoulder of Stùchd on Lochain, providing the perfect belvedere for a cattleherd.

Stob Grianan in Glen Etive was supposedly the bower of the legendary Deirdre, lover of Naoise. It was the spot where she dwelt in happiness before being tricked away to her fate in Ireland. In her farewell lament she speaks wistfully of ". . . flocks of sunbeams crowd thy fold".

leac, leacann

This means a large flat stone, from a bare rock on a hillside to a bare hilltop. Stonehaven's **Leachie Hill** is from this word, and **Creag Leacach*** above Glenshee, while **An Leacainn*** by Inverness is from the related *leacann*, the broad (slabby) side of a hill.

Creag Leacach – krayk **lyech**koch
Dùn a'Chaisteil – doon *a* **chash**ty*a*l
Dùn a'Bhuilg – doon *a* **vool**k
Dùn a'Choin Dhuibhe – doon *a* choyn **ghoey***a*   gailbhinn – **gala**veen[y]
Gulvain – **gool***a*van   Beinn a'Ghuilbhein – b**Yn** *a* **goola**vyn
An Grianan – *a*n **gree-***a*nan   An Leacainn – *a*n **lyech**kYn[y]

leitir

A slope – often running down to the water's edge (hence *leth-tìr*, half-land) – this often appears in settlement names like Letterewe, as well as in hill-names like **An Leitir*** (the slope) near Sligachan in Skye where the hill takes the form of an evenly-rising slope tapering to a broad ridge; the slope on this one *is* the hill. The Ladder Hills feeding the upper Don are possibly from this word too. The similar-looking but unrelated word *leathad* also means a slope, and the well-known peak **Clachlet** above Rannoch Moor is *clach leathad*, the stone of the slope.

màm

This, the word for a breast, has moved from anatomy to topography to describe a round hill of breast-like form. Found all over the Highlands, it lies especially down the western seaboard area between Mull and Skye. (It is fully discussed in the chapter on the Body of the Land). Màm can also apply to a pass in the hills, as in Màm Ratagan on the road to Glenelg, probably from the shape of the saddle between two breasts.

maol*

Like *màm*, *maol* has moved from body to hill. It means bald head. Peaks like **Maol Cheann-Dearg***† (the bald red head) in Torridon are very well-named steep-sided flat-topped lumps where the vegetation straggles to survive on top. **A'Mhaoile** in Sleat is simply the bald one, or blunt one. A related word *maoilean* means either a bald person or the bleak brow of a hill, as in **Na Maoilean*** near Oban and the Munro called **Maoile Lunndaidh**.*

meall

Mealls have a bad press. One Gaelic dictionary defines them as 'lumps, or knobs', another source as 'heaps, hills, eminences or mounds'. The word can apply indeed not just to hills but also to banks of clouds, swellings in general and even to buttocks! Skye author Alexander Forbes goes so far as to refer to Meall hills as 'heaps, or almost shapeless lumps'.

Certainly, half of the Munro Mealls are in Perthshire where the hills often have the lumpy bumpiness of middle age – these and the uninspiring but ski-famous **Meall Odhar*** at Glenshee are enough to give a *meall* a dull name. But what about the **Meall Garbh*** (rough hill) on Ben Lawers plunging down hundreds of cliff-metres into the depths of Lochan nan Cat, or Aonach

---

An Leitir – *an* **lyay**tyeer   maol – moe:l
Maol Cheann Dearg – moel chy*an* **dy**erek
Na Maoilean – n*a* **moe**-eelan
Meall Odhar – myowl **oa**ar   Maoile Lunndaidh – moel*a* **loon**dee
   Meall Garbh – myowl **g**arav

Eagach's rocky ridge which ends on the craggy **Meall Dearg**[*]? And whilst Glen Lyon's **Meall Buidhe**[*] (yellow hill) is truly a grassy lump, Knoydart's **Meall Buidhe** is a bare rocky mass with grass struggling in crevices to survive like late spring snow. So the charge against *meall* that it is a 'lump' that lowers the tone of Scotland's mountains must, on the evidence, be found 'not proven'.

What is true is that a *meall* alongside a *beinn* is a hill amongst mountains, lower in height. There are nearly as many *mealls* in Scotland as there are *beinns* – approximately a thousand – yet *beinns* outnumber them nearly three to one among the higher peaks as listed in the Munro and Corbett tables. In the top hundred mountains there are only four **mealls,** and the highest (Meall Garbh of Ben Lawers) is 33rd in the rankings, against nearly thirty *beinns* and their top two spots. Outside of its Perthshire heartland most *mealls* are lowly hills, but common enough except in the old Viking areas of the north and in the islands of the west: here it seems to be substituted by the similar word *maol*, a 'great, bare, rounded hill', and *mòl* in Lewis. (This word has a Welsh cousin *moel*, as in Moel Ysgyfarnogod in the Rhinogs – besides which Gaelic names like Maol a'Bhàird (hill of the bard) seem easy to pronounce!) Some corrupted hill-names in the south-west and north-east such as **Meaul, Millbawn** and **Milldown** probably come from the same ancestry, while **Mull of Miljoan** hill near Girvan should probably be the meall of Milton, the hamlet at its foot.

monadh

This is a very old word meaning mountain. It comes from the same linguistic root as Welsh *mynydd*, Breton *menez*, Latin *mons* and mountain itself. Sadly in Scotland it has fallen from grace for is used in modern Gaelic to indicate simply dry upland moorland (contrasting with wet boggy *mòinteach*). At one point in the past, about thirteen centuries ago, Monadh referred to the entire Highland area. A ruler who died in 560 AD was described as the King of Monadh, and there are references in literature to Sliabh Monadh and Monadh Druim-uchdair, mountain of the high ridge (now Drumochter). Gradually the word's application was focussed down on more specific locations, often plateaux or mountain blocks. In the south-west we find **Monadh Leacach**[*] (slabby) near Inveraray, once described as:

> ". . . verie dangerous to travel in time of evil stormy weather, in winter especiallie, for it is ane high Mountaine"

Other "high mountaines" include **Am Monadh Dubh**[*] above Rannoch Moor, now literally translated as The Blackmount. Other hues show up in **Monadh Bàn**[*] (white) and **Monadh Gorm**[*] (blue) west of Loch Lochy, and the

---

Meall Dearg – myowl **dyer**ak   Meall Buidhe – myowl **booy**a
Monadh Leacach – mon*agh* **lyech**koch   Am Monadh Dubh – *a*m mon*agh* **doo**
Monadh Bàn – mon*agh* **baan**   Monadh Gorm – mon*agh* **gor**om

Monadh Liath*, **Monadh Mor*** and **Monadh Ruadh***, the grey, big and red *monadhs* on either side of the Spey Valley. Interestingly there is no mass duplication of the colours in the way that there are many examples of Càrn Gorm or Meall Buidhe, for instance. This might suggest that the *Monadh* blocks were originally named to distinguish different masses within the whole Highland chain, whereas later 'coloured' peaks picked out local variations, and underlines the fact that *monadh* referred to sizeable blocks of hill country – the word might best be translated, in its original form, as 'mountain-land'.

Later the word seems to have been diluted, applying either to mere shoulders of a hill like **Monadh Odhar*** (dun-coloured) in Glen Artney. In the Loch Arkaig region there are four *monadhs* all referring to the shoulders of hills, **Monadh Gorm, Beag, Ceann-arcaig** and **Uisge Mhuilinn** – respectively blue, small, end of Arkaig, and mill-stream (properly *Uisg' a'Mhuilinn*).

To the east and south the word *monadh* became anglicised, into mounth, mont, mond or mon. The plateau south of Lochnagar is **The Mounth,** and there's another area of this name north of Inverness. Scotland's most easterly Munro is **Mount Keen** (from *caoin*, gentle) and out on the eastern Buchan lowlands are fishermen's landmark **Mormond Hill** (*mòr-mhonadh*, big *monadh*), and **Fourman Hill** near Huntly, from *fuar mhonadh*, cold *monadh* – where the snow lies late. **Monameanach** Hill near Glen Shee is *monadh meadhonach*, the middle mountain. And there are many other Mounts, Monds, and Monts, like **Dechmont** hill (*deagh mhonadh*, fine *monadh*), all from this root.

mullach

Mullach means a height or summit, usually inferring a rather undistinguished top at the highest part above some more interesting feature. Most of the high *mullachs* are 'tops' rather than separate Munros – **Mullach nan Coirean** (summit of the corries) being an exception – their full names often referring to a corrie or slope at whose head they stand. **Mullach Coire Mhic Fhearchair*** (Farquhar's corrie) and **Mullach an Rathain*** (pulleys) in Torridon, **Mullach Fraoch-choire*** (heathery corrie) and **Mullach Lochan nan Gobhar*** (goats' lochan) are examples of this. The mass of *mullachs* are spread down the western seaboard of the Highlands, and this mainland pattern is mirrored in others on the islands from Arran to Harris, and as far out as St. Kilda's Mullach Bì. In the far south-west is **Three Mullach Hill,** a partial translation of an older Gaelic name.

Monadh Liath – mon*agh* **lyee**-u   Monadh Mòr – mon*agh* **moa:r**

Monadh Ruadh – mon*agh* **roo**-*agh*   Monadh Odhar – mon*agh* **oa**ar

Mullach Coire Mhic Fhearchair – mooloch **kora** veechk era*char*ʸ

Mullach an Rathain – mooloch *an* **rahan**ʸ

Mullach Fraoch-choire – mooloch **froe:ch** cho*ra*

Mullach Lochan nan Gobhar – mooloch lochan n*an* **gowar**

òrd

An *ord* (genitive form *ùird*) is in Gaelic a hammer, but also a steep rounded hill (of comparable shape), usually not very high. More often it is applied to an area of ground with morainic hummocks, rather than to individual hills – The Ords in Shetland and Muir of Ord near Inverness suggest this. The **Ord of Kessock** at 633 feet (193m) overlooking the A9 road bridge is the site of a large Stone Age fort. In Angus, **Ordies Hill** is *òrd deas*, southern hill: this name indicates what the location of other *òrds* show, that they are often near boundaries. In the Borders the word *urd*, as in **Ladyurd Hill, Lochurd Hill** and others, may well be related: for while these hills, near Blyth Bridge, may be named after farms at their feet, the farms in turn may well have been named after the knobbly hills near them. Their connection with Gaelic *òrd* is underlined by the fact that there are a couple of hills within a mile or two whose names appear to be translations of its other meaning, such as **Hammer Head** above Broughton.

ploc

A *ploc* (or *pluc* – pronounced ploochk) means a small lump, or plug – and every schoolboy knows what a 'plook' is! Above the confluence of the rivers Findhorn and Mazeran stands **Ploc Mòr⃰** (big), but better known is **Am Ploc** (the lump) above the picture postcard village of Plockton. Originally a *ploc* was a lump of earth, or clod. Equally expressive is **Am Bulg⃰** in Angus from *bulg*, a bulge or belly.

sàil⃰

Sáil means a heel of a hill. This is detailed in the chapter on the Body of the Land.

sgàirneach

Sgàirneach means a quarry, a scree, or stony hillside, or even the sound of falling stones, and is applied to hills by way of comparison, as in **Sgàirneach Mhòr⃰** above Drumochter.

sgòr, sgòrr

Sgòrs are found mainly in the eastern Grampians, where it indicates a rocky-topped hill. *Sgòr* is sometimes used interchangeably with *sgòrr* or even with *sgùrr* (to which it is closely related) in maps and books, but a Gaelic dictionary says that a *sgòr* sometimes has the nuance of a rock cleft or notch. (Indeed there is a similar Scots word *skur* meaning a cleft or chasm in a rock.) **Sgòr na h-Ulaidh⃰** above Glen Coe has a deep gully cleaving its northern face right to

---

Ploc Mòr – plochk **moa:r**   Am Bulg – *a*m **bool***a*k   sàil – saal
Sgàirneach Mhòr – skaarnyoch **voa:r**   Sgòr na h-Ulaidh – skor n*a* **hoolee**

the summit. The Cairngorm's **Sgòr Gaoith***, windy peak, above Loch Einich stands at the head of a deeply seamed granite rock face. It can also mean simply a sharp steep hill, or a little height upon another mountain.

sgoran

A 1988 issue of *High* magazine carried a fine story of a winter expedition above Loch Einich under the intriguing sub-title "What is a Sgoran?" . . . but furnished no answers to the question! The answer is that it is the diminutive form of *sgòr*, suggesting a little rock or tor, and is found mainly in the eastern Highlands. **Sgoran Dubh Mòr*** above Loch Einich is the big dark *sgoran* and has a summit granite tor, and there is an **An Sgoran*** near Cromdale on the eastern flanks of the Cairngorms. On Ben Rinnes above Dufftown three granite tors around the top are called the Scurran – the **Scurran of Wells**, of **Morinsh** and of **Lochterlandoch** – obviously a local dialect word for *sgoran* and signifying a tor or rock on a hill (the 'sg' of Gaelic is pronounced 'sk'). As one John Brown, shepherd, explained to the local Round Table in 1873:

> "I had thocht mony a time about that mysel fin' I wis herdin sheep and lookin
> at the scurrans o' the hillheid. The top o' the mountain has been worn down by
> the weather leaving this scurran as a remnant."

There is also a related word *sgoraban*, small pointed rock, found mainly in Wester Ross.

sgùrr*

A Gaelic dictionary tells us that a *sgùrr* is 'a large conical hill'. One description in a walkers' magazine, of a traverse of the switchbacking Mamores range, praises its peaks as 'real Sgurrs', implying a sterner test of mountaineering than is offered by mere *beinns*. And on Skye the Cuillin ridge, rockiest mountain range in Scotland, is dominated by *sgùrrs*, with nine of the ridge's ten Munros. This might suggest that a *sgùrr* is a "mountain's mountain" while a *beinn* is of more pedestrian character. And there is a general belief among walkers that a *sgùrr* is a jagged rocky peak (like a German *horn*) while a *beinn* is more rounded, if higher. The savage sharpness of any *sgùrr* in the Cuillins contrasted with the broad shoulders of Ben Nevis seen from the south provide the stereotypes by which others are judged.

Sgùrrs are confined mainly to the west of the Great Glen, excluding the far north, and to Skye. A few also lie east of the Great Glen in Lochaber – in the Grey Corries, the Mamores and by Ballachulish – within a few miles of Ben Nevis. In the west, and in Lochaber, steep-sided narrow ridges run westwards to the Atlantic whose sea-lochs bite deep into the land. To the east where

---

Sgòr Gaoith – skor **goe-ee**   Sgoran Dubh Mòr – skoran doo **moa:r**
An Sgoran – *a*n **skoran**   sgùrr – skoo:r

there are no *sgùrrs*, the land is by contrast a great rolling plateau, most obvious in the Cairngorms. The overall pattern seems to confirm the idea of youthful thrusting sgùrrs compared with round-shouldered old beinns.

The case for *sgùrr* as a hard rocky peak is well presented by Gaelic poet Sorley Maclean in his paean to Sgùrr nan Gillean in the Cuillins:

> ". . . Ach Sgùrra nan Gillean sgùrr as fheàrr dhiubh,
> An sgùrra gorm-dhubh craosach làidir,
> An sgùrra gallanach caol cràcach,
> An sgùrr iargalta mòr gàbhaidh,
> An sgùrra Sgitheanach thar chàich dhiubh."

> ". . . Sgùrr nan Gillean the best Sgùrr of them,
> The blue-blacked gape-mouthed strong sgùrr,
> The sapling slender horned sgùrr,
> The forbidding great sgùrr of danger,
> The sgùrr of Skye above the rest of them."

Sgùrr nan Gillean

Sgùrr appears therefore to be a word of the clans of the west. Perhaps they sculpted it from the Old Norse word *sker*, a rock, as in skerry (a sea-submerged rock) or the related Gaelic *sgeir*. Like a primeval creature it may have crawled from the ocean onto the land and developed there: after all, the word *cleit* in Uist means a sea-rock, while in Lewis it is a rocky hill. (In Islay i‏ even means a healing rock with a hole in it!) Or perhaps its specifically Scottish roots lie on the island of Eigg, just off the west coast near Mallaig. This isle, once part of the Norse-controlled northern Hebrides, is dominated by a giant molar of basalt rising almost vertically from the ocean to 390 metres (1300 feet) at its southern lip. Known as **An Sgùrr** (*the sgùrr*) or as the **Scùrr**

of Eigg, it may very well come from the Norse word *sguvr* or *score* – appearing also in the Uist hill **Scurrival** – meaning an edge or cliff (and related to the English scar and Scots scaur). The distinctive name of this striking peak, An Sgùrr (the definite article 'the' indicates its importance) may then have been adopted by the western seaboard Gaels who took it up to name the rocky conical peaks typical of the west. Within sight of Eigg's Sgùrr are the *sgùrr* peaks of the Skye Cuillin, and on the mainland the striking rocky cone of **Sgùrr na Cìche,** as well as many others.

The aptness of the word led to its adoption right across to the Lochaber area, but its spread further east and south was stymied by the generally rounder peaks there and the inertia of the established word *beinn*. *Sgòrr* is an alternative spelling of *sgùrr* in Lochaber (such as **Sgòrr Dhonuil** above Ballachulish), and even on the isle of Rhum just beside Eigg. There's a diminutive, **An Sgùrran,** the little *sgùrr*, in Skye.

Sgùrr's failure to be widely adopted into Scots (apart from the rare word *skur*, a gashed rock outcrop), unlike other Gaelic words like *beinn*, *gleann* and *càrn*, may be due mainly to its failure to reach the southern Highlands, the contact zone with the Scots lowlands.

sìdhean, sìthean

Usually spelt *sìdhean* (or *sìdh*) inland and in the south, and *sìthean* in the north and on Skye, it is prounounced, 'shee:han'. It means a fairy hill, or one shaped that way. The air of Celtic folklore is thick with fairies good and bad – indeed fairies were often known simply as 'the people of the hollow hills' – and there are as a result numerous small hills throughout Gaeldom called *sìthean*. For instance two knolls known simply as **Sìthean** lie by Loch Morlich, reputed to be the home of Dòmhnull Mòr, King of the Fairies, who once did the locals a good turn by driving away some unwelcome outsiders. Another **Sìthean** near Bernera in Lewis was reputedly a hill where lived fairies who borrowed the locals' pots and pans on a rather careless basis. One angry housewife, seeking her pans, walked into the hill by a door which appeared on its side, and was pursued home by a fairy dog for her pains. In Argyll **Cnocan Sìthean** is known as "Crockiver's Fairy Hill", and its legend that an old chief was buried on top was confirmed by excavations last century – he was probably the 'Ivor' whose Gaelic name was in this Cnoc Iomhair.

Usually *sìthean* conform to the nursery image of little knolls – like the glacial sand hummocks that give Glen Shee its name – but **Sìthean Mòr** (big fairy hill) at 403 feet (123m) on Handa might suggest big fairies. Bigger still however are Strathyre's 1871 foot (570m) **Beinn an t-Sìthein,** Loch Monar's **An Sìdhean** at 2661 feet (814m), the 2864 feet (873m) **Ben Hee** in the north-

---

Sgùrr na Cìche – skoor n*a* **kee:**cha   Sgòrr Dhonuil – skor **ghawil**ʸ
An Sgùrran – *a*n **skoo:**ran
Sìthean Mòr – shee:-han **moa:r**   Beinn an t-Sìthein – bYn *a*n **tshee:**hin
An Sìdhean – *a*n **shee:**-han

west, and finally **Schiehallion*** (fairy hill of the Caledonians), a Perthshire Munro. **Ben Tee** near Loch Ness may be from *tigh*, a house, but it is probably *beinn an t-sìthein*, because it has a very sharp cone shape, especially from the west. In giving these names the shape or outline was of course more important than the occupants!

sliabh

Pronounced 'shlee-uv' (as in the modern Irish hill-word *slieve*), this Old Irish Gaelic name meaning mountain or extensive tract of moorland, never really caught on in Scotland. Most *sliabhs* are found in the south-west, often within view of the Emerald Isle. Nearest landfall Machrihanish is overlooked by **The Slate** hill, a plausible derivation. **Sliabh Gaoil*** (hill of love) is in Kintyre, (its story is told in chapter 11) and there are many in Galloway, sometimes anglicised to *slew*. Interestingly, most of the few *sliabh* names outwith the south-west are on upper Speyside, a geographical leapfrog away, hills like **Sliabh Loraich*** – from *lorgach*, extensive – which refers to a hill slope rather than to a top, for nearby a low summit is called **Cnoc an t-Slèibh***. There may well be a connection with Irishman St. Columba who founded a chapel at Ruthven near Kingussie, and whose men may have brought hill-words as well as the new religion from the south-west to this locality. The rare adjective *sléibhteach*, mountainous, may be the root of **Sleiteachal Mhòr*** in Lewis.

socach*

A snout, this is detailed in the chapter on the Body of the Land.

spìc*

A *spìc* is a spike of rock.

spidean

A word of the north-west – where it may be a dialect version of *bidein* – it usually applies to points above distinctive features, like corries. Torridon's Liathach mountain has **Spidean a'Choire Lèithe*** (grey corrie) and neighbouring Beinn Eighe has **Spidean Coire nan Clach*** (stony corrie). **Spidean Mialach*** above Loch Quoich appears to translate as the lousy *spidean* (in the strictly biological sense!), although originally in Gaelic it meant animals in general, here perhaps referring to deer.

There's an old Highland game "spidean", similar to pitch and toss, in which a small stick called a *spid* is placed in the ground for the players to throw at: this 'spiky' image is the one used for the hill-name.

Sliabh Gaoil – shlee-uv **goe-eel**   Sliabh Loraich – shlee:uv **loreech**
Cnoc an t-Slèibh – krochk *a*n **tlay:v**   Sleiteachal Mhòr – slaytochal **voa:r**
spìc – spee:chk   Spidean a'Choire Lèithe – speedyan *a* chor*a* **lyay:**h*a*
Spidean Coire nan Clach – speedyan kor*a* n*a*n **klach**   socach – **soch**koch
Spidean Mialach – speetyan **mee**-aloch   Schiehallion – shee**hal**y*a*n

sròn*

Sròn is a nose, another word that has moved from anatomy to landscape. It is detailed in the chapter on the Body of the Land.

stac

A relatively uncommon hill-name confined largely to the north-west on account of its Norse origin and famed because of the spectacular hill of **Stac Pollaidh***, the stack at the pool, often anglicised as Stack Polly. (**Beinn Stack** near Kylesku is another case of the word being anglicised on the map). To the Vikings *stakkr* mant steep or precipitous, and was applied to sea 'stacks' like St. Kilda's Stac Lee (*stakkr hlìdh*, sloping steep rock) as well as to hills. To the Gaels it meant steep, columnar rock formations – such as compose Stac Pollaidh's stunning pinnacled ridge – or a steep conical hill like **An Stac** in the west. The name of the hill called the **Stack of Glencoul** is a mapmakers' anglicisation; local Gaelic, even in translation, had no such name, for them it was simply the local *stac* without need of qualification. In the north there are several hills called **Ruadh Stac** (red steep hill), while **Ruadh Stac Mòr*** (big red steep hill) in the Fisherfield Forest has recently been elevated to full Munro status.

stob

This mountain-word leads a double life east and west. Literally meaning a short stick or upright post (in Gaelic and in Scots), it rings with the English 'stub', and in the hills can aptly suggest a short stubby top. Thus in the east, in the Cairngorms, a *stob* often crowns the highest point above a corrie bowl like a skelf on a roughly-cut thumbnail, as in **Stob Coire an Lochain***. In the west however a *stob* is a peak, not a mere point: Lochaber, home of many *sgùrrs*, also boasts a fine chain of *stobs* that make up the Grey Corries range, as well as those which blacken the setting sun from Rannoch Moor, like **Stob Ghabhar*** (goat peak), **Stob Dearg*** and **Stob Dubh***, the red and black peaks (now known as the Buachailles). Nearly two-thirds of the high *stobs* – and there are a very few lower ones – lie in Lochaber, and they usually have full Munro status, whereas their eastern cousins in the Cairngorms are normally mere subsidiary tops of larger mountains. Above Balquhidder is a simple **The Stob,** part of a group clustered round Stobinian (or Stob Binnein).

streap*

A verbal noun meaning the act of climbing or scaling – or simply a climb –

---

sròn – strawn   Stac Pollaidh – stachk **polee**
Ruadh Stac Mòr – rooagh stachk **moa:r**
Stob Coire an Lochain – stob kora an **loch**Yn^y
Stob Ghabhar – stob **ghow**ar   Stob Dearg – stob **dyer**ak
Stob Dubh – stob **doo**   Streap – strehp

this is a nicely expressive description of the steep **Streap** hill above Strathan in the far west.

stùc

Stùc means pinnacle or steep conical hill, or a projecting hill steep on one side and rounded on the other, and appears to be related to the Old Norse word *stac*. Unlike *stac* however *stùc* is found all over the Highlands, from **An Stùc**[*] (the *stùc*) near Ledmore junction in the far north-west to another steep hill of the same name in the Ben Lawers chain in the south. Probably the best-known *stùc*, by sight, if not by name, is **Stùc a'Chroin**[*] (hill of the sheepfold) lying near the southern edge of the Highlands and thus visible over a wide area of the central belt of Scotland.

Similar words *stuaic* (a projecting rounded hillock), *stuic* (the anglicised form – as in **The Stuic** on Lochnagar) – and *stùcan* (the diminutive) are all related cousins. But while *stoc* differs by only one letter there is no connection: the hill **An Stoc-bheinn**[*] by Lairg probably means the tree-trunk hill.

Stùchd is another form of *stùc*, according to a Gaelic dictionary, although its dozen examples are geographically confined to the southern edge of the Highlands, and tend to be distinctive in shape with flat-topped summits. The *stùchd* spelling may on the other hand simply reflect the spelling peccadilloes of the original O.S. surveyor in this area. The Perthshire mountain **Stùchd an Lochain**[*] (affectionately known as the Stui) has a flat summit ridge scooped around a splendid corrie lochan down to which it throws grassy gullies and rocky ribs. Further south **An Stuichd**[*] is a flat-topped shoulder south of Loch Voil, and there's an **An Stùchd** in Kintyre. One Gaelic dictionary says that a *stùchd* is "a little hill jutting out from a greater one, steep on one side and rounded on the other" . . . but Stùchd an Lochain can hardly be described as that, since it is the highest in its chain.

suidhe

A seat. The concept is best expressed in Arran's rocky bower **Suidhe Fheargais**[*], Fergus' seat (its story is told in chapter 9, under Arran). There are **An Suidhe**[*] hills above Inveraray and on Speyside, but the most photographed yet unrecognised must surely be **Meall an t-Suidhe**[*], hill of the seat, the mere 2300 feet (700m) flank of Ben Nevis above Fort William. It is sometimes spelt in anglicised form (roughly as it is pronounced) Melantee Hill. High above Applecross, **Carn an t-Suidhe** is said to be where Saint Maelrubha's body lay, while his pall-bearers rested, on his last journey from Loch Maree to the sacred burial ground below; bed or bier rather than seat being the meaning here.

An Stùc – *an* **stoo:chk**	Stùc a'Chroin – stoo:chk *a* **chro-an**[y]
Stuchd an Lochain – stoo:chk *an* lochain	An Stoc-bheinn – *an* **stochk** vYn
An Stùichd – *an* **stoo:chk**	Suidhe Fheargais – sooy*a* e**rageesh**
An Suidhe – *an* **sooya**	Meall an t-Suidhe – myowl *an* **tooya**

Suidh' Fhinn[*] in Skye, a knoll on the shoulder of **Beinn na Grèine** (mountain of the sun) above Portree, is where Fingal sat to watch his Fionn warriors hunting in Glen Varragill below. Above Tarbert, **Cnoc an Suidhe** (properly *Cnoc an t-Suidhe*) was the 'council hill' where justice was dispensed, and people even condemned to death – here the 'seat' was the seat of justice. In the east the word has become Suie, as in **Suie Hill** in Grampian Region.

tiompan[*]

Tiompan is a rounded one-sided hillock: it is probably of Norse origin. The word also means a musical instrument. The Clach an Tiompain (stone of the lyre) near Strathpeffer was so-called because when struck it made a hollow sound. It featured in a prophecy of Còinneach Odhar, the Brahan Seer, that one day the sea would flood the land so that ships could ride anchored to the stone!

tom

Of Irish origin, it initially meant a copse of woodland, and this is the meaning it had in south-west Scotland, its original beachhead. But as it marched Birnam-style across the country it changed to mean a hillock or knoll – perhaps because it was often only on agriculturally-useless hillocks that trees were left standing. Mere knoll it may have been, but it has several Munros to its credit: the summit of **Tom Buidhe**[*] (yellow knoll) at 3140 feet (940m) above Glen Doll is a gentle hillock barely noticeable amidst the wide plateau of the Mounth. But by the time it reached the far north it took on still grander forms like **Tom na Gruagaich**[*], the first mighty summit of Beinn Alligin above Loch Torridon. The intriguing **Naked Tom** hill near Forfar is a partial translation of *tom nocht*; and the several hills of the south-east called **Corum** are from *corr-thom*, pointed knoll. The word is found all over the Highlands except in the south-west where the original sylvan meaning was retained, although the low hill in Inverness city **Tomnahurich**[*], *Tom na h-Iùbhraich*, hill of the yew-tree, might suggest that the 'tree-roots' remained. This hill is also known as **Tom nan Sìthichean,** knoll of the fairies, and the Brahan Seer had prophesied that the day would come when the hill would be under lock and key to stop the fairies doing their mischief: and, indeed, long after his death, this hill became the city's cemetery, protected by a fence and a padlocked gate.

Suidh' Fhinn – sooy **een**[y]   tiompan – **tyowm**pan

Tom Buidhe – towm **booy**a   Tom na Gruagaich – towm n*a* **groo-***a*geech

Tomnahurich – Gaelic: Tom na h-Iùbhraich – towm n*a* **hyoo:**reech

tòrr

In Gaelic, or in the Scots versions 'tor' or 'tore', this is a mound or a low conical hill, as **The Tor** above Loch Alvie clearly shows. In distant Cornwall, the virtually-extinct Celtic language had the word *tor* for the granite rocks that outcropped on the great moors, like Wild Tor on Dartmoor. Both languages may have taken their inspiration from the Latin *turris*, a tower, but it was the Cornish version which won its place in the English language to the extent that the granite outcrops of the Cairngorms are often referred to as the tors – of Ben Avon, etc. – even though there is a Gaelic word *bad* for these features. Among Gaelic speakers the word was used mainly for lower hills, such as **An Torr** at 613 feet (187m) above Loch Caolisport, or **Tore Hill** above Boat of Garten. Above the village of Pennan, made famous by the film *Local Hero* is the Tor of Troup, which topples over in big cliffs into the North Sea.

The *tòrr* hills are thickest on the ground in the south-west and the west coast up to Skye, becoming fewer in number moving inland towards Inverness. Indeed apart from some overlap near the Great Glen the names *tòrr* and *tom* are almost mutually exclusive.

tolm

A rounded hill, or a knoll, deriving like *tulach* from the root *tul*, a hillock. **Sgùrr Thuilm*** (the genitive form) near Glenfinnan is distinctive in outline, for it is far less rocky or pointed than its neighbours, and has the gentler shape of a lowland hill. On the other hand the Skye Sgùrr Thuilm is a more pointed peak, with scree slopes, but compared to its rugged Cuillin neighbours it offers, as one guidebook says, an 'easy walk back to the valley'.

There is a tradition that tulmen hills (from the Gaelic diminutive *tolman*, plural *tolmain*) were knolls concealing fairy palaces that resounded to continuous revelry, pre-modern disco palaces!

tulach*

The word *tulach* means a hillock, a knoll, or a 'little green eminence'. Obviously it applies mainly to lower hills, but it is featured in **Beinn Tulaichean***, a Munro above Loch Voil, a summit ringed by small crags and boulders. Because it is mainly a word of lower ground, particularly in the south, it has suffered the same fate as *bàrr* and *àirde* – swallowed up into settlement names (as in Tulliallan or Tillicoultry), corrupted by non-Gaelic speakers (as in the Touch Hills south-west of Stirling), and having to carry a tautological translation as in Brechin's **Tullo Hill**, Blair Atholl's **Tulach Hill** or Tayside's **Tulich Hill** (all meaning 'hill hill'). It is found almost entirely in the southern and eastern fringes of the Highlands on lower hills, apart from a

---

Sgùrr Thuilm – skoor **hool**am   tulach – **too**loch
Beinn Tulaichean – bYn **too**leech*a*n

46

few specimens in Easter Ross. Professor W.J. Watson suggests that it is a substitute for the south-west's *bàrr*, for low hills, north of the Forth-Clyde area.

uchd*

Uchd can mean a bosom or breast, and by bodily analogy the face of a hill. (See chapter on Body of the Land).

Chapter Four

The Ranges

Hills, like people, all have individual names. Some are also better known as members of a group, or range. But what makes a 'range' in Scotland? Is Ben Lawers a simple mountain as its name implies, or a range, with its six Munros, each with separate names? Are the Five Sisters of Kintail a range, as their English name suggests, or a single mountain as the Gaelic name Beinn Mhòr (big mountain) suggests?

Indeed the Five Sisters, or Beinn Mhòr, gives us a clue to the use of a "range" term, for most of the range names seem to have been given by English speakers, not Gaels. The densest collection of range names is, as the map shows, in the south and east of Scotland, where Gaelic was weakest; and even where Gaelic is the foundation of the range name, as in the Cairngorms or Mamores, the plural form is entirely English, or is a translation of a singular Gaelic term, as in The Blackmount for Am Monadh Dubh. It is also very striking that in the dense mountain areas of the north and west Highlands, beyond the Great Glen, there are hardly any range names at all apart from the English 'Five Sisters' and the newly-coined 'Torridons', used in books. The ancient name for the main watershed, Druim Alban (the ridge of Scotland) is no longer used, but it too was singular. This suggests that it was English and Scots speakers who brought the idea, and thus the names, of ranges. One of the earliest attempts to identify 'ranges' was by English-speaking map-maker Dorret, who in 1750 "identified" such now-lost ranges as the Cuinak Hills (Quinag), and – in the Mounth – the Scairsoch Mountains (An Sgarsoch), the Minigeg Mountains and the Mountains of Benchichins (Lochnagar, formerly Beinn nan Cìochan)!

Like the very terms 'hill' and 'mountain' the term 'ranges' is variously applied: as criterion of 'range' we will accept the existence of a name implying a plural, like 'The ----s' or 'The ----- Hills', and also those names that imply a group like The Blackmount, or Argyll's Bowling Green. We indeed begin our ABC of Scots ranges with this latter ABG!

Argyll's Bowling Green
This name is not on the O.S. map, but is well-known amongst locals and walkers. Travellers on the West Highland Railway edging along above Loch

Cromalt Hills

Fannaichs

Torridons

Cuillin

Five Sisters of Kintail

Cuillin of Rum

Hills of Cromdale

Convals

Monadh Liath

Kincardine Hills

Lodder Hills

Cairngorms

Coreen Hills

Grey Corries

Easains

Mamores

Grampians

Coyles of Muick

Mounth

Black Mount

Sidlaws

Formont Hills

Arrochar Alps

Trossachs

Lomond Hills

Ochils

Touch Hills

Cleish Hills

Cullaloes

Campsies

Kilpatricks

Paps of Jura

Renfrew Heights

Pentlands

Braids

Moorfoots

Lammermuirs

Leadhills

Uplands

Eildons

Southern

Lowthers

Minto Hills

Cheviots

Minnigaffs

Rhinns

Long look west to a knobbly peninsula between lochs Long and Goil, a ruckled piece of land. The inappropriateness of the soubriquet Bowling Green to such a spot is in the Scots' tradition of self-deprecating humour, like the equally famous and unmapped Highlanders' Umbrella (the railway bridge over Argyle Street in Glasgow). Names lying within it include **Clach Bheinn*** (stony peak), the simple **Garbh*** (rough) and **Tom Molach*** (rough hill). Irony may have been the origin of the current name – it is of less than 200 years vintage – but it probably had a straightforward Gaelic origin in *Buaile a'Ghrianain*, cattlefold of the sunny hillock, *grianan* being a fairly common Gaelic hill-name; the whole area of course belonged to the Duke of Argyll. The name, in its English corruption, originally applied to a spot on the drier eastern slopes of Saddle hill, but now applies to the whole area.

Many miles north, the summit of Beinn Tee (west of the Great Glen) was known last century as Glengarry's Bowling Green, even although, as Victorian writer Edward Ellice says, there is "scarcely a square yard of green of any sort" among its summit rocks.

Arrochar Alps
A few jack-lengths from Argyll's Bowling Green lie the "Arrochar Alps". Containing Munros Beinn Ìme, Vane and Narnain, they are however dominated in fame and feature by the slightly lower peak of Ben Arthur, the Cobbler. This, with its three peaks jagging the sky, could well be a 'horn' in the Bernese Oberland when under snow and the name Arrochar Alps is the acceptable face of the Scots 'Wha's like us?' syndrome. It was apparently given to it in the 1930s by climbers from the Clydeside unemployed who escaped there for weeks on end from urban misery. Articles on the area in the Scottish Mountaineering Club Journal at the turn of the century never used the term 'Alps', referring instead to 'the Arrochar group' or 'the Arrochar mountains' which, wrote to W.W. Naismith in 1895, "will probably have been brought (by the new railway) within a couple of hours from Glasgow." The term 'Arrochar Alps' was first used in print in 1946 by author and climber Ben Humble, and although the 1950s SMC Guidebook was too strait-laced to use this new coining, the name caught on and is now widely used.

Blackmount
The Blackmount is the narrow-spined but wide-limbed plateau lying west of Rannoch Moor and encompassing such peaks as Stob Ghabhar and Meall a' Bhùiridh. It is a straight translation from its Gaelic name **An Monadh Dubh***, the colour in its name coming perhaps from the dark peat and heather of Rannoch Moor which it overlooks – including the **Black Corries** hills

---

Clach Bheinn – **klach** vYn	Garbh – **garav**
Tom Molach – towm **mo**loch	Am Monadh Dubh – *a*m mon*a*gh **doo**

(formerly A'Chruach, the heap) at its centre and the Blackwater River draining it westwards. The Blackmount is deeply gouged on its northern flanks by corries, one of which, Corrie Bà, is reputed to be Scotland's largest in terms of cubic 'bite': this casts deep shadows in the evening, another possible source of its name. Facing as they do north and east, they hold snow late, and one of them is the site of a major ski development known, ironically, as the White Corries. At the foot of the ski road, to complete the Russian Doll effect, is the whitewashed Black Rock cottage.

Braid Hills

The Braids lie along the southern side of Edinburgh, a gentle first wave of hills before the real crest of the Pentlands beyond. Two golf courses are able to run parallel along its slopes, and the name could well be from the Scots word 'braid' meaning broad. The name first appeared in the 12th century as Brade and it may derive from Gaelic *bràighe*, a height. Another suggestion was that it is from the Gaelic *bràghad* (which can be a genitive of *bràighe*) which can mean a throat or neck or gully: J.B. Johnston says that such a gully lies north across the valley of the Braid Burn on the slopes of the nearby Blackford Hill. There certainly is a gash on that hill but this hardly explains the name of different hills lying some distance away. Alternatively, *bràghaid* is the locative case of *bràighe*, as in Breadalbane (the uplands of Alba, Scotland), and this might be the best Gaelic meaning. However Gaelic was in decline by the 12th century in the Lothians, while the Scots 'braid' certainly sits well on these hills' wide shoulders.

Cairngorms

Probably Scotland's best-known range as far as media Britain is concerned, on account of its ski developments, it takes its modern name from one mountain, Cairn Gorm. This peak at 4084 feet (1245) m) is the lowest of the range's quartet of four-thousand-footers, and lies at the northern edge of the massive plateau. The name Cairn Gorm is not unique, for there are several examples of **Càrn Gorm*** (blue cairn) some 50 miles to the north-west in Ross; but what does make it unusual among Scottish mountain ranges is that one individual peak's name has spread out like a ripple in a pond to become the name of the whole range, in the process submerging its Gaelic name of **Am Monadh Ruadh***, the red mountain-land. This name was from the pink colours of the Cairngorm granite, in contrast to the grey schists of the Monadh Liath range west across Strathspey. This name was lost together with much of the once-great Speyside Gaelic culture during the 20th century.

Also submerged by the 'ripple effect' was the old name of another mountain in the range lying four miles south of Cairn Gorm, another Cairn Gorm; there

---

Càrn Gorm – kaarn gor*a*m
Am Monadh Ruadh – *a*m mon*a*gh roo*a*gh

was no room for two of the same name when one had become so famous. So the southern, lower one is now known as Derry Cairngorm. Both Cairn Gorms were originally named An Càrn Gorm, the blue hill . . . or perhaps the green hill. If blue, it is in appreciation of the apparent colour when seen from the distant habitations at Linn of Dee and Aviemore, for distance and dust tend to leave blue light after absorbing the red wavelengths. And if green, from its grassy slopes (in contrast to the dark cliffs or gravel spreads elsewhere in the range) – the name was of course given before the ski developments scarred the green. And since the range had these *two* Cairn Gorms, this may have helped the growth of the new collective name for the whole range.

The ripple effect of its name spread even beyond the Cairngorms proper, to include in some books all the mountains north and east of the A9 and the Angus glens. In 1928, Henry Alexander, editor of the SMC Guidebook on the area, defended the book's title *The Cairngorms* for the whole area just mentioned on the grounds that the correct name 'the Grampians' had never found popular favour and conjured up 'no distinct mental picture', whilst 'the Cairngorms' was the name being used more and more widely as descriptive of the whole area. He does concede that the 'true' Cairngorms are limited to the mountains between the Dee and the Spey.

Although the individual mountain Cairn Gorm has retained its two-word form, the range is generally referred to as one word Cairngorms. This was not always true. For David Thomson, author of *Nairn in Darkness and Light,* writing from his notes of early this century tells of days when:

". . . the calves of my legs (were) stronger – perhaps from climbing the Cairn Gorms so often"

By the 1920s however the name was commonly used in its modern one-word form.

Campsies

This layer-cake of lava flows is well seen looking north from the Clyde Valley, presenting a steep-sided but flat-topped appearance like an Arizona mesa. It is also commonly known as the Campsie Fells, a name which first appeared in print in the 1790s Old Statistical Account, where the Reverend Gibb of Strathblane parish told us of "that part (of the hills) known as the Campsie Fells". As the Reverend went on to indicate, the Campsies are properly only the higher and southern part of the whole mass of hills, an 'island' between Blane, Forth and Kelvin valleys; but the other groups like the Touch and Kilsyth Hills have been swallowed up in the 'Campsies' name.

The word 'fell' is of Norse ancestry (from *fjall*, a mountain) but English parentage, for the word was born and brought up in Cumbria. A few lower hills in south-west Scotland adopted the name, but the Campsie "Fells" is very much the late baby of the family, and probably reflects the growing status of English among the Scots gentry . . . like the Reverend Gibb.

Earlier references, from the 13th century, are simply to Camsy or Kamsi (probably to the hillfoot village rather than the hills), a name that crops up elsewhere in Scotland, for instance on Tayside. J.B. Johnston interprets this as from the Gaelic *cam sìth*, crooked hill, or knoll; but another possibility is *cam suidhe*, the latter word meaning a seat or sometimes simply a level shelf. Certainly the 'level shelf' best suits the hills' description, with the crook being the deep gash cut by the burn where the Campsie Glen descends the steep slopes and then angles away across the lower ground.

This flat-topped range is dimpled by the sharp cone of the **Meikle Bin,** Scots for big hill (from the Gaelic *beinn*), and its junior, **Little Bin.** Less distinctive but a few metres higher is the range's highest point **Earl's Seat,** named probably from the Earl of Lennox whose castle stood on the southern flanks of the hills. Other Scots or English names in the range include **Black Hill** and **Brown Hill, Hart Hill** and **Holehead** (at the end of a 'hole', Scots for hollow): and the **Laird's Hill** and **Laird's Loup** above Kilsyth where legend tells of a horsebacked Highland laird falling fatally while fleeing for his life.

Gaelic names include **Slackdhu,** from *slochd dubh* the dark pass or summit, and **Tomtain** from *tom an teinne*, hill of fire. The curious name of **Clachertyfarlie Knowes** in the west of the range, (spoken like the clickety-clack of a train?) may well be from *clach an fhàirleois*, the stone on the skyline – when seen from nearby Dumgoyne there does appear to be a large boulder here on an otherwise smooth horizon. Dumgoyne's name leads us back in time, to the days when a Scotsman's home was his castle . . . or else! For the several hills beginning with Dun or Dum, indicate a hilltop fort. (*Dùn* usually changes to *dum* before letters b, p, f or m.) **Dundaff** and **Dumbreck** are the dark and speckled forts, **Dungoil** and **Dunmore** forts of the strangers and the big fort – this latter, on the edge of the northern corrie crags, has an authenticated fort identified on the O.S. map. The outlying western hills of **Dumgoyne** and **Dumgoyach** are perfect defensive sites, with steep slopes on all sides; the higher one, Dumgoyne, is probably from *dùn gainneach* (pronounced **gan**yoch), fort of arrowheads. The little knobbly peak on its side is **Dumfoyne,** perhaps *dùn foinneach*, wart-like hill-fort.

Cheviots
The Cheviots, and **The Cheviot** hill, mark the present Scottish border and lie largely within England. The name is probably better known in Scotland as a breed of sheep held responsible as agent of the hated Clearances, a foreign intruder into Gaeldom. The sheep took its name from the hill area, and it lies too far south-east to be of Gaelic ancestry, so it is Sassenach in every sense of the word. The earliest references are to Chiuiet, Chyviot and to Montes (mountains) Chiueti and Chiuioth. W.C. MacKenzie in his *Scottish Placenames*, claims that their meaning is 'watching hills', but gives no evidence in support, although they do lie in ever-vigilant Border country.

Another suggestion from J.B. Johnston is from the French *chevet* meaning a pillow, appropriate to their gentle swelling shape perhaps, but a bit unlikely in linguistic terms. The most likely origin lies in the Welsh (originally Brittonic) word *cefn*, a ridge – places like Chevening and Chevin in England come from this word, and so probably does Cheviot.

Cleish Hills
The Cleish Hills lie above the flat moorlands of western Fife near Loch Leven, south of the village of the same name. In the 13th century the names Kles and Cleth were recorded, from the Gaelic *clais*, a ditch or furrow. The mosses to the north are ditched for drainage but this would only have been possible technologically much later than the 13th century. The hills have some prehistoric forts on them. **Dumglow** (misty fort) and Dummiefarlane, and when seen from the south (from Knock or Saline Hills) the top surface of the hills has a furrowed appearance. This may indicate an ancient ridge-and-furrow farm practice, common in Scotland even at this height in the gentler climate of those days, and these furrows may explain the hills' name.

Conval Hills
Above the whisky distilleries of Mortlach on Speyside stand Little and Meikle Conval Hills, outliers of the Ben Rinnes massif. Their names have similarities with many other hills in the north-west called Conival or Con' mheall. These hills are often shoulders of bigger mountains, and the name probably derives from a root *con* meaning with or together. So the Conval Hills name means probably a pair of adjoining hills.

Coyles of Muick
A trio of hills above Deeside where it is joined by Glen Muick (glen of the pig), it comprises the Coyle of Muick (the wood, *coille*, of Muick), Meall Dubh (dark hill) and the Craig of Loinmuie.

Correen Hills
This little group of hills above Alford in the north-east forms a horseshoe cradling a corrie which sends forth a well-fed burn to make its way to the River Don, and Correen is probably from Coire Uaine, the green corrie, which lies at its heart.

Cromalt Hills
The Cromalt Hills of Assynt in the north-west are an anglicisation of Crom Allt, crooked stream, that flows off their northern slopes. Rather undistinguished hills, functioning as a natural viewing platform (from the Knockan Nature Trail) for their famous western neighbours Stac Pollaidh and Cùl Mòr, it is perhaps appropriate that they take their name from a mere

burn. The name, Knockan, from *cnocan*, means little knolls, indicating their stature. Another, single hill with an almost identical name and meaning is **Cramalt Craig** in the Borders (above a stream called Cramalt Burn): and near to it is the Scots-named **Long Grain Knowe**, which means the knoll of the long (stream) valley.

Cromdale Hills

The Hills and Haughs of Cromdale lie east of the hamlet of the same name, which in turn is from *crom dail*, crooked field or meadow, from the shape that the water-meadows have been carved into by the wide meanders of the River Spey.

Cuillin

Possibly the most famous mountain range in Scotland, this spectacular rocky horseshoe in the Isle of Skye has almost as many spellings of its name as it has separate peaks. It can be singular (the Cuillin) or incorrectly plural (the Cuillins), and has been spelt Coolin, Cuillin, Culinn, Culen, Cullen, Cullin, Cuilfhionn, Cuidhean, Cuilian, Cuilluelun, Culluelum, Gulluin, Quillen, Quillin and Cuchullin; the first two are in most general English use today. In Gaelic the range is An Cuilfhionn or An Culthionn, *The* Cuillin.

There is a tradition that the range is named after Cùil Fhionn, the hiding place of Fingal, Celtic hero and leader of the Fingalians, who pops up in several places in Scotland. Another tradition attributes the name to Cuchullin, an Ossianic hero who is reputed to have built a fort at Dunscaith near Loch Eishort and kept the Norse at bay. Sir Walter Scott, for whom romantic legend was the very stuff of historical analysis, wrote:

> "Coolin the ridge, as bards proclaim,
> From old Cuchullin, chief of fame"

If this were true, it would make the range unique in Scotland in being named after a historical character or legend, and would not accord well with island naming traditions.

Attempts at linking the name to the Gaelic have included Thomas Pennant's "narrow dark hollow" (presumably from *caol*, narrows, as in Kyle of Lochalsh), and another writer who took the meaning to be 'fine corner' (from *cúil*, a corner). But the main Gaelic claim is for *cuilionn-mara*, the sea-holly whose blue flowers' outline the jagged peaks are said to resemble; or simply *cuilionn*, the prickly holly-tree itself. In 1897 Professor Norman Collie – not a native Gaelic speaker – wrote an article in the SMC Journal on the range entitled "A'Chuilionn", thus staking its claim . . . but getting its gender wrong in the process (it should be An Cuilionn).

There are a few holly-trees in the vicinity of Glen Brittle, and the Cuillins' jagged outline could spark off in the mind the image of a holly wreath: and there are parallels, for there is a **Meall a'Chuilinn*** near Strontian on the west coast some 45 miles (75 km) distant, and a **Cnoc a'Chuilinn** in the Irish Macgillycuddy Reeks. In an earlier SMC Guidebook to the island, the holly's claim to the name is supported with the statement that "the Highlanders nearly always name their places from their appearance or local peculiarity . . ." While this is true in general, other Gaelic mountain names relating to trees or flora do not come from their *appearance*. The many hills with a tree name – usually birch, pine or rowan – refer to nearby specimens growing there. Holly rarely gets a mention in hill-names, because unlike the Scots pines and the rowans, it is rare to find an isolated and therefore distinctive specimen growing alone in a corrie. Also, when a mountain *is* named after a tree, it is usually prefixed by one of the Gaelic hill-words like *beinn* or *meall*. So the case for holly is not very strong, although we can't rule out the Gaels calling it their holly-peak using *their* nearest word to the Old Norse name that we're about to meet.

The Cuillin

Colin Phillip, in the SMC Guidebook mentioned, refers to two gentlemen with whom he discussed the name: the first a Welshman who said to him "We have an old Celtic word *coolin* meaning worthless" – apt enough for its stony wastes; the second, a Dane, suggested that the name might be Old Norse, since (he said) *Kjolen* meant high rocks. The Dane is probably right, for there are several reasons why the Norse connection is the most likely.

Firstly, there is the fact that almost all the main hill-names in Skye are Norse, sometimes with the Gaelic word ben prefixed – from Ben Volovaig in

---

Meall a'Chuillin – myowl *a* **choolyeen**[y]

the north to Ben Cleat in the south, from Hartaval and the Stòrr in the east to Healaval and Ben Idrigill in the west. For a seafaring people like the Vikings the hills' function as landmarks was all-important, which is why they identified and named all the high points on Skye, Rum and the Outer Hebrides. And since the range – or from the maritime viewpoint the single large mountain that the Cuillin is – is so high that it can hardly have been missed out, the name too must surely be Norse.

Secondly there is the fact that the Norwegian name for their high plateau, from whose fiords the Vikings sailed, is the Kiolen Mountains. Like all colonisers they brought names with them that reminded them of home, and several Hebridean hill-names have doubles in Scandinavia; a range as striking as the Cuillin, high point of the Hebrides, would have been a worthy holder of this 'high rocks' name from home.

Thirdly there is the fact that the Norse names are by and large prosaic, referring usually to their more obvious features. Thus in Skye **Healaval** (flagstone fell) describes exactly its flat top while **Ben Tianavaig** is simply peak above the bay. In this context the other suggestion of a Norse derivation from *kjolr* meaning keel or keel-shaped is inappropriate (in spite of **Druim nan Ràmh***, ridge of the oars); whilst the name *kiolen* meaning high rocks fits perfectly this bare rocky range with scarcely a blade of grass to be seen on their gabbro sinews, and perfectly described by Thomas Pennant as "a savage series of rude mountains."

Lastly there is the fact that the nearby isle of Rum also has a range called the Cuillin, similar in rocky outline, and this suggests the possibility of a generic name, rather than one based upon a unique historical figure. The name Cuillin therefore reflects Norse powers of observation rather than Celtic legend or Gaelic imagination.

(The names of the individual Cuillin peaks are described in the chapters on Islands (under Skye) and on Characters (under climbers).

Cullaloe Hills

The old form of the name of this little group of Fife Hills was Culzelauche (the 'z' representing an old Scots letter which was pronounced 'y'), and is from the Gaelic *cùl dhà locha*, at the back of two lochs. Today, there are a couple of reservoirs sheltering in the crook of these hills.

Easains

A very small range consisting of just two large mountains rising out of Loch Treig. They take their name from the higher one, **Stob Coire Easain***, peak of the corrie of the little waterfalls, spilling down the steep slopes to the loch.

Druim nan Ràmh – drim n*a* ra:v
Stob Coire Easain – stob kor*a* esYn^y

The other half of the range is **Stob a'Choire Mheadhoin**[*], peak of the middle corrie. Although comprising only these two summits, the ridge they crown is 7 miles (10 km) long.

Eildon Hills

This trio of conical hills above Melrose in the Borders has captured the imagination for centuries. Almost two millenia before Sir Walter Scott chose it as his favourite view – to the eternal gratitude of the Borders Tourist Board – the Romans from their nearby camp at Newstead referred to it as **Trimontium,** literally the three mountains. In legend its shape was put down to the Devil cleaving it in three on the challenge of a local wizard. Other legends tell of King Arthur and his warriors sleeping below 'in Eildon's Caverns Lost': while a local man, Thomas of Ercildoune, foolishly followed a fairy down a secret passage into the hills to the court of Faery, and paid the penalty of seven years capture.

But long before the Romans, the northern peak was a hill-fort capable of sheltering up to 2,000 people in times of crisis. And there can be little doubt that the '-don' part of the name is from *dùn* (or *din*) meaning a hill-fort in Brittonic or Gaelic. The oldest forms of the name go back to Aeldone in 1120 and Eldune in 1143, and the Gaelic *ail* (a rock or cliff) has been suggested for the first part of the name. But there is not really a cliff on the hills, and more importantly the hills are outwith the main Gaelic-speaking areas: Brittonic (Old Welsh) or Old English are more likely origins, and the Old English *eld* (or *aeled*) *dun* meaning old hill-fort seems apt linguistically and historically. Only a few miles to the west just beyond Peebles are two hills with similar names, the **Black** and **White Meldon**s. They too have hill-forts on their summits, and may originate in the old Brittonic words *maol din*, bare hill-fort (although *maol teinne*, bare hill of fire, has been suggested). Melrose village itself, at the foot of the Eildons, is believed to be from Brittonic *maol ros*, bare moor.

Fannaichs

This chain of Ross-shire mountains appear to take its group name from the large loch, Fainich in Gaelic, washing their southern feet, and the deer forest running from shoreline to skyline. The origin of this name is obscure, and while there is a Gaelic word *fàn* indicating a gentle slope, it would have a longer 'a' sound, and in any case seems inappropriate for these swooping Munros. There are two **Druim Rèidh**[*] names in this group, meaning level ridges, contrasting with the steeper slopes around them. (There is a Gaelic word *fannaich* meaning to grow faint or feeble, as Munro-baggers perhaps feel on the ninth and last of the group!). **Meall a'Chrasgaidh**[*] (possibly Meall

---

Stob a'Choire Mheadhoin – stob *a* chora **vee**on^y
Druim Rèidh – drim **ray**:   Meall a'Chrasgaidh – myowl *a* **chras**gee

a'Chrasgaich) is perhaps the hill of the crossing, guarding as it does the northern entrance to a hill-pass that lets travellers and herds cross the Fannaich ridge from north to south: on the face of it however, the name is literally hill of the box or coffer.

Five Sisters of Kintail

Lying above Glen Shiel, at the head of the sea-loch Duich, the view of them from the west is almost an 'industry standard' for Scottish pictorial calendars. Perhaps this is because its skyline resembles a young child's idealised drawing of a mountain, with a series of sharp points linked by swooping and regular curves. In reality it is not a range but one long mountain ridge, as indicated by its original Gaelic name of **Beinn Mhòr***, the big mountain. Each separate peak has a Gaelic name: **Sgùrr na Mòraichd***† (majestic or mighty peak), **Sgurr nan Saighead*** (arrows peak), **Sgùrr na Càrnach*** (rocky peak), **Sgùrr na Cìste Duibhe*** (peak of the dark chest), and **Sgùrr Fhuaran*** (ostensibly, peak of springs – but it is locally said to be Sgùrr Ùrain, which either means wolf peak from *odhar-choin*, or small stream peak from *our*, an old term for water).

Just why it has the name Five Sisters is not very clear. The Gaels certainly did not call it this, so it is not a translation. Nor is it a very old English name, for Dr. Johnson and Boswell, passing through Glen Shiel on 1st September 1773, referred only to "prodigious mountains on either side". The term was however being widely used by the late 1930s. Hamish Brown in his book *Hamish's Mountain Walk* hints at the possibility that the shape of their peaks is pap or breast-like, which would make sisters the appropriate term; but again there is no record of local use of the common Gaelic name-words for breast or nipple, *cìoch* or *màm*, to suggest this. And the marked sharpness of the Five Sisters lacks the slight summit rounding appropriate to *cìoch* or *màm*, as can be seen on Sgùrr na Cìche 10 miles (15 km) away.

The tendency to see hills as 'sisters' may have begun on the English chalk cliffs The Seven Sisters, and in Scotland the buttresses of Bidean nam Bian above Glen Coe became known as the **Three Sisters of Glencoe,** after a dramatic and famous painting by MacCulloch, which hangs in Glasgow's Kelvingrove Art Gallery. And down in the Central Lowlands near West Calder a group of shale bings has long been known as the **Five Sisters** (of Westwood)! Further up Glen Shiel, continuing the same mountain ridge, are the less-famous siblings, the **Three Brothers** of Kintail – a rarely-used name –

Beinn Mhòr – bYn **voa:r**   Sgùrr na Mòraichd – skoor n*a* **moa:**reechk
Sgùrr nan Saighead – skoor n*a*n **s**Y*at*
Sgùrr na Cárnach – skoor n*a* **kaar**noch
Sgùrr na Ciste Duibhe – skoor n*a* **keesht**y*a* **doey***a*
Sgùrr Fhuaran – skoor **oo**–aran (correctly Sgùrr Ùrain – skoor **oo:**ran[y]

consisting of **Saileag*** (little heel), **Sgùrr an Fhuarail*** (cold peak) and **Sgùrr a'Bhealaich Dheirg*** (red pass peak). But the 'family name' for these brothers and sisters is definitely English, not Gaelic.

Formont Hills

This range of hills in Leslie parish in Fife is, like **Fourman Hill** near Huntly, a corruption of the Gaelic *fuar mhonadh*, cold hill. Why cold? Colder soil, making them difficult for farming, may have been due to late-lying snow or to waterlogging, or simply to the breezy exposed position. Above Loch Ness a hill called **Meall Fuar-mhonaidh*** has the same meaning.

Grampians

This is a huge range, that in some atlases covers the entire Highlands east of the Great Glen. But is its name genuine? Author W. Douglas Simpson, in his *Portrait of the Highlands*, wrote of this range's name:

> "It is greatly to be wished that the word 'Grampian' should disappear from our atlases and from books dealing with the Central Highlands"

Why? Because like a rainbow, the name appears to shift around the mountains and in close-up vanishes altogether. Some books and atlases apply it to the whole Highland area east of the Great Glen, putting Ben Nevis as its high point; others confine it to the area east of the A9 road, and south of the River Dee, whilst others cross the A9 west into Perthshire. A 1940 book on British Mountains said that the term "Grampians":

> ". . . may be held to apply to the whole mountain barrier stretching between the lowlands and the Great Glen. However it is often applied to the range east of the Tay valley and south of Deeside."

F. Fraser Darling's book on the natural history of the Highlands adopts a compromise position, with Rannoch Moor as the eastern boundary of 'the Grampians': Bartholomews' *Grampians* map sheet covers the central rather than the eastern Highlands; and to add to the confusion the modern political name Grampian Region includes only the north-east part of these mountains plus a huge area of Buchan lowland, headquartered in Aberdeen.

The generally-accepted modern limit of the term is to the hills east of the A9, but south of Deeside. A 1970s book called *Grampian Ways* is an account of the hill-paths across this area, that was and still is known as the Mounth – a name derived from the Gaelic *monadh*, mountain-land. Atlases however still play fast and loose with the word Grampian, scattering it across the map of Scotland with the abandon of modern art painting.

Sàileag – **saa**lak   Sgùrr an Fhuarail – skoor *an* **oo**areelʸ
Sgùrr a'Bhealaich Dheirg – skoor *a* **vya**leech **yay**rak
Meall Fuar-mhonaidh – myowl **foo**–ar vonee

But the broad sweep of the 'Grampian' canvas has no near view . . . the 'rainbow' has no pot of gold at its end. Nowhere within its supposed domains do local people point out 'the Grampians' in the way that the Cuillin, Cairngorms or Pentlands might be indicated to a visitor. Not that this has prevented expatriate Scots from exporting the name 'The Grampians' to Victoria, Australia.

Nor has the elusive nature of the name deterred speculation about its origin. A Celtic word *grug* has been proposed, supposedly meaning curved or rounded, fitting the modern perception of the hills' shape compared to the western Highlands, and the Old Welsh word *crup* meaning a heap is said to come from this source. As such it would be like the Gaelic *cnap* (pronounced krahp) meaning a hillock. And there was also, according to Professor W.J. Watson, a Celtic word *crouc*, the root of *cruach* meaning a heap or hill – but this is a long way from the word Grampian. Equally 'far away' is another European root-word *gra-ug* which was said to mean a hill-like place as in the Graian Alps, but in fact these are named after Hercules the Greek (*graecus* in Latin) who was reputed to have carried out some of his Labours in these Italian mountains.

There is also a theory that the name came from a printers' mistake in the transcription of the Roman scribe Tacitus' *Life of Agricola,* where the battle-site Mons Graupius or Craupius became Grampius, a mistake later compounded by Hector Boece, a 16th-century Aberdeen historian, writing it as Grampians. The new name – for there are no earlier references to it – was immortalised in Blaeu's 17th-century map where the words 'Grampius Montes' appear across the Highlands. It is not very clear where the A.D. 84 battle of Mons Graupius, where the Romans defeated the Picts, was – authorities differ between a site near Inverness and one in the Aberdeen area – and whether the Mons was one hill or a range (*montes* is plural of *mons*, but the Appenine chain in Italy was known simply as Mons Appeninus).

Hector Boece claimed in his books that the locals called it, in the vernacular, Granzebain, and one contemporary translation of his work speaks of the "mountains of Granyebene", stretching from 'Loch Lomond to the mouth of the Dee'. Later he refers to the Tay rising "far beyond the mountains of Granyebene". If this name *was* authentic, and if the last part is -*beinn,* then the meaning remains obscure since *beinn,* especially in the eastern Highlands, normally comes before an adjective. So although the adjective *griangheal* (pronounced **gree**-un-yal) seems appropriate becaue it means sun-bright and perhaps refers to the sun glinting off the late-lying snows . . . however it should really be *beinn griangheal* rather than *griangheal-bheinn* to be convincing as an origin. One Gaelic dictionary does have the word *gruaim-bheinn,* meaning gloomy mountain or dark hill, another possibility.

But is it possible that the Romans have made up the name *Mons Graupius* themselves – after all they 're-named' the Eildon Hills in the Borders as the

'Trimontium' (three mountains) from their shape – or did they base their Latin word Graupius on a local people's name? Certainly any local name cannot have been of Gaelic origin, for that language came to Scotland centuries after the Legions left. And the Picts who ruled that part of Scotland left us so few words altogether that it is impossible to say. However the fact that Grampians is not a locally-used name today – unlike other ancient names that have survived, like the Ochils and Pentlands – must cast doubt on its authenticity. So its origin and meaning must lie as mystery-enshrouded as the site of the famous battle site of Mons Graupius!

Grey Corries

This is the chain of high mountains that runs along Glen Spean, eastwards from the Ben Nevis area. The ridge sheds long slides of ash-grey scree to north and south and the northern corries in particular have a bing-like bareness to them, weeping grey. Geologically these mountains are a mixture of quartzites (a whitish rock that also explains the name of nearby **Stob Bàn***, white peak) and greenish-grey mica-schists, and some limestone, three apparent sources of 'grey'. On close examination, however, much of the summit quartzite is tinged and veined with a rose pink, and much of the greyness seems to be due to the lichens growing over the surface of the stones. The Gaelic name **Na Coireachan Lèithe***, formerly used by the peoples of Glen Spean, does not appear on maps, only the English translation. A similar anglicised fate befell An Monadh Dubh a few miles south at The Blackmount. And The **Black Corries** range, also a few miles away, is not even a translation, for this long low hill was **A'Chruach*** in Gaelic, or indeed Cruach Rainich (fern-covered hill – Rannoch Moor, encircling it, comes from this word.)

Kilpatricks

This low and rather undistinguished hilly moorland was named from an ancient settlement at its foot – Kilpatrick means the church of Saint Patrick – which stood on the banks of the Clyde where Irish missionaries could have made a landing. The highest point is **Duncolm,** hill-fort of (Saint) Columba, one of Patrick's patrons. On the north slope of these hills lies **The Whangie,** a deep rock fissure popular with rock-climbers, said to have been caused by the Devil flicking his tail as he flew past. The rock formation allows people to walk through long narrow clefts behind the main rock face, and the name may derive from Gaelic *uinneag*, a window, or possibly from the diminutive of Scots *whang*, a leather thong or strap, from the cliff's appearance from below.

Stob Bàn – stob **baan**
Na Coireachan Lèithe – n*a* kor*a*ch*a*n **lyay:**h*a*
A'Chruach – *a* **chroo:**ach

Kincardine Hills

This small range above Loch Morlich, an outlier facing the mighty Cairngorms, has a name reflecting the life of the valleys rather than the mountans. For it comes from Gaelic *cinn* (the locative case of *ceann*, and anglicised to kin) meaning at the end of, and *cardann*, meaning a wood. The highest hill in the group is **Meall a'Bhuachaille***, hill of the herdsmen or shepherd, and the other tops are named after cliffy outcrops – **Creagan Gorma***† (blue crag), **Craiggowrie** (goat crag) and **Creag Ghreusaiche*** (cobbler crag).

Ladder Hills

Professor W.J. Watson says that the name of this north-eastern hill range is a literal translation of **Monadh an Àraidh***, and backs it up with a reference to the Irish use of *àradh* (a ladder) to hills with tranverse ridges. Some twenty miles away **The Fara** hill above Loch Ericht is probably from *fàradh*, ladder, for its summit ridge is described by Hamish Brown as a "long undulating crest" as you'd expect of a ladder lying on the ground. However in Gaelic the term *tarsuinn* is usually used for such tranverse ridges, and in any case the key word *monadh* rarely disappears completely in translations (eg – The Blackmount, from Am Monadh Dubh), as it has done if the 'ladder hills' are a translation. It is also possible that it is from the Gaelic word *leitir*, a slope. In the western Highlands the word often appears in placenames as 'letter' as in Letterewe: indeed, on the western slopes of these hills is a shoulder called Letterach. The north-east, where this range lies, is the home of many 'corrupted' Gaelic words – *monadh* becomes mount, *creag* becomes craig, *càrn* cairn and so on – and a change from *leitir* to ladder would not be surprising.

Lammermuirs

Over 1000 years ago these hills were mentioned in documents as Lombormore, and later as Lambremor. There is a definite similarly with Gaelic's *lompair mòr* (big bare surface), and it would fit the landscape. However these low south-eastern hills, merely rippling Lothian's horizons, are on the very fringe of former Gaelic-speaking areas. The Old English words *lombor* and *lambre*, meaning lambs, fit the name and the hills' agriculture well. Indeed there are hills within the range called **Lamb Hill**, **Lammer Law**, **Wedder Law** and **Hog Law** (wedders are castrated rams, and hogs are unshorn yearling sheep), for they made good pasturing country, being not too high (maximum 1760 feet, 537m) nor too cliffy for the sheep.

Meall a'Bhuachaille – myowl *a* **voo***a*cheely*a*
Creagan Gorma – krayk*a*n **g**orom*a*
Creag Ghreusaiche – krayk **ghree-***a*seech*a*
Monadh an Àraidh – mon*a*gh *a*n **aaree**

Leadhills

In southern Lanarkshire the village of Leadhills stands amid the hill range known as the Lowthers, though the immediately surrounding ones are the Leadhills. They are pitted with small mines, worked from the 13th century until early this century. The individual hills' names probably predate the lead mining for they bear very un-mineral titles like **Dun Law, Broad Law** and **Hart Law.**

Lomond Hills

Not to be confused with Ben Lomond above Loch Lomond (out of which flows the River Leven), the Lomond Hills of Fife rise steeply above Loch Leven. Is there a connection? Are the eastern and western Lomonds cousins, and do the names Leven and Lomond come from the same parent? The case for the family tree was well put by W.J. Watson in his book on Celtic place-names. Quoting from a 10th-century document which speaks of a great lake Lummonu in the land of the Picts (Fife), 'called in English Loch Leven', he attributes the names to the pre-Gaelic *llumon* meaning a beacon or fire, with the loch- and river-names being derived from the mountain. The location of both Ben Lomond and the Lomond Hills would suit a beacon role admirably, rising suddenly up from plains as they do: the Fife Lomonds are visible from Edinburgh to Dundee, while Ben Lomond can be seen from many parts of the Lanarkshire and Glasgow area. And from Stirling Castle Rock both the Lomond Hills and Ben Lomond can be seen.

However, dissenting voices blur the clarity of this message, arguing the case for a root in the Gaelic *leamhan* (pronounced leven) meaning elm, or *loman*, a banner or shield. This seems unlikely for three reasons. Firstly, while there are often trees in Gaelic hill-names, these names' form is usually of the possessive "*a*' (or *an*)" form (as in Beinn a'Chaoruinn or Cnoc an Iubhair), which Ben Lomond does not have. Secondly, the Lomond Hills fall more within *pre*-Gaelic hill-name areas (the Ochils, the Pentlands), while Ben Lomond is on the Highland fringe. And finally it would require quite modern thinking to "see" a shield here. Since Fife was one of the flagships of the Pictish kingdom, and the Lomond Hills its mainmast, the beacon hills would be both functional and appropriate.

Within the range **Bishop Hill** refers to the Bishopric of St. Andrews which owned all the land hereabouts. **Maiden Castle** on the shoulders of **West Lomond** may be an Arthurian name referring to an old fort, while **Maiden's Bower** by tradition represents a spot where a jilted girl pined her life away.

Lowther Hills

Dominated by the Green Lowther hill with its high radio beacon for aircraft navigation, the meaning of its name is obscure. Reverend J.B. Johnston suggests an origin in early Irish *lothur* meaning a canal or a trench, though it's difficult to see the connection unless it refers to the north-south route up the Nith valley.

Mamores
This chain of Munros starts across Glen Nevis from 'The Ben' and uncoils east for several miles, rearing and falling and throwing out several spurs. A full traverse is a major mountain day even in summer, and in this context Johnston's suggested *"magh mòr"*, the big plain, is completely out of place. Much more likely is *màm mòr*, big breast-shaped hills: indeed the second-highest hill in the range is **Sgùrr a'Mhàim***, and the large southern outlier is **Màm na Gualainn*** (shoulder), both based on this same word *màm*.

Minnigaff Hills
These hills above Newton Stewart in the south-west are believed to be from the Gaelic *monadh a'gobhainn*, or the Brittonic *mynydd-y-gof*, both of which mean hill of the smith.

Minto Hills
These hills near Roxburgh take their name from the Brittonic *mynydd*, a mountain (cousin of Gaelic *monadh* and Scots mount), plus *howe*, Scots for a hollow, producing the hill above a hollow. The earliest references are to Munethov in 1166.

Moorfoots
This name if taken at face value would be contradictory. For a place at 'the foot of moors' would obviously be a plain or valley, not hills. The contradiction is resolved by the oldest occurrence of the name in 1142, when it was referred to as Morthwait or Morthuweit. The second element is of Norse origin in *thweit*, in common use in Yorkshire and northern England as thwaite meaning place or farm. Thus the whole name means simply place on the moors, a prosaic description of the reality of a high moorland fit for grazing.

Mounth
The Mounth is the historic name for the east-west ridge of mountains that hinders north to south road and rail travel in the eastern Highlands, forcing the ribbons of steel and tarmacadam out onto the North Sea coastal plain, or west into the Drumochter cleft.

Travellers on foot fare better with a selection of Mounth passes between these two trade routes, but these lonely ways are treated with respect by walkers. Such respect was not always accorded the old name, for atlases and books refer to the hills as the Grampians; Mounth, the older name, comes

---

Sgùrr a'Mhàim – skoor *a* **vaa**-eem
Màm na Gualainn – maam n*a* **goo***a*leen[y]

from the Gaelic *monadh*, literally a mountain mass. In north-east Scotland many Gaelic names changed – *càrn* to cairn, *creag* to craig – and the shift from *monadh* to moneth, mounth, mound, mond and mount (all extant usages) would not have been difficult. Further north the Ord hill near Inverness, a long ridge, was also known earlier as the Mounth, since *monadh* is a generic term.

In an old Latin document the name Muneth is recorded, being crossed by holy men with relics en route to convert the King of the Picts; perhaps the mountain called **Càrn an Rìgh**[*] (cairn of the king) near Braemar commemorates this king, while the **Hill of St. Colm** near Tarfside more definitely commemorates the first missionary to the area. And in 1400 a chronicle records the pursuit of Macbeth ". . . our the Mounth thai chast hym than, til the wode of Lwnfannan" (Lumphanan – where they killed him).

Within the range the name still lingers on in The **White Mounth** (the plateau behind Lochnagar) and the easternmost Munro of **Mount Keen** (from *caoin*, gentle or smooth in the sense of being unbroken by cliffs). The Cairn o'Mounth pass, **Capel Mounth** (mare or colt mounth), **Firmounth** and **Tolmount** and **Mounts Blair** and **Battock** are also survivors of the name that originally stretched over the whole of this east-west ridge from the coastal plain to the edge of Rannoch Moor, where it was called Monadh Druim-uachdair, the mountain of the upper ridge.

Ochils

This name dates back to before Gaelic times, from *uchel* meaning simply 'high' in the ancient language of Brittonic. The earliest references are to Cindocellun (*cind ochil*) in AD 700, Sliab Nochel in 850, Oychellis in 1461 and Ocelli Montes in 1580. An ancient Irish tract says that St. Serf had his cell somewhere between 'Mount Ochel' and the Firth of Forth.

To the early peoples of central Scotland these hills would seem mountainous, being higher than the Campsies, Pentlands or Lomonds. From a distance they rear up from the Forth plains with the steepness and straightness of an ocean breaker, but on closer inspection they are revealed as a series of quite distinct hills prised apart by deep wounds of glens. One of them **Dumyat,** standing slightly proud of the group, means 'the fort of the Miathi', the ancient tribe who took to it for defence.

Although the range's name, and Dumyat, are pre-Gaelic the individual hills have Gaelic or Scots names. The highest point **Ben Cleuch** has a Gaelic first name followed by the Scots word for gully, with its southern slopes falling steeply and evenly down into the deep gash of the Daiglen. (Gaelic origins suggested for cleuch include *cliotach*, a gully, and *gliuthachadh*, exalting, but neither is very convincing. In 1840 it was spelt Benclough.) **Ben Ever** is, in

---

Càrn an Rìgh – kaarn *an* ree:

Scots, upper hill, though some say it is from Gaelic *eibhir*, granite – which the rock is certainly not. **Ben Buck** is from *boc*, Gaelic for a buck deer, while **Tarmangie Hill** is from *torr na mainge*, fawn's hill. **Craig Leith** above Alva, is the grey crag, while over the range above Glendevon **Ben Shee** is the fairy hill from *sìthean*. **Mellach Hill** in the east is from *meallach* meaning lumpy (or *mullach*, summit), and **Meikle** and **Little Corum** are from the root *corr* meaning pointed. **Whitewisp Hill** is where snow lingers late in the season, while **Lady Alva's Web** on Ben Cleuch is another sign of spring snow.

Above the steep southern edge is a top with the splendid Scots name **The Nebit**, literally the nosed one, a name more complimentary than **Scad Hill** to the north which appears to be from the Scots sca'd meaning scabbed. **Andrew Gannel Hill** sounds like a man's memorial but is believed to be a corruption of the Gaelic *an sruth gainmheail* meaning the sandy stream, while **Mailer's Knowe** is *not* some kind of postman's knock but a similarly garbled form, of Meall Odhar, the dun-coloured hill! Last but not least **Wood Hill** above Tillicoultry may sound ordinary as well as merely English, but there's nothing ordinary about the fine ribbon of beech and Scots pines that fights its way up the packed contours to 1500 feet (450m).

Paps of Jura

A pap is an old Scots word for a breast, and the island's three hills in this range are aptly-described. The name was originally given by sailors, for whom they were a clear landmark in the south-western coastal waters. The earthy mariners' idea for their name was perhaps too much for the author of *The Placenames of Scotland*, the Reverend J.B. Johnston, who could only bring himself to say of them that "They are so-called from their shape".

Martin Martin in his guidebook, printed in 1703, said that the term 'The Paps' referred to the two highest hills, but a more recent poem by A. Young gives the correct count:

> "Before I crossed the Sound,
> Storm-shattered and sharp-edged,
> These breasts rise soft and round,
> Not two but three."

At least Martin Martin got the spelling right, for Blaeu's map of 1600 had them marked as the "Papes of Ijura"! Today the Paps are landmarks for walkers from many tops in the southern Highlands. (See also the chapter on Islands, paragraph on Jura)

Pentlands

The Pentlands run north-eastwards from the Biggar area, starting as a gently swelling moorland, rise to its high point Scald Law in a switchbacking ridge, and end suddenly with the steep drop of Caerketton's northern screes falling away towards Edinburgh city. (Its ridges and its dramatic 'north wall' have earned it the affection of many hillwalkers who grew up in the capital, as the titles of books like *The Breezy Pentlands* (1910) and *The Call of the Pentlands* (1927) indicate.)

A thousand years earlier, the hills' striking height and shape ensured them a name. The name first appears in written form in 1150 at Pentlant, and a century later took on its modern form of Pentlands. Is there a connection with the name of the Pentland Firth 200 miles to the north, the sea strait between Scotland and the Orkneys, named by the Vikings meaning Pict-land firth? This name appeared about the same time historically; but there are no Norse names anywhere near this part of Scotland, and the normal southern limit of Pictish names, usually starting with *pit* (as in Pittodrie and Pittenweem) is Fife.

The people of central and southern Scotland spoke Brittonic, the ancestor of modern Welsh. The Ochils and the Lomonds probably also have Brittonic names, and the most likely origin of this range is from *pen llan* – with *llan* pronounced 'chlan' as in modern Welsh – meaning height above the enclosed land. The element *pen* is common in Wales, with hills like Pen-y-fan (the height of the slope) in the Brecon Beacons. At the Pentlands' foot lies *Pen*icuik, and some miles south lie the hills of **Penvalla** and **Penveny** near Stobo. Another possible Brittonic source is *pen glan* meaning the clear or holy hill; a bit fanciful perhaps, but apparently Druids used to hold religious ceremonies on the top of **East Cairn Hill** in the southern Pentlands. Finally the fact that there is a **Pentland Hill** near the border with England suggests a semi-generic term describing a common landscape feature.

Two of the highest hills in the range also have Brittonic names. **Caerketton** is fort (*caer*) of the refuge or the retreat, and **Carnethy Hill** above Penicuik is probably Caer Nechtan, the fort of King Nechtan of the Picts. Carnethy is pipped by 10 feet (3 m) for the position as highest hill by **Scald Law,** Scots for scabbed hill, referring to the smears of scree in its eastern corries. (There are several hills of this name, or Scaw'd Law, in the Borders). However Will Grant's book *The Breezy Pentlands* states that its name means poet's or bard's hill, from its past – the Skalds were Scandinavian bards – but he produces no evidence for this claim, and it is besides outwith the main areas of Old Norse names.

The most striking hill in the southern Pentlands has a Brittonic name, for **Mendick**, distinctive with its two-stepped summit ridge, is from *mynydd*, a hill – the word is still used in the original form in many Welsh hills. Good plain Scots hill-names like law and mount, kip and rig, feature in other Pentland Hills, while English has altogether unromantic names like **Black Hill** (named for its heathery cover) or **Turnhouse Hill** (from the hamlet at its foot).

Renfrew Heights

Not so much a hill range, more a rumpled block of high moorland south of Greenock in the crook of the Clyde estuary. There are few habitations within it, and no local name for the area. The designation Renfrew Heights has the chalkdust air of old geography textbooks to it. Its individual high points all have Scots or English names, with only a few corrupted Gaelic names like **Knock More** (from *cnoc mòr*, the big knoll). The names are largely unimaginative, like **Misty Law** or **Brown Hill,** though the intriguing **Cockrobin Hill** may well be the site of a famous murder! The highest point at 1712 feet (521m) is the **Hill of Stake,** that may come the Scots word for the stalk (after deer), or just possibly from the Norse *stakkr*, steep, although there are few Norse names here. Nearby is **Irish Law,** watching over to the Emerald Isle across the mouth of the Clyde, where its role is echoed by **Paddy's Milestone,** the nickname of Ailsa Craig.

Sidlaws

First mentioned in 1799 as the Seedlaws, this is the low range of hills behind Dundee and its famous Law. Indeed the second element of the range's name obviously comes from the same Scots word for a hill. The first element of the name may come from the Gaelic *suidhe* meaning a seat, or level shelf, or from the common hill name *sìthean* or *sìdh* meaning a hill in the shape of a fairy knoll. This possibility is reinforced by the name of one of the hills in the range, made famous by Shakespeare's "Macbeth", namely **Dunsinane,** probably *dùn an t-sìthein**, fort of the fairy knoll. The usual Dundonian pronunciation of the range's name as the **Seedlees** adds to this reinforcement. The highest hill in the range **Craigowl** is from *creag gabhal* (forked cliff) or *creag gaothail* (windy cliff), the latter fitting the scenery better.

Southern Uplands

A dry geographical term now taken up by the long-distance footpath called the Southern Uplands Way, these are really several smaller ranges of hills (the Lammermuirs, the Eildons, the Lowthers, and so on) which form the barrier between Scotland and England – southern uplands for the central Scots, but northern uplands to the English.

Torridons

Several books published in the 1980s – among them an edition of the *Munro's Tables* – make reference to 'the Torridons', and although mapmakers do not yet recognise such a range, it may well be a name for the future. At present the Torridon name applies to the glen and to the area in general. Professor Watson thought from the sound of the Gaelic *toirbheartan* that it meant place

---

Dùn an t-Sìthein – doon *an* **tshee:hin**

of portage, where boats were carried across a narrow strip of land: such places normally are called *tarbert*, a related word (and there are several places Tarbet or Tarbert in Scotland) but there is no obvious isthmus here for this carrying to take place, and it's a long way to haul a longship to Loch Maree!

Touch Hills
The Touch Hills lie south-west of Stirling, part of the Campsies range. Their name, locally pronounced the 'Tooch' Hills (the ending as in 'loch'), is a corruption of *tulach*, meaning a knoll or hill, a Gaelic word (from an Old Irish root *tul*) that is common in the southern Highlands and very often has the English 'hill' appended to it.

Trossachs
The name is sometimes applied to the hills within this popular tourist area, but it properly only refers to the low-lying area between Lochs Achray and Katrine, where boats presumably could be hauled across, for the word originates in Na Troiseachan meaning the crossing places. Normally hills that 'cross over' or are transverse to the grain of the land are called *tarsuinn*, as in the several called **Beinn** or **Meall Tarsuinn***.

Beinn Tarsuinn – bYn tarsYn^y

Chapter Five

Colours

Colours. What colours? For homesick English soldier Edmund Burt, posted to Inverness in 1720, there were but two. In a letter home, he described the mountains thus:

". . . of a dismal gloomy brown drawing upon a dirty purple."

But then he *was* an English soldier, far from home. Many Scots know the refrain of the song "A Scottish Soldier", popularised by singer Andy Stewart. In it, facing death in a faraway European battlefield, the soldier cries:

"O, for these green hills are not Highland hills,
Not the Island hills, they're not my land's hills,
And fair as these green foreign hills may be,
They are not the hills of home"

The refrain was perhaps more accurate than it perhaps intended for the Scots mountains seen through Gaelic eyes are generally *not* green, let alone the Englishman's brown and purple. Green is only one of nearly a score of Gaelic colour words commonly used to describe the hills. Brown is a rare shade and purple is present only in 'purple prose' about the hills!

Colours are not immediately obvious to the untrained eye in the hills. Dr Samuel Johnson on his autumn tour through the Highlands to the Hebrides in 1773 saw none:

"(The hills) . . . exhibit very little variety; being almost wholly covered with dark heath . . . What is not heath is nakedness . . . An eye accustomed to flowery pastures and waving harvests is astonished and repelled by this wide extent of hopeless sterility . . ."

Modern eyes may be more used to brighter, primary colours, but in the Highlands the long distances from the tops, the gentler lights from a sun lower in the sky, the moisture and haze in the atmosphere, all tone the colours down to subtle pastels.

To distinguish certain peaks or corries, slight differences in hue were noted, which is why Gaelic 'colour' features are often in groups. Thus **Meall**

Corranaich* of Ben Lawers has corries Odhar, Ban, Gorm, and Liath – respectively the dun, white, blue and grey corries – taking chunks out of its sides.

Often colour names are found where rock types adjoin each other to form a contrast. For instance there are five peaks all called **Càrn Dearg*** (red cairn) immediately beside Ben Nevis, whose central mass is composed of the *grey* andesite rock. An Teallach in mainly of reddish sandstone, but where small caps of whiter quartzite tip the points a name like **Sàil Liath** (grey) is found. All this indicates the sensitivity of the Gaelic eye in picking out these subtle colours, and their intimate knowledge of the high tops – for instance **Càrn Dearg** in the Monadhliath doesn't look at all 'red' from any distance, but if you traverse it, small outcrops of reddish-veined rock are found near the lower summit.

There are literally hundreds of Scottish hills, mountains and corries named after their colours or hues. In the *Munro's Tables,* the classic list of the 3,000-foot Scottish tops, nearly one quarter of its 550-odd peaks contain a Gaelic colour word. Similar proportions obtain among lower hills. And although the greatest concentrations of colour words are found in the northern Highlands and in the Cairngorms, they can be found in every area, although *sgùrrs* in the west have fewest colours.

Of course other nations and peoples have given their hills colour names . . . Mont Blanc, the Schwartzhorn and the Blue Ridge Mountains of Virginia, to name but three. But these are mere flecks of paint compared to the kaleidoscope in the Gaelic Highlands, where the sheer number of 'colour' peaks, and the wide range of the colour spectrum used are outstanding compared to other upland groups. Why should this be?

The answer lies in the geology, plants and weather of the Scottish Highlands. Compared to many other hill areas in Europe, the Highlands are a very complex geological area, since they once lay at the interface between European and North American earth plates, and suffered massive pressures, faulting, tilting and episodes of volcanic activity. This produced the present complicated jigsaw of rock types, which weather out in various colours. Scotland's position on the edge of the Atlantic Ocean with its mild climatic effects, but also within reach of cold northerly airstreams, has therefore a wide range of micro-climates, from the palms at Inverewe Gardens in the north-west to the Arctic tundra of the Cairngorms. This, in association with the varied rock types, produces a wide variety of vegetation of different hues. And, although some peaks are not far short of the height needed for glaciers to form, permanent snows do not lie to give the mountains the monochromatic white on black effect seen in ranges like the Alps.

Meall Corranaich – myowl **kor**aneech   Càrn Dearg – kaarn **dye**rak

In the Gaelic hill-name colour spectrum the hues are subtle rather than dramatic, pastel rather than primary, gentle rather than bold. Indeed in Gaelic, the words *odhar, glas, uaine, fionn* and *bàn* can also mean simply pale, wan or drab. Gaelic is more precise than English in its distinction of the Highlands' hues. The very overlap of colours on any one hill or range is recognised in words like *glas* or *gorm*, and by the word *breac*, indicating the dappling of a hillside with different colours. So Gaelic helps us to "see" both the colours and the patterns on the face of the hills.

Gaelic Colours

airgiod
There are a couple of 'silver' hills (in the mineral sense) from *airgiod*, like **Airgiod Bheinn*** above Blair Atholl, and the **Airgiod-Meall*** above Glenmore. The latter lies on a ridge of granulite at the northern edge of the Cairngorms' granite plateau: granulite contains the mineral mica, whose thin translucent flakes give its rocks a silvery glint, and indeed the word mica comes from the Latin *micare*, to glitter.

bàn
White. There are three "whiter shades of pale" in Gaelic, with *bàn, fionn* and *geal*. Often translated simply as white, they have in fact distinct nuances. While both *bàn* and *fionn* mean pale, white, wan or fair – and *fionn* hints also at the colour lilac and at the condition cold – *geal* (pronounced 'gyal') means white, clear or bright.

White is the world's commonest and oldest element in mountain names: Mont Blanc, Aconcagua, the Weisshorn, Elbruz, Mauna Kea, the Cordillera Blanca, and many more are 'white peaks' in other tongues, but mainly on account of snow and ice. However the main cause of a white appearance in the Scottish summer hills is either whitish rock or lighter vegetation. **Sgùrr Bàn*** (on Beinn Eighe) and **Stob Bàn** in the Mamores both occur where bands of whitish quartzite rock spill down the slopes in long scree curtains, and are often mistaken from afar for snowfields by summer tourists. Quartzite is chemically too pure to provide many nutrients as a basis for soil and vegetation to grow, so it often appears naked on the weather-whipped hill summits.

Bàn is the commonest of the three Gaelic 'whites' in mountain names and, like *fionn*, is overwhelmingly a word of the western Highlands and inner islands, with examples of **Beinn Bhàn*** and **Càrn Bàn** stretching from Applecross to Arran. In the south the word often appears in the corrupted form in hills like **Tombain**.

Airgiod Meall – er*a*kit myowl   Airgiod Bheinn – er*a*kit vYn
Sgùrr Bàn – skoor **baan**   Beinn Bhàn – bYn **vaan**

breac

Meaning dappled or speckled, it is applied to hill-slopes where patches of scree and heather, greys and greens and browns, break out from under each other. Thus the **Beinn Bhreac** in the Cairngorms has a heathery hillside patterned with great weeping grey scars of scree; and there are fifty-four other mountains called Beinn Bhreac in Scotland. **Ben Vrackie** in the Trossachs, **The Brack** near Arrochar, the several **Dumbreck** hills also come from this word – and so perhaps does **Beinn Bhraggie** in the north. Another Ben Vrackie near Killiecrankie is geologically a whirl of black schists, grey micaschists, white quartzite and greenish epidiorite, all with characteristic screes, soils and therefore plants to give it 'speckle'. Approaching it on the 'tourist path' you face a patchwork of grey screes, dark heather, and light grasses on its south-western slopes.

One authority on Gaelic folklore says that there is a hag-like creature in Gaelic legend called Cailleach Beinn a'Bhric, the "spirit of the speckled mountains", who was said to disguise herself in deer-hides and be able to be a good friend or a mortal enemy to lone travellers. Perhaps the many a Beinn Bhreac and the several **Beinn a'Bhric** hills were named in order to appease her.

Another, rarer, word for speckled is *bailgeann* (from *bailgfhionn*): **Tom Bailgeann** in Stratherrick is composed of conglomerate sandstone, in which various pebbles were geologically pressed into a sandstone bed, giving it a three-dimensional speckled appearance. And *lap,* as in **Beinn nan Lap** at the edge of Rannoch Moor, is also said to mean dappled, since *lap* refers to a defective colour spot, in textiles.

buidhe

Yellow. Not the modern bright yellow of the some walkers' fluorescent jackets but the soft tones of the dried grasses and bents that mat to form the mellow yellow sward on the many a **Tom Buidhe** and **Meall Buidhe** – there are at least 28 hills with this latter name. One of this large family, Meall Buidhe above Glen Lyon, stands at the western end of a chain of dark heather-covered hills, and is by comparison pale yellow in tone. This colour is most commonly found on hills along the western seaboard, especially on the south-west coast and islands. Since grasses rather than heathers tend to colonise the wettest hill-slopes (heather being therefore commoner in the drier east), this pattern may reflect the heavier rain falling on these Atlantic coasts. In the east however there are some, for **A'Bhuidheanach Bheag** above Drumochter is

---

Beinn Bhreac – bYn **vrechk**   Tom Bailgeann – tom **bala**gan^y
Beinn Bhraggie – (properly, Beinn Bhràgaidh) – bYn **vraagee**
Beinn na(n) Lap – bYn n*a* **lahp**   Tom Buidhe – towm **booy***a*
Meall Buidhe – myowl **booy***a*   A'Bhuidheanach Bheag – *a* vooy*a*noch **vayk**

74

the little yellow place (and there is a Bhuidheanach slope on Cairn Toul). This Gaelic colour also peeps from anglicised hill-names like **Drumbuy, Ben Bowie** and **Cairnbowie,** while **Monthboy** and **Monawee Hill** in Angus are from *monadh buidhe.*

dearg
Dearg is a blood-red colour with a hint of crimson, and is found with *beinn, càrn* and *meall* in over twenty Munros especially in the Glen Coe and Ben Nevis areas, and altogether over a hundred hill-names contain *dearg.* There are a dozen instances of **Càrn Dearg** in upper Deeside alone, for they are often found where a hard granite rock intrudes through layers of grey schist. Granite with a high content of the mineral feldspar appears reddish, and for instance **Càrn Mòr Dearg*** screes show pink in contrast with neighbour Nevis' dull grey andesite rock. **Stob Dearg** (better known as Buachaille Etive Mòr) is tinged with pinkish rhyolite rock.

Mullach na Dheiragain* may come from *deargan* or *deargan-allt,* the kestrel, literally the red one from the distinctive sheen of its feathers. In a more corrupted form the colour peeps out from anglicised hill-names like **Drumderg** or **Craigie Darg** in Aberdeenshire, and **Corrieyairack Hill** is from *coire dearg.*

donn
This, the colour brown, is found almost exclusively on lower hills around the Clyde estuary, the earliest Gaelic-speaking area. There are two pairs of **Meall Donn*** and **Cnoc Donn,** one on either side of the Kilbrannan Sound in Arran and in Kintyre. **Maol Donn,** the brown headland on Arran, refers to the colour of its Old Red Sandstone rock, but the other hills of this colour are on granite and so it may be that their 'brown' refers to the tangle of heather on the hillsides. It's surprising that there aren't more *donn* names in a country where heather is second only to the thistle as the national plant. Even the Lowlander Rabbie Burns noted the colour:

> "We'll sing auld Coila's plains and fells,
> Her moors red-brown with heather bells."

There is a **Beinn Donn** near Oban on grey schist rock, and the colour probably comes from its heather; the hill seems to mark the northern limit of hills with *donn.*

Càrn Mòr Dearg – kaarn moa:r **dye**rak
Mullach na Dheiragain – moolach n*a* **ye**r*a*kan[y]
Meall Donn – myowl **down**

dubh

Dubh means dark or black. This is by far the commonest Gaelic shade with over two hundred hill-names to its credit. Over a dozen major tops include Sgùrr Dubh, Meall Dubh and Tom Dubh, and in the west there's a trio of hills called **Ciste Dhubh***, literally dark chest (or more ominously black coffin!). The dark or black may refer to the heather which covers some hills more than others, or to the blacker rocks that outcrop on it, or to the way the light falls on a particular hill or corrie. For instance **Aonach Dubh** in Glencoe is a steep north-facing wall, with the sunless black cleft of Ossian's Cave on it barely visible in its shadow. While **The Dubhs** at the southern end of the Cuillin ridge – a relatively easy day, celebrated in the poem's alliterative line:

". . . They call it not 'climbing' but 'doing the Dubhs' "

. . . are where the giant slabs of gabbro, a darker volcanic rock, are most noticeable. Several other *dubh* hill-names incorporate *creag* or *coire* (crag and corrie), naturally shadow-filled features, as in **Beinn Dubhchraig** or **Stob Coire Dhuibh*** (of Creag Meagaidh). In southern Scotland the word dubh has been altered to the less pleasing duff – as in south Edinburgh's **Torduff,** and the **Tarduff** hills in the Ochils and the Campsies – and is often found paired with a **Torfinn,** white hill.

The Vikings had 'dark hills' too – **Murkle** in Caithness is from *myrk-holl,* the root of our word murky.

fionn

White, fair, or light-coloured. *Fionn* is found mainly in the cold, sharp watery light of the north-west and on Skye, as in the Fannaichs' **Fionn Bheinn***. Fionn Bheinn's name seems to come from its long damp slopes above Achnasheen covered in light grasses and mosses, in contrast with the dark moors south of it. Curiously, although *fionn* is an uncommon colour word, it is one of the few which often *precede* the hill name, as in **Fionn Àrd, Fionn Mhàm** and **Fionn Aoineadh***, suggesting that the colour is a very old name-element. In southern Scotland the word often appears as 'fin', as in Fife's **Drumfinn.**

Elsewhere it may be confused with Fionn, the Celtic hero, as in **Suidh' Fhinn** on Skye, but Fionn or Finn's name was in fact itself derived in Irish legend from the Irish Gaelic word for fair or white. Elsewhere it has been suggested that the pinnacle **Sgùrr Fiona*** (of An Teallach), usually translated as from *fionn*, may in fact come from *fiòn* meaning wine, and while this may seem unlikely – in this the heartland of whisky! – wine was in fact a common

---

Ciste Dhubh – keeshty*a* **ghoo**   Stob Coire Dhuibh – stob kor*a* **ghoey**
Fionn Bheinn – **fyown** vYn
Sgùrr Fiona – skoor **fee***ana*   Fionn Aoineadh – **fyown** oe:n*a*gh

drink of the Highlands, through the French connection, until the early 19th century. Indeed 18th-century traveller Thomas Pennant wrote that "These crags are called Sgur-fein, or hills of wine". Perhaps the local people saw in the array of pinnacles a resemblance to the necks of the stone wine pitchers imported by ship.

Sgurr Fiona

geal

White. Although *geal* is a common Gaelic word, it is only used in hill-names in the Spey and Laggan valleys. In this area a walker who sets out to climb Geal Chàrn will have 19 hills all called **Geal Chàrn*** to choose from, and four of them are Munros. These four lie within a radius of ten miles, and all visible from each other, and are rounded grassy peaks. Their fair, pale colour is a result of late-lying snow (here in the central Grampians they are a long way from the Atlantic's thawing influences), for this prevents the growth of the darker heather at the expense of the lighter grasses. Heather needs a snow-free growing season of at least six months. Another interesting example of this is the **Brown Cow Hill** on Donside where a late-lingering crescent of snow, known as the **White Calf,** melts off in mid-summer to leave a crescent of light-coloured grasses stencilled into the surrounding heather.

There are also several hill-names incorporating the phrase *clach geala*, white stone: the northern Munro **Eididh nan Clach Geala*** means nest or web of the

Geal Chàrn – **gyal** chaarn
Eididh nan Clach Geala – aytyee n*a*n klach **gyal***a*

white stones, describing the intricate patterns of quartzite blocks shifted into geometric shape by frost movements.

Only two or three of Scotland's hill features are named by reason of permanent snow, unlike the famous 'whites' abroad, Mont Blanc and the Weisshorn. There is a top in the Monadhliath called **Sneachdach Slinnean*** (properly Slinnean Sneachdach) snowy shoulder, a shoulder indeed of the aptly-named Càrn Bàn. Similarly Cairngorm has a **Fiacaill** and **Coire an t-Sneachda,** snowy ridge and corrie. **Cuidhe Crom***, atop Lochnagar, translates as the crooked snow wreath (properly *cuithe chrom*), describing the white crescent there that often lingers into early summer. In the Borders lies the splendidly-named **Gathersnow Hill,** at a mere 2,260 feet (689m): but at that height, as one 19th-century writer noted . . .

   "The white-croon'd law blithe spring can thaw."

. . . and perhaps that is its winter name, shed in spring, for it is indeed also called Glenwhappen Rig!

glas
Glas, means grey (or green, when applied to new spring grass) or indeed grey-green – *liath* can also have both meanings. It may seem strange that grey and green may inhabit the same word. To town man, green is the bright colour that we expect in our manicured lawns and summer city parks, while grey is the lowering belly of a cloud on a dreich winter's day. But on windswept hillsides the grasses that survive, poking from amongst the grey rock screes, are not the light bright city softie variety but a darker hardier race. The overall effect of the blend of these plants and rock is grey-green. The best-known is surely **Beinn Ghlas*** of Ben Lawers, its slopes facing the south-west spilled with screes, crumbled from grey schistose rock. **A'Ghlas-bheinn*** in Kintail is simply the grey-green hill, while further north in Assynt, **Glas Bheinn's** grey gneiss screes threaten to overwhelm the heather moors at its foot.

gorm
Gorm can mean green when applied to grass, but more usually indicates the colour nearby on the spectrum, blue or azure. There are several Gorm Lochs, and several specimens of **Càrn** or **Meall Gorm*** across Scotland, and they are found especially to the west of the Great Glen. Ironically, while there are five

---

Sneachdach Slinnean – (properly, Slinnean Sneachdach) – shleenyan **shnech**koch
Cuidhe Crom – kooy*a* **krowm**   Beinn Ghlas – bYn **ghlas**
A'Ghlas-bheinn – *a* **ghlas** vYn   Meall Gorm – myowl **gorom**

examples of Càrn Gorm in Ross-shire, it is the lone one east of the Spey, and now corrupted to **Cairn Gorm,** that has become best known through lending its name to the mountain range. Indeed this Cairngorms range, literally the blue mountains, was known for centuries as Am Monadh Ruadh, the red mountain! – as it still is in Gaelic. It has been suggested that the 'blue' colour stems from the rocks – two Meall Gorm hills on Deeside are said to have blue-grey boulders on their slopes – but such colours would more likely be *liath* to the Gael. More probably the blue colour in the name *gorm* stems from the fact that *all* hills seen at a distance through the atmosphere take on a bluish tinge due to the properties of light, as the red wavelengths are absorbed by dust and the land. There are blue hills world-wide, such as Australia's Blue Mountains and the Blue Mountain in Jamaica, and poetically it is expressed in the poet A.E. Housman's memorable phrase . . .

". . . What are these blue remembered hills? . . ."

Indeed there is a Gaelic proverb which runs:

"Is gorm na cnuic a tha fada bhuainn"
("Blue are the hills that are far from us")

According to Adam Watson, contemporary expert on the area, Cairngorm itself looks blue when seen from Nethy Bridge (but not from Aviemore), while some miles south Derry Cairngorm looks blue from Inverey on Deeside. As walkers in the area know well, the distances to the peaks here are long, and this distance from habitation and therefore from perception may be responsible for the concentration of 'blues' here. Ironically the famous semi-precious Cairngorm stone, collected for jewellery, is usually not blue but a brown or yellow colour.

Another famous 'blue' mountain in Scotland is Skye's **Blaven***, a hybrid of Norse *blà* and Gaelic *beinn* producing blue mountain. The old pronunciation, and spelling, as Blaavin, is more Norse than the sometimes-suggested Gaelic version *blàth bheinn,* mountain of bloom.

liath

Grey. Among many hill-names bearing *liath*, the main concentrations are in the north-west and north-central Highlands. The best known are Liathach in Torridon and the Monadh Liath range above Kingussie. **Liathach*** is from *liath-ach*, greyish one: it is a square-shouldered lump of a mountain rising steeply from the glen – grey from the colour of the quartzite rock that forms

---

Blàven – (properly, Blàbheinn) – **blaavYn**
Liathach – **lyee***a***hoch** (locally, pronounced **lee***a***ghach**)

its protective hard cap over the softer sandstones, and from the trailing clouds that catch and tear on its ridge, and from its grey-weathered plunging cliffs. As Thomas Pennant wrote of it in 1774:

". . . an amazing mountain, steeply sloping, composed of a whitish marble so extensive, glossy and even, as to appear like an enormous sheet of ice . . ."

That *liath* in a name often indicates such screes should be health warning enough for walkers, for instance on the ankle-twisting quartzite boulder slopes of **Sàil Liath*** of An Teallach.

The **Monadh Liath*** – the grey mountain, or moorland – is a massive outcrop of grey mica-schist rock, so-called to contrast them with the Monadh Ruadh – the red mountain – across the Spey. They are also grey in the sense of dull and uninteresting, being described in an HMSO Forestry Guide as:

"They don't afford much scenery but offer hill-track access to the Great Glen"!

In the east is **Cairnleith Hill,** using the genitive form of the colour, and it may originally have been Cnoc a'Chairn Leithe. However *lì*, as in Mullach Lì in the west, is not a short form of *liath*, but means instead coloured or hued. There's an intriguing name in the Fannaichs, the mountain **Beinn Liath Mhòr a'Ghiubhais Lì***, big grey hill of the colourful pine. Other *liaths*, for instance **Càrn Liath** above Blair Atholl, mark sites of greyer metamorphic quartzite and schist rocks.

odhar

Odhar means dun or tawny, a greyish brown colour and is pronounced 'oa-ur', (roughly as in the corrupted name of **Ben Our**). This colour name is found throughout the Highlands, though commonest in Kintyre and upper Speyside. One example, **Meall Odhar***, is very familiar to thousands of hill-users, though they will not recognise this colour easily, for most of them see it in the form of the winter-white lump trussed up like Gulliver in a tangle of ski-wires on the east side of the Glenshee car-park. It is mainly composed of a grey schist rock, while the brown element of the colour dun will be from the heather that grows thick on these eastern hills.

òr

There is a hill of gold (in the mineral sense), **Beinn an Òir***, the middle of the famous trio of the Paps of Jura. As discussed in the chapter on Islands under Jura, it may be from local occurrences of fool's gold, iron pyrites. In Glen

---

Sàil Liath – saal **lyee-u**   Monadh Liath – mon*agh* **lyeeu**
Beinn Liath Mhòr a'Ghiubhais Lì – bYn lyee-u **voa:r** *a* yoo-*a*sh **hlee:**
Meall Odhar – myowl **oa–**ar   Beinn an Òir – bYn *a*n **aw-eer**ʸ

Geldie in the Cairngorms, the **Cnapan Òir**[*†] (little knob of gold) is supposed to be where Mackenzie, a local laird, hid stolen gold under a stone. (The Golden Valley near Achnashellach is obscure – it's certainly not a translation from Gaelic.)

riabhach

Grey or speckled but in a streaked manner, like a rain-blotched water colour, it appears in **Braeriach** (*Am Bràigh Riabhach*), Scotland's third highest mountain. **An Riabhachan**[*] near Loch Monar means simply 'the grey one' – although the name is close to being An Riabhach Mòr, the Devil! Sometimes the word is anglicised, as in **Sròn Riach.**

ruadh

Ruadh refers to those russet soft-brown colours we choose to call red, as in red-haired or Old Red Sandstone. It is found in **Ruadh-stac Mòr**[*], big red stack, and others in the north-west where the softer tones of the Torridonian sandstone provide a warmer colour in a bog-green and peat-black landscape.

Another reddish hue is rust, and although the Gaels lived on the land they were familiar with rust on their tools and weapons.

Càrn Mairg[*] in Perthshire perhaps comes from the Gaelic word for rust, *meirg*, a colour typical of the bracken slopes in autumn, as the old year's brackens sours in the cold rains and crumbles in the frosts. Also in Perthshire, Creag Roro is from *ruadh-shruth*, the russet stream, a rather interesting name.

uaine

There is a Gaelic word for the bright green we recognise in the Lowlands, *uaine*, as in Glenshee's **Meall Uaine**[*]. But it is rare in Gaelic hill-names, with less than a dozen examples: the word *glas* meaning grey-green is commoner, because it is a more accurate description of the colours involved. Curiously, five of the very few Gaelic 'green hills', all called Meall Uaine (three in the lower Grampians between Killiecrankie and Glenshee and a further two near Fort William) all lie within a few miles of the one line of latitude.

Sometimes a top with *uaine* is named after a subsidiary feature, as in the Correen Hills on upper Donside (from Coire Uaine), and **Sgòr an Lochan Uaine**[*] (peak of the little green loch) on Cairn Toul. The Cairngorms have in fact four examples of Lochan Uaine, the most dramatic and yet easily accessible of which is the one in the Ryvoan Pass just beyond Glenmore

---

Cnapan Òir – krahpan **aw-eer**[y]   An Riabhachan – *an* **ree***a*vochan

Ruadh-stac Mòr – roo*a*gh stachk **moa:r**   Càrn Mairg – kaarn mar*a*k

Meall Uaine – myowl **oo**–any*a*

Sgòr an Lochain Uaine – skor *an* lochYn-[y] **oo**-any*a*

Lodge. Its striking green, almost a Mediterranean turquoise, is set beneath grey screes and surrounded by dark Scots pines; the colour comes from underwater plants and algae. Legend, less scientific, has it that the colour comes from the fairies washing their clothes in it. The curiously-named **Laidwinley** hill in Angus is probably a corruption of *leathad uainealach,* the greenish slope.

English and Scots colours

In central Scotland, hills with Scots or English names have a limited range of colours compared to Gaelic, for while there are enough Black Hills and White Hills to almost make a chessboard, all the other colours together would struggle to make up a team of pawns. Black Hills are the commonest: the Pentlands near Edinburgh have two Black Hills, a Black Mount and a **Black Birn,** as well as a White Hill. (A birn is an area of springy grass, or a summer sheep pasture – the Lothian equivalent of a Highland shieling.) **Black Hill** above Balerno, was described by writer George Reith in his 1910 *The Breezy Pentlands* in this way:

> ". . . the Black Hill descends abruptly towards us (in the Green Cleuch) in what looks like cataracts of road metal." . . . (and from Scald Law) . . . ". . . the steep dark sides of Black Hill, looking for all the world like a dirty patched gipsy tent."

Today, nearly a century later, the hill is still clearly darker than its neighbours, because of these dark grey screes. The **Black Mount** near Dolphinton is blanketed with heather and thus clearly darker than the rolling fields and improved sheep-grass at its foot. Probably the Black Hill whose name is most familiar to the man on the three-piece suite is the transmitter of that name near Airdrie in central Scotland where his STV programmes are beamed from; its name comes from the dark volcanic rocks that outcrop near the top. **White Knowe** near Broughton is covered in pale bent grasses in contrast to the dark heather tangle on nearby Brown Dod. The Ochils have the mellifluous **Whitewisp,** named from its late-lingering snows.

For the rest of the colour spectrum the Renfrew Heights, the Kilpatricks and Campsie, Ochils, Lomonds and Sidlaws, Pentlands and Lammermuirs can collectively only muster half a dozen **Brown Hills** (mainly in the west) and a few **Green Laws.** There's also a **Blue Hill** above Aberdeen marking the eastern fringe of the Mounth, a **Blue Mull** in Shetland, and a **Pinkstone Rig** near Douglas in the Borders (possibly a corruption of pin stane rig, pin meaning a hill-top). A handful of **Dun Rigs** or Laws completes the range, which is hardly the Gaelic colour rainbow, even though they once spoke the language here too . . . hills like **Drumfinn** (from *fionn,* white) and **Tarduff** (from *dubh,* dark) in the Ochils and Campsies are faint echoes of the old tongue.

In the Highland areas proper few English colour names exist, obviously due to Gaelic's influence. There are several Brown Hills in the drier north-east, generally from their heather cover. On Skye the **Black Cuillin** appear to be geologists' terms adopted by climbers (the earliest reference to the term was in 1896), to distinguish the dark gabbro and basalt rocks of the main Cuillin cirque from the granites of the Beinn Dearg group, whose red scree slopes are Nature's superior imitation of the Lothian oil shale bings! The **Red Cuillin** was apparently a local name, Na Beinnean Dearga, but the 'Black-labelled' Cuillin was never a local Gaelic name . . . and indeed the range includes not only a Dubh (dark) name, but a Sgùrr Dearg (red) and a Sròn Bhuidhe (yellow). In Angus, twin hills two miles apart, the **Brown Caterthun** and **White Caterthun** are old hill-forts (from *cathair*) whose rubble ruins are respectively heather-covered, and bleached bare.

Lochnagar was generally known by its Gaelic name, Beinn na Cìochan, or by the Scots name the **White Mounth** from its capacity to carry snow late into the spring due to its height and its cold easterly position. But this is being very prosaic, and romantic poet Lord Byron, remembering his Aberdeenshire youth, saw the mountain quite differently:

> "England! thy beauties are tame and domestic
> To one who has roved o'er the mountains afar:
> Oh for the crags that are wild and majestic!
> The steep frowning glories of dark Lochnagar!"

Lochnagar

The soubriquet 'Dark Lochnagar' has passed into the collective perception of this hill, daily confirmed by the fact that from Royal and Tourist Deeside its tall cliffs will always seem dark against the sun to the south. Beyond these cliffs lies the 'forgotten' White Mounth, visible only to the walkers who forsake douce Deeside.

White Mounth's name 'pair', the **Blackmount,** lies some 60 miles (85km) away, rising west of Rannoch Moor. It is a plateau too, also much favoured by cross-country skiers; it is simply a translation of the Gaelic name Am Monadh Dubh. Thomas Pennant on his 1769 tour speaks of a Black Mountain here, but places it between Kinlochleven and Kingshouse, a mile or two north of the Black Mount, in the vicinity of the ridge known as the Devil's Staircase. Ironically perhaps the ski developments on The Blackmount are in the name of the White Corries company, from the late-lying spring snow.

The newest area to be developed for skiing has also, coincidentally, an English colour name, for the Aonach Mòr ski development stands at the western end of the **Grey Corries** range. This is also a translation of an old Gaelic local name, Na Coireachan Lèithe, from the ash-greyish colour of the quartzite screes and indeed one of the peaks is **Stob a'Choire Lèithe***, peak of the grey corrie.

But it is down in the Border hills where English colour names come into their own, with green and grey, black and brown and white hill-names liberally scattered above its quiet hopes and lochs. And there are some distinctive Scots names too, like the several hills called **Scawd Law,** Hill or Bank (from scaw'd meaning scabbed or dappled in the manner of the Gaelic *breac*) and the simple **Faugh Hill** near Moffat is Scots for dun, or pale-red, hill.

Stob a'Choire Lèithe – stob *a* chor*a* **lyay:**h*a*

The Cioch, Skye

Chapter Six

The Body of the Land

Rocks have faces, hills have heads, mountains have shoulders. On the rocky skeleton of the hills, names have fleshed out a whole 'person', drawing on comparison with different parts of the body. In the Borders there are hills like **Croft Head, Rough Shoulder, Fell Shin,** and a mysterious **Snickert Knees** (nicked or notched knees); and the little dip just beside Tinto's summit is known as **The Dimple.** These names are unusual, although not perhaps as distinctive as **Broken Back** and the **Crown of Scotland** near Moffat, but Gaelic names in the Highlands go much further, and over a score of body parts are used as common generic hill-names, producing a comprehensive anatomy.

aodann and **aghaidh**
(Pronounced **oe:**tan and **oe-ee** respectively) These, the Gaelic for face (so commonly used in English descriptions of rocky hills or cliffs) make relatively few appearances. The best-known is probably **Ben Aden*** (*beinn aodainn*) above Loch Quoich, and nearby are **Aodann Chlèirig***, minister's face, and **Aodann an t-Sìdh Mhòir***, face of the big fairy hill. Elsewhere a corrie wall on Aonach Beag called **An Aghaidh Garbh*** is the rough face, from *aghaidh*. And while English uses the term 'beauty spot' for both a scenic tourist attraction and for a focal mole on the female complexion, the nearest Gaelic equivalent is the unflattering **An Guirean*** near Fort William, a little hill translating as the pimple or pustule!

beul
(Pronounced **bee**-ul) A mouth. This Gaelic word also came to mean a common pasturage, or lying place for cattle, and it is understandable how a protected scoop in the hills might invite comparison with the shelter provided by the mouth. **Beinn Bheòil*** above Loch Ericht is derived from this word, as is

Ben Aden (properly Beinn Aodann) – bYn **oe:**tan
Aodann Chlèirig – **oe:**tan **chlay:**reek
Aodann an t-Sìdh Mhòir – **oe:**tan *a*n tyee: **voa:r**ʸ
An Aghaidh Garbh – *a*n **oe-ee** garav
An Guirean – *a*n **gooran**   Beinn Bheòil – bYn **vyaw-eel**ʸ

Beinn Bheula* near Lochgoilhead – most of the few names using this word lie in the south-west or in the Western Isles. Sometimes the word is used in the more literal sense, such as **Beul Coire nan Each***, mouth of the corrie of the horses.

The Devil's Point

bod

(Pronounced bawd) A penis. By contrast with the breast – found in *cìoch* and *màm* – the male sexual organ hardly lends itself to comparison with hill shapes in the British Isles, excepting the vertical sea stacks known by the probably euphemistic names of **Old Man – of Hoy, of Stoer,** and the like. However the Devil's Point in the Cairngorms, a sharp peak of scaly black slabs above the Lairig Ghru, was originally called **Bod an Deamhain***, or demon's penis. In the early 19th century it was sometimes known as Poten Duon, a corruption of the Gaelic possibly with the intention of providing some modesty through opacity! Early writers ducked the problem of translating the offending word into cold print, referring to it as "the devil's ——", or simply as "a literal translation". The 'problem' of its name was solved by the Victorian clerics and professors, the early mountaineers, whose demure English translation of *bod* into 'point' made hillwalking safe for decent people in the area, draping a veil of modesty across the name! (The Gaels were not alone in identifying a penis in their hills, for the Himalayan peak Shivling means the god Siva's penis.)

Beinn Bheula – bYn **vee-ul***a*
Beul Coire nan Each – bee-ul **kora n***a*n **yech**
Bod an Deamhain – bod *a*n **dye**veen

It is possible that the rare hill-name *biod* found in lower hills in Skye, may be related to this word. And there is an obvious connection with *bodach*, an old man, for there are several **Am Bodach*** hill-names around the Highlands. **Slat Bheinn*** in the west means rod (or just possibly penis) mountain, less direct than *bod* in its metaphor.

bràighe

(Pronounced bra:ya) This can mean a neck or throat and geographically refers to the higher places, or upper parts, on a hill. **Braeriach***, the third highest Scots mountain, is from *Am Bràigh Riabhach* (dappled neck), and other examples include **Bràigh a'Choire Bhig*** (the neck of the wee corrie) and, in Scotticised form, the ubiquitous Braes (as in "o' Killiecrankie" or "o' Loch Lomond').

ceann

(Pronounced kyown) The whole head itself, in Gaelic *ceann*, is most often found in its anglicised version 'kin' applied to low-lying villages such as Kingussie and Kinlochleven. Indeed the only clear example in *Munro's Tables* is **Ceann Garbh*** (rough head), a top in the north-west. However there are two separate mountains called **Maol Cheann-Dearg*** and **Maol Chinn-Dearg**, literally bald red head, which is especially apt in Torridon where sparse tufts of grass cling desperately to its steep sandstone sides but give up on its bare windswept pate. ('Bald' is at any rate a more flattering desription than those summits sniffed at by Englishman Edward Burt in 1754, as having ". . . the disagreeable Appearance of a Scabbed head.") **Ganu Mòr***, the summit of Foinaven in the north, is a corruption of *ceann mòr*, big head. The Norse *skalli* for skull is found in island hill names like **Scalla Field**, while near Elgin is a hill called **The Scalp**.

Not all hill-heads are bare: the **Bads of Ben Avon** – local name for the granite summit tors – are from *bad*, which can indicate a Tintin-style tuft of hair on the head. Head cover is also provided by *sgulair*, a large old hat (**Beinn Sgulaird***), **Sgùrr na Boineid*** (bonnet) and **Sgùrr na h-Aide*** (hat). **Sgùrr Sgùmain** in the Cuillin is probably from *sgùman* meaning a headscarf (formed by folding over a square piece of cloth), for it is a pointed peak, a shape inappropriate to the usual meaning given to it of boat bailer, also *sgùman*. However, a round-bottomed boat bailer *is* appropriate for **Sgùman Coinntich** near Loch Long.

Am Bodach – *a*m **bo**toch   Slat Bheinn – **slaht** vYn
Braeriach – (properly, Am Bràigh Riabhach) – *a*m brY **ree-***a*voch
Bràigh a' Choire Bhig – brY *a* chor*a* **veek**
Ceann Garbh – kyown **garav**   Maol Cheann-Dearg – moe:l chy*a*n **dyer***a*k
Ganu Mòr – ganoo **moa:r**
Beinn Sgulaird – bYn **sgool***a*rt   Sgùrr na Boineid – skoor n*a* **bon***a*d^y
Sgùrr na h-Aide – skoor n*a* **had**y*a*

cìoch

(Pronounced kee:ch) A nipple or breast. Gaelic society, at the time when most hills were given names, was not inhibited by the prudishness in body matters that was later imported into the Highlands by the English language and Presbyterian church. Sexual parts of the body, taboo to the incoming 'culture', are referred to quite openly in names. The words for nipple and breast, cìoch (or cìche, 'of a breast') and màm, are widely used in the mountains, while uchd another word for bosom or breast, is rarer. Màm has come to have the alternative meaning of a rounded hill, while cìoch mountains generally come to a point, either in the apex of a cone, or in the nipple-like summit tors. Thus **Sgùrr na Cìche**[*] in Knoydart has a conical shape (although a little rounded just at the top) while **Màm Sodhail**[*] above Glen Affric has a more rounded appearance overall. In granite hill areas like the Cairngorms the summit tors, granite rocks that protrude sharply out of the flat plateaux, bear names like the **A'Chìoch**[*] on Beinn a' Bhùird, and Beinn nan Cìochan (the mountain of the little nipples – the original Gaelic name of Lochnagar), suggesting the shape. Arran too is a granite island, and its **Cìoch na h-Òighe**[*] (the maiden's breast) clearly outlines the combined breast and nipple shape when seen from North Glen Sannox – as does the **A' Chìoch** on Mull's Ben More.

Ironically one of the best known, and certainly the most aptly-named of the cìochs was discovered by an English speaker, Professor Norman Collie. He explored much of Skye's Cuillin range at the turn of the century, and one evening in Coire Lagan noticed a giant shadow swelling across the slabs as the sun declined in the west. On investigation next day he discovered and climbed **The Cioch,** a rock breast protruding from the steep slabs and tipped by a stone nipple. Its existence had not previously been suspected, for the glen-living native Skyemen would have little use for such high rock gymnasiums in this bare corrie. It was however a Skyeman, John MacKenzie (Collie's guide) who christened it in his native tongue the following day in 1906. Since that day this dramatic rock has become like the great Black Stone of Mecca for rock-climbers in Skye, an object of pilgrimage and devotion. However while Skye thus gained a cìoch, Glen Coe has effectively lost one: for **Sgòrr na Cìche**[*] at the west end of the glen is now more often known by the equivalent Scots name The **Pap of Glencoe.**

Not every cìoch is on the high tops, for the Cìochan of Beinn Laoigh (Ben Lui) are well down its northern slopes, while the **Cìoch Beinn an Eòin**[*] is on a easterly spur of the Coigach mountains.

Sgùrr na Cìche – skoor na kee:cha   Mam Sodhail – maam soaal
A'Chìoch – a chee:ch   Cìoch na h-Òighe – kee:ch na hawya
Sgòrr na Ciche – skor na kee:cha
Cìoch Beinn an Eòin – keech bYn an yaween[y]

claigionn
An Claigionn* on Deeside is literally the skull and is, as you would expect, a rounded hillock.

corrag
(Pronounced korrak) A forefinger, or 'pointing one'. **Corrag Bhuidhe*** of An Teallach means yellow finger, and is one of the fistful of rocky pinnacles poking into its skyline.

druim, drum
(Pronounced **droe**-eem) A back. This is a common Gaelic placename word referring in the body to the back, and in the hills to a long ridge-shaped mountain. The spine in Gaelic is *cnàimh an droma*, literally the bone of the back, *droma* being the genitive case of *druim*. Indeed there is a hill rising gently above Loch Cluanie called **Druim nan Cnàmh*** (ridge of the bone or spine) with gentle rumples on its ridge reminiscent of the spinal vertebrae. There are many Lowland ridges bearing the anglicised prefix *drum* as in Drumchapel, Drumbryden and Drumclog, to name but three which are now covered over by human settlements. In the Highlands two of many hill examples are found in Glen Shiel's **Druim Shionnach*** (ridge of foxes) and Perthshire's **Drummond Hill** (from the plural *dromannan*, also the origin of the common Scottish surname). The ancient Gaelic name Druim Alban, the ridge of Alba (Scotland), referred to the whole dorsal ridge that runs north from Lochaber to the far north, separating the Scots in the west from the Picts in the east. Drumochter, the famous rail and road pass where the snow gates are often shut in winter blizzards, is **Druim Uachdair,*** high ridge.

fiacail
(Pronounced **fee**-*a*chkil) A tooth. (Plural *fiaclan*). Many mountains around the world bear a resemblance to and the name of a tooth, as in Switzerland's Dent Blanche or North America's Moose's Tooth, and so it's not surprising to find them in Scotland. There are several **Càrn nam Fiaclach** hills in upper Deeside, and a **Fiaclach*** (toothed ridge) on Ben Wyvis. On the sandstone Skye peak of Marsco is **Fiaclan Dearg,** red teeth, from the rock's colour.
   The subtlety of the dental description can be seen, for instance, from the Mallaig train, passing beneath the long **Druim Fiaclach** ridge west of Loch Shiel: looking up at the ridge against a blue sky, you can see the delicate and compacted serrations that typify human teeth, not the leaping fangs of an animal. However in the east, Cairngorm's eastern Coire an t-Sneachda (the

---

An Claigionn – *an* klagin^y
Corrag Bhuidhe – korrak **voo**y*a*
Druim nan Cnàmh – drim n*a*n **kraav**

Druim Shionnach – drim **hi**noch
Druim Uachdair – drim **oo**-*a*chk*a*r
Fiaclach – **fee**-*a*chkloch

snowy corrie) has a toothed ridge leading up on either side of its steep headwalls – **Fiacaill a'Choire Chais**[*] (steep corrie) and **Fiacaill Coire an t-Sneachda**[*]. Just when you thought it was safe to go back on the rocks . . . jaws!

There are jaws in the Border hills too, for that is precisely the meaning of the Scots second element of **Carrifran Gans** hill by Moffat.

glun

Glun Liath, a top on the northern spur of Bodach Mòr (big old man) in the Freevater Forest, is the old man's "grey knee" or "grey joint."

gualainn

(Pronounced **goo**-uleen) A shoulder. There are about a dozen instances of this body-name in the Scottish mountains, mainly in the south-west and far west. The mountain called **Màm na Gualainn**[*] above Loch Leven, really a southern outlier of the Mamores, means hill of the shoulder, describing its shape and its lower height than the main range. More mysterious is **Gualainn nan Osna**[*] in the far west, translating as the shoulder of sighing or blubbering. Does it refer to the wind moaning through the gap in the hills, to a long-forgotten tragedy . . . or was this 'a shoulder to cry on'?

làmh

(Pronounced la:v) *Làmh* is a hand, and on Speyside, the fortified knoll of **Dùn-dà-làmh**,[*] the fort of the two hands, is said to be from the way that two ridges splay out on either side of the main *dùn*.

lurgann

(Pronounced **loo**roogan) The shin. **Lurg Mhòr**[*] near Loch Monar is the Gaelic for 'big shin' or 'long shank', an apt name for a mountain so far from the nearest road end! This mountain's form is of an extensive ridge throwing a long sinewy spur east towards Loch Monar. The few other *lurg* hills are mainly in the south and east of the Highlands.

màm

(Pronounced ma:m) A breast. Originally meaning simply a breast, it came through common use in mountain names to signify a round-topped hill of that shape. The more rounded *màm* hills are often less conically striking than the

---

Fiacaill a' Choire Chais – **fee-**achkil[y] *a* chor*a* **chash**
Fiacaill Coire an t-Sneachda – **fee-**achkil[y] kor*a* *a*n **tnech**ka
Mam na Gualainn – maam n*a* **goo-**aleen[y]
Gualainn nan Osna – goo-uleen n*a*n **osn**a
Dùn-dà-làmh – doon **daa laav**   Lurg Mhòr – looroog **voa:r**

cìochs (also meaning breast or nipple, see above). **Màm Sodhail** above Glen Affric is one of the highest examples.

The **Mamores** are one of the hillwalker's favourite mountain chains, with large rises and drops between each of its ten Munro summits, giving nearly 10,000 feet (3000m) of ascent and re-ascent. Although the finer detail of its peaks, with steep narrow ridges and scalloped corries, hardly fits the well-rounded sense of *màm*, the overall outline from a distance suggests that the name must come from *màm mòr* (*mòr* meaning large); and one of the principal peaks in the range is indeed **Sgurr a'Mhàim***, while outlying is **Màm nan Gualainn.**

In parts of the south-west Highlands there was a recorded tradition that for the healing of swollen glands (*màm*), a gifted person would pass a steel blade over the affected part then point it at a hill called *màm*, rather than the usual *beinn*, so transferring the sickness from the person to the swelling of the hill!

Màm can also refer to a pass in the hills, like the well-known **Màm Ratagan** on the road to Glenelg. This meaning comes from the idea of a pass as the dip between two hills as between two breasts. And while the Cairngorms' **Càrn a'Mhàim*** may be cairn of the breast (seen from Glen Luibeg it has a nipple-like rock outcrop on its crest), it's more likely to be the cairn above the pass, for it stands guardian at the southern end of the famous Lairig Ghrù .

meur

(Pronounced mayr) *Meur* means a finger, as found in the rather clumsy Cairngorms' names of **East** and **West Meur Gorm Craig.** In Galloway the same word is the root of **Merrick**, from *meurach* referring to the branching of a hand's fingers. Perhaps it was responsible for delivering the **Meikle Knypes**, a hill near Sanquhar meaning big punches or blows!

ruigh

(Pronounced ree) The Gaelic word *ruigh* for forearm has passed into the description of topography, referring to the outstretched base of a hill or the sheiling ground for summer pasturage. One can easily imagine the comparison between a forearm resting on a table, and a ridge leading down from the tops. In the Cairngorms, **Ruigh-àiteachain*** bothy in Glen Feshie, from where painter Landseer worked on his famous stag pictures, stands at the foot of this the 'ridge of the small place'. **Druim Righeannach** in the west is the ridge of the outstretched bases, from *ruigh*. **Meall Ghaordie*** (sometimes Meall Ghaordaidh) may come from *gàirdean*, the upper part of a shoulder or arm,

---

Sgùrr a'Mhàim – sgoor *a* va:-eem
Càrn a 'Mhàim – kaarn *a* va:-eem
Ruigh-àiteachain – ree **a:**tyocheen^y
Meall Ghaordie – myowl **ghoe:**rdee

and a similar limbed comparison may exist in **Beinn Udlamain*** near Loch Ericht, possibly from *udalan* (pronounced **oo**talan), a ball-and-socket joint.

sàil

(Pronounced sa:l) Gaelic for a heel, *sàil* is found in examples such as **Sàil Mhòr*** (big heel) of Beinn Eighe and in **Sàil Liath*** (grey heel) of An Teallach. Both are long slopes running down from tops which themselves round off a chain of peaks, like the heel at the end of a loaf. **Sàileag*** (little heel) is a steep grassy hill linking its more rugged neighbours in Glen Shiel, and not far away **Sàil Chaoruinn*** (heel of the rowan-tree) rounds off a northern spur. Another well-known example is **Sàil Gharbh*** (rough heel) at the end of Quinag. *Sàil* seems therefore to be a word favoured by the Gaels of the north-western Highlands. The actual summits bear the name, but the *sàil* is probably the long slope that falls away from them, for it is that which makes them distinctive among hills.

slinnean

(Pronounced **shlee**nyan) A shoulder-blade. Walkers often refer to the shoulders of a hill, the ridges leading out and down from its top, and yet the word has not passed into English or Scots hill-names. There is only one Gaelic instance on O.S. maps, **Sneachdach Slinnean*** (the snowy shoulder-blade) of Càrn Bàn – though this shoulder is 'back-to-front', since the adjective should follow the noun to give *slinnean sneachdach!*

slugan

(Prounounced **sloo**gun) *Slugan* refers to the throat or more precisely the gullet, hinting expressively at narrow mountain defiles such as the Cairngorms' cleft of Gleann an t-Slugain, and the several hills called **Meall an t-Slugain.***

sròn

(Pronounced **strawn**) Whereas English uses 'shoulder' for the ridges falling from a hilltop, Gaelic generally goes for *sròn* meaning nose, and by extension a promontory; apt because, like a nose, such a ridge may be concave or convex, rough or smooth, broad or narrow, but always projects out from the hill face. Because it is a hill*side* rather than a hill*top*, there are few actual summits with this name, and those that there are taking their name from the slope they top,

---

Beinn Udlamain – bYn **oot**laman[y]

Sàil Mhòr – saal **voa:r**	Sàil Gharbh – saal **garav**
Sàil Liath – saal **lyee**-u	Slinnean Sneachdach – shleenyan **shnech**koch
Sàileag – **saal**ak	Meall an t-Slugain – myowl *an* **tloogan**[y]
Sàil Chaoruinn – saal **choer**Yn[y]	

like *sàils*. **Sròn a'Choire Ghairbh** (nose of the rough corrie) near Loch Lochy is the only separate mountain in *Munro's Tables*, while other tops in the Tables including two cases of **Sròn Gharbh** (rough noses) are the subsidiary tops of bigger mountains. There are over 250 *sròn* hill-names, covering all the Highlands except for the eastern Grampians.

Strone is one anglicised version of the word, with **The Strone** hill in Angus, and **Stronend** in the Fintry Hills as examples, while Harris' **Sròn Ulladal** cliffs which plunge down for over 1,000 feet (300m) must be one of the most magnificent specimens (it is Strone Ulladale on older maps). Outwith Gaeldom in the Ochil Hills, the splendid Scots-named hill **The Nebit** means the hook-nosed one.

teanga

(Pronounced **tyoegha**). A tongue. The tongue-like ridges of **Teanga Mhòr** and **Teanga Bheag** in the Red Cuillin of Skye clearly protrude like rounded glacier snouts down to the valley. There are over a dozen hill-names with *teanga*, mainly found in Mull and Morvern, and in Lochaber near the solitary Munro of the species, **Meall na Teanga** above Loch Lochy. Not far away is the intriguing **Teanga gun Urrain**, literally the tongue without a responsible person . . . a gossip, perhaps? In the Renfrew Heights there is a broad ridge called simply **The Tongue**, a simple translation into English of an original Gaelic name. And another 'tongue', that of Old Norse, was at work in the Hebrides in hill-names like Barra's **Ben Tangaval**.

uchd

(Pronounced oochk) This means a bosom or breast, and by analogy a steep hill. **Uchd Mòr** in Skye is the big hill, while **Uchd a'Chlàrsair** is the harper's hill in Atholl. **Creag Uchdag** near Ben Chonzie may be from *uchdach* meaning steep.

Animal features

Having spotted the human frame in so many hill features, not surprisingly Gaelic also found space for the likenesses of animal bodies. Thus we have several **An Socach** hills, meaning a snout of the porcine variety, while near Sanquhar in the south-west is **Dalzean Snout** hill. There's also a fine Scots description for "piggy-backed" hills – a 'soo's back'! Gaelic for a wing, *sgiath*, as in **Sgiath Chùil** near Crianlarich, also means a sheltered spot, hinting at

---

Sròn a'Choire Ghairbh – **strawn** *a* chor*a* **gharav**
Sròn Gharbh – strawn **gharav**   Sròn Ulladal – strawn **ool**ut*a*l
Teanga Mhòr/Bheag – tyoegh*a* **voa:r/vayk**   Uchd Mòr – oochk **moa:r**
Uchd a'Chlàrsair – oochk *a* **chlaar**sayrʸ   Creag Uchdag – krayk **ooch**kak
An Socach – *a*n **soch**koch   Sgiath Chùil – skee*a* **choo:l**ʸ

94

the wing's protective crook, and it usually applies to long narrow ridges, running at right angles to the westerly gales – like the group of three hills on Skye's Sleat peninsula called *sgiath-bheinn*. **Ladhar Bheinn***, hoof mountain above Loch Hourn (Loch Hell), suggests a bovine or perhaps a devilish imprint on the landscape, while **Sgùrr an Ùtha*** near Glenfinnan is peak of the udder, the animal version of Sgùrr na Cìche.

With so many parts of the anatomy and physiognomy covered in their hill-names, no wonder the Gaels went on to personify so many peaks, naming them after real or legendary people or professions. We meet them in the chapter on Mountain Characters.

Ladhar Bheinn – **loe-***a*r vYn
Sgùrr an Ùtha – sgoor *an* **oo:-***a*

Chapter Seven

Kips and Laws –
Scots generic hill-names

Most of Scotland's hills have Gaelic names, either in original or corrupted form. But in the Borders and in many lowland areas of east and central Scotland, their names are from the Scots language.

The Scots language originated as one of several branches of English with common roots in the Germanic Anglo-Saxon of Britain's eastern invaders. Each region had its own variations: in England the East Midlands variety came to predominate as so-called 'standard English' and to a large extent erased many of the northern English varieties. While this linguistic genocide proceeded at full pace in England's own backyard, the process was less thorough north of the Border, because of the barrier of Border hills and the Scots' nationalistic pride. Their linguistic resistance has ensured that Scots hill-names have preserved words long vanished from the northern English hills.

That many of the Scots hill-names have Northern Old English connections does not mean that the poor, dependant Scots had to import English words to describe the hills for them. Many of the Scots hill-names are original developments of Old English words (for instance hlāw became law) and Scots has also drawn upon its northern Gaelic reservoirs (for instance *cnoc* became knock) to brew its distinctive mix.

There are also Scots words fashioned from Old Norse or Gaelic material – like fell and cairn – and we inherited, neat, some Old Welsh names, from the centuries when the Britons spoke the language that is the ancestor of modern Welsh. Names like *din* (hill-fort), *pen* (head, summit) and *bar* (top) all still exist in Welsh. In the Border hills they remain like a tidemark of history in names like **Din Law** and **Skelfhill Pen** near Hawick (both complete with Scots translations!), and **Carter Bar** on the actual border.

bell
In Scots a bell is a bubble or blister, and it seems to have entered hill-names probably on account of their shape. There are several shoulders of hills, and

one isolated hill called by the apparently generic name **The Bell** (for instance on the side of Mendick hill), in southern Scotland and just over the border with England, as well as one or two in the English Lakes. **Yeavering Bell**, **Bell Craig** and **Bell Hill**, all in the southern Borders, add to this family.

ben

This is the anglicised version of the main Gaelic hill-word *beinn*. On maps nearly a quarter of the one thousand Highland peaks properly called Beinn are shown as Ben, especially those more popular with tourists like Ben Nevis, Ben Lomond, and Ben More.

The word was first used in Scots-English in the mid-19th century, but only in the way we often use foreign words to refer to foreign things. Thus a Professor Shairp wrote a poem in 1864, attacking the advent of railways into the Highlands:

> "Land of Bens and Glens and Corries,
> Headlong Rivers, clean floods,
> Have we lived to see this outrage,
> On your haughty solitudes?"

The use of the word as a properly adopted Scots word appears to be less than a century old, the first recorded reference being in 1898:

> "An' the white snawdrifts sunlicht-kissed on the great bens". (from a book called, paradoxically, *In Glasgow Streets!*)

So the word ben that is now seen as quintessentially Scots is in fact a relative newcomer in common usage. This recency is confirmed by the fact that very few hills outside the Gaelic Highlands carry the name. In the Central Lowlands hill-ranges it is found mainly in the Ochils near Stirling, sometimes taking a Scots rather than Gaelic language mate as in **Ben Ever** (upper). There are a few bens in the south-west where they are corruptions of original Gaelic, such as **Benyellary,** from *beinn na h-iolaire*, mountain of the eagle.

bin, binn

Almost as common as ben in southern Scotland is the other Scots corruption of *beinn* in the form of bin. In the north-east we find the **Bin of Cullen** and its sidekick the **Little Bin,** and plain **The Bin** near Huntly. In the Ochils lies **Binn Hill** (a Scots-English tautology) and nearby is the politically-famous **The Binns,** mansion house and estate on the low hills near Linlithgow, home to crusading Labour M.P. Tam Dalyell. **Byne Hill** by Girvan, first ascent for many young holidaymakers, may come from this word too or more probably from the Scots bine meaning a wash-tub, to which upturned it has a resemblance (and the local pronunciation of byne, as in bind, confirms this). But the best-known of all the 'bins' is surely the Campsies' **Meikle Bin**, Scots for the big hill. Seen from the grey guddle of urban Clydeside it tapers to a sharp cone peeping above the flat plateau of its hill-range, a Mount Fuji of weekend promise. Certainly it's the only top in the Campsies sufficiently meikle or peak-shaped enough to deserve the accolade of 'bin', this very Scots word for mountain. (And interestingly, there's an ancient name Mons Bannauc, which Professor W.J. Watson located at the head-waters of the River Carron (here in the Campsies): based as it is on the root-word *banna* meaning peaked, could it be this same Meikle Bin?)

cairn

The Gaelic word *càrn* for a rocky hill has been appropriated by Scots as cairn for a hill, and indeed has passed into English as the term for the summit pile of stones. Quite a few of the Cairngorm mountains, including the flagship **Cairn Gorm** itself, have been scotticised in this way, and among other eastern Highland hills **The Cairnwell** of Glenshee, and **Cairn o' Mount,** are almost as well known; the second name-element of the last two has been scotticised too, from the Gaelic respectively *bhalg* and *monadh*. In the Pentlands near Edinburgh we have an **East** and **West Cairn Hill** both with widely sprawled cairns on top, supposedly the remains of Bronze Age Druidic cairns for sacrificial celebrations. The name is relatively recent for there is an older name for the hill, **Harperrig,** which is reputed to refer to the harp-players at the Druidic ceremonies, centuries before English-speaking came to the area.

Most cairns are in the north-east, in Grampian and Tayside Regions, or in Dumfries and Galloway, both areas where the original Gaelic names were often corrupted by Scots or English speakers.

cock

In Lowland Scotland, from Deeside to Lothian and the Renfrew Heights, are many hills called **Cock Law** (or Hill or Rig). It may well refer to the cock birds or moorfowl, but in Scots the word cock can mean a cap or headwear, sitting on one's topmost part. As such it may have links with the Old English *coc* meaning a hill, or with the Gaelic *cochull* meaning a hood or cowl, as used in **Cockleroy** (*cochull ruadh,* red hood) above Linlithgow.

comb, coomb

The Border hills, known to geographers by the soulless term the Southern Uplands, are rich in Scots hill-names with a family connection south of the Border, as we would expect. Comb in England means crest: in the Border hills we have two Comb Heads and a **Comb Hill.** The similar word coomb means, in Scots place-names "a bosom in the hill" (the dictionary's version of the Gaelic *coire!*), and so we have hills like **White Coomb, Coomb Dod, Coomb Fell** and **Law.**

curr

This rare Scots hill-name, possibly derived from the Gaelic *corr* meaning pointed hilltop, is found near Kirk Yetholm in **The Curr** and **Blackdean Curr** hills.

dod

A dod or dodd is "a bare round hill", and is related either to the Old English word *dodden* (to pollard or cut), or to the Old Norse *toddi* meaning a foothill, or slight elevation near a mountain mass. This second explanation, while not very flattering in suggesting a mere 'doddle', is the more likely, for the name dod is found in sizeable numbers in the English Lakes, reservoir of Norse words. In Scotland there are dods in the eastern Borders – **Deuchrie Dod** and **Wester Dod** in the Lammermuirs, **Moll's Cleuch Dod** and **Garelet Dod** near Moffat, for examples – and there's a **Dodd Hill** in the Sidlaws. There are at least a dozen plain **Dod Hills** in the Borders. The still-used Scots phrase "a dawd o' tatties" for your plate conjures up nicely the shape of these lumpy hills.

edge

Of Northern English origin (as in the celebrated Striding Edge of Helvellyn), the word edge is used to describe the tilted slope of a hill, as in **Spartleton Edge** and **Blythe Edge** near Abbey St. Bathans in Borders Region.

fell

This is a name that straddles the border with England, and in Scotland is found particularly in the south-west within view of the Lakeland Fells. The name originated both in the English Lakes, where the Viking settlers had brought *fjall*, a mountain, which their descendants made into fell, and in the Galloway hills in Southern Scotland. The higher hills in this area have Gaelic names, with the fells generally being lower, as poet Rabbie Burns observed:

> "The Partridge loves the fruitful fells,
> The Plover loves the mountains."

. . . thus indicating the relatively lower height of the fells.

In Dumfries and Galloway Region there are four specimens of **Fell Hill,** and several hills called Fell of . . . (as in **Fell of Fleet**), as well as a simple **The Fell.** The term spread north into the Borders with names like **Hart Fell** (reputed home of Merlin, who could turn himself into a deer or hart), **Capel Fell** and **Larrington Fell** in the east.

It has also been used – unsuccessfully – to describe Highland hills. When Borderer James Hogg, the famous Ettrick Shepherd and poet (1772-1835), saw the supposedly haunted Ben Macdhui during a Highland journey, he wrote of a man he'd met who had "beheld the fahm (the 'Grey Man') o'er the fell.": but the name did not catch on in the Highlands.

Two of the best-known 'fells' are furth of the Borders: the Campsie Fells and Goat Fell in Arran. Both 'fells' appear to be relatively late arrivals in their area. (See the Campsies in The Ranges chapter, and Goat Fell in the Islands chapter).

heugh

A heugh is a cliff or "rugged steep", and in the southern Borders are **Hart Heugh** and **Peniel Heugh**. They are perhaps derived from the Old English *hōh*, a heel. The similar-sounding but unrelated names of **Broughton Heights** (above the village of that name) and **Tamond Heights** come from heich or heicht, Scots for a height.

kip

Kip means a sharp-pointed hill, as in the distinctive clean-cut lines of the **East** and **West Kip** in the Pentlands, or a jutting-out point on a hill, sometimes found in the Borders. Thus an early 19th-century Borders writer says:

> "I saw the bit crookit moon come stealing o'er the kips o' Boweshope Law."

Near Peebles the **Makeness Kips** are the only pointed set of peaks amongst the rounded hills of the area, their tops on the plateau like rock tips peeping above the gentle sea swell. Near Dolphinton is the splendidly-named **Keppat Hill,** a small sharp-pointed hill of sand and gravel, from the adjectival form kippit. Just as fine, if not so descriptive, is its alternative local name as 'The Deil's Riddlins', where the legend is that the Devil himself sieved out the soil of a nearby hill, dumping the rocks in Biggar Moss and the sand here!

There are only a few kips, including five called simply **The Kip** or Kipps, but they have a wide family network abroad. Its distant language relatives include the Old English *copp* – there's a **Cop Law** near Ettrick – the German *Kopf*, the Dutch and Afrikaans *kop* and indeed the Gaelic *ceap*, all meaning 'head'.

knock, nock

Cnoc is a Gaelic word for a lower hill, a knoll rather than a mountain. The Scots form is knock (or more rarely nock) and it usually describes isolated, cone-shaped hills. There are enough Knocks in Scotland to fill a "Who's There?" page, and one Galloway writer counted two hundred in his native county alone. Among the many are **Knock Hill** near Huntly – with its splendidly-named hillfoot farm Yondertown of Knock – and elsewhere **Big Knock, Meikle Knock,** and **Knock More** (all meaning the same thing in English, Scots and Gaelic!), whilst **Great Knock** in the Manor Hills tries to outdo them all! There are a dozen examples of **Knock Hill** – including one in Fife best known for the racing circuit at its foot – four simple hills called **The Knock,** and a **Knock Hills** range near Carter Bar on the border.

knowe

A knowe is the Scots version of the English knoll. However, while south of the Border the knoll betokens a small hillock suitable for fairies to dance around, here in Scotland a knowe is made of sterner stuff, rising to as high as 2,650 feet (809m) in **Fifescar Knowe** in the Manor Hills. As one of Rabbie Burns' songs suggests, a knowe was big enough to be a sheep-farm and complete eco-system all rolled into one:

> "Ca' the yowes [ewes] tae the knowes,
> Ca' them where the heather growes,
> Ca' them where the burnie rowes,
> My bonnie Dearie"

Knowes are found especially in south-western Scotland, and are also a prominent feature in Orkney and Shetland where they take the name-form Knowe of . . . (as in **Knowe of Setter**). Other specimens include the alliterative **Nickies' Knowe** near Moffat, and Edinburgh's Silverknowes and Kingsknowe.

law

This is surely the archetypal Scots hill-word, its answer to Gaelic's *beinn*. This fine word is found in some small measure in the western hills (in the Renfrew Heights and Campsies) but it is mainly a word of the east and south where Gaelic was not an alternative. There is the Sid*law* range in Tayside, which is a backdrop to **Dundee Law**, which in turn is one of a kenspeckle group including **Largo Law, Traprain Law** and **North Berwick Law**. This quartet owe their fame to their situation as steep-sided isolated hills rising like shark's fins above the surrounding sea of farmland or (in Dundee's case) housing. They confirm to the shape and situation suggested by the Scottish National Dictionary's definition of a law as:

> "a rounded hill generally of a somewhat conical shape, and frequently isolated or conspicuous among others".

Some of them are by geological origin volcanic plugs, stoppering up the neck of a dead volcano, and left standing by the erosion of surrounding crumbly rock. As such they were ideal defence sites in the pre-nuclear age; Dundee Law has an ancient hill-fort on top – *dùn* is a Gaelic word meaning fort and the town therefore takes its name from this hill – while Traprain Law's earlier name was Dun Pelder, the fort of the spear shafts. Both Dundee and North Berwick Laws have giant arches of whale jawbone on top, in the former's case because the town was the home port of many whaling ships.

Although some of the Borders' laws fit the definition of isolated – like **Yetholm Law** above the village of that name – many other laws are less distinctively-shaped. Such 'bye'-laws were well described by Borderer James

Hogg who wrote over 150 years ago:

"The common green dumpling-looking hills commonly called law"

Among the many will be found the Pentlands' **Twin Laws** and **Castle Law** (another defence site, with its Stone Age earthwork), the Manor Hills' **Broad** and **Dollar Law,** the simple **Law** near Elvanfoot, and five plain names **The Law.**

The word law is Anglo-Saxon in origin: there was an old English word *hlāw* meaning hill or mound, but this word is now obsolete south of the Border and the Scots are now 'a law unto themselves'!

mount, mounth

The Gaelic word *monadh* (and its Welsh cognate *mynydd*) meaning a mountain or high moorland has ancestral links with the Scots mounth and mount. **The Mounth,** formerly the name for all the high ground now referred to as the Grampians, now refers only to the east-west ridge south of Deeside; it contains **Mount Keen** (from the Gaelic *caoin,* meaning gentle or pleasant), **Mount Battock,** and the **White Mounth** (Lochnagar's broad shoulders).

In Fife there is a **Mount Hill,** while further south in the Pentland Hills we find **Mount Maw** and plain **The Mount,** which at only 1762 feet (537m) is a dwarf of the genus mountain. **Mount Skep** near Galashiels is from the Scots word for a basket, or beehive, from its shape. In parts of Scotland, a **munt** refers to a low tree-covered hill. However, the nickname of **Mount Misery** for the 576 feet (176m) high Knockour Hill (*cnoc odhar,* dun-coloured knoll) by Loch Lomond has a spurious air to it . . . only the most wretched urbanite could find this little climb, up to a stunning viewpoint over Loch Lomond, 'miserable'!

naze

This means a promontory, according to the Scots dictionary. There are a couple of hills a few miles apart in upper Nithsdale in the western Borders, called **Rough Naze** and **Herd Naze.** Both are slightly rising tops in the middle of long plateau-like ridges, so the dictionary's meaning seems appropriate, and parallels the shape of a sea headland of the type commonly called ness. This suggest a Norse origin, and the location of **Naze Hill** near Langholm in the south-west confirms it in an area of Norse influence; or it may simply be the Scots equivalent of the Gaelic *sròn.*

pap

Pap is another Scots word with Northern English connections – the **Maiden Paps** near Hawick is but a few miles from the Border – but it is from a Norse root, perhaps via the Lake District. Indeed another **Maiden Pap** in Caithness in the north is in old Viking territory. ('Maiden' in Northern England can signify a hill-fort). Pap means a breast, or nipple, and unusually for Scots words it has penetrated into Gaelic territory, which has its own perfectly good word *cìoch*. Several Gaelic mountains have kept their original *cìoch* (genitive, *cìche*) but others have been ousted by this incomer. The distinctive Sgorr na Cìche at the mouth of Glen Coe is now widely known in English as the **Pap of Glencoe,** probably due to the linguistic pressure of the tourists who visit this area.

The famous **Paps of Jura,** a landmark of any hill-view in the south-west Highlands, were also named by Scots or English speakers, for according to Martin Martin's 1703 book *A Description of the Western Isles:*

". . . the two highest (hills) are well known to *seafaring men* by the name of the Paps of Jurah." (my emphasis)

The native Gaels had quite different individual names for Jura's peaks (see the Islands chapter), and while the Scots mariners' phrase is felicitous as regards their well-rounded shapes it rather overlooks the fact that there are a *trio* of peaks of roughly equal size, just as Glencoe's Pap is a singular example of the species! At least Lochnagar's **Meikle** and **Little Pap** summits achieve the desired number. These Scots names are the translation of the old Gaelic name Beinn nan Cìochan, the mountain of the little nipples, for like other Cairngorm tops the granite rocks have weathered to produce tors which stand proud of the swelling plateaux like nipples. One of the few examples of Pap in southern Scotland is the **Pap Craig** on the southern slope of Tinto Hill, a cliff whose profile is distinctly mammary when seen from the east.

pen, pin

From the Brittonic or Old Welsh language that was spoken in southern Scotland in pre-Gaelic and pre-English times, there remain words like *pen* and *pin* meaning a head or hilltop. In present-day Welsh *pen* is still in use, as in Pen-y-Fan (the head of the slope) in the Brecon Beacons. In the Scottish Borders **Pennygant Hill** south of Hawick is clearly Welsh in sound. More Scottish in name, but of Welsh lineage, are **Ettrick Pen** and **Skelfhill Pen** near Hawick (a skelf being in Scots a splinter or a ledge on a hill). **Penvalla** and **Penveny** Hills above Stobo are *pen fah law* (head of the fair hill, in Old English) and *pen faen,* head of the stone; **Penbane** near Durisdeer is from Welsh *ban,* a peak. The Pentland Hills come from the same root, with two Welsh elements *pen + llan:* however **Pinbreck Hill** (and **Penbreck** hill near Daer) have a Gaelic second element (*breac,* speckled), and **Pin Stane** hill near Elvanfoot has a Scots second element.

pike

This word is usually associated with the English Lake District, with its

Langdale Pikes, and its roots lie in the Old Norse *pik*, a peak. There are several hills in the southern Borders, with names like **Pike Fell** and simple **The Pike**.

rig, rigg

The word rig or rigg has both Old English and Old Norse connections. It means a ridge, usually a straight, steep-sided one. In the English Lakes there are one or two instances, like Loughrigg (the ridge above the loch), while southern Scotland has many examples such as **Rig of the Shalloch** in Ayrshire, **Mid Rig** and **Firthhope Rig**. **Rig of the Jarkness** is another splendid name near the head of Glen Trool, possibly meaning the ridge of the turbulent waterfall. In central Scotland the word has got mixed up with an old Scots term referring to the run-rig system of farming, practised communally with a series of long parallel ridges or furrows. Lanarkshire hamlets like Limerigg and Stanrigg, standing at nearly 800 feet (240m) above sea level, could derive their name either from their farm history or from their airy situation on the edge of the Slamannan plateau.

seat

Seat, as found in Edinburgh's **Arthur's Seat** and the Campsies' **Earl's Seat** expresses the idea of a high throne for the powerful in the land. That's why the other common name using this term is **King's Seat,** also referring to the mighty in the land – there are hills of this name in the Ochils, the Sidlaws, and near Dunkeld. Its language root is the Old English *soeti*, and the hill-word side – as in the Borders hills of **Faw Side** (faw or faugh meaning mottled) and **Hummel Side** (hummel, low-lying) in the Borders – probably comes from the same source.

tap, top, tip

Obviously meaning a hill-top, this is found in a few names in the farthest south-west and in the north-east, but not in between. In remote Galloway lies a hill called **Tops of Craigeazle,** the highest point of a branch of the Rhinns of Kells. While in Grampian Region above the village of Rhynie stands a summit, site of an old hill-fort, called **Tap o' Noth.** One writer has derived its name from the Gaelic *taip a'nochd*, meaning (according to him) the top of searching or observation – in other words a lookout post for the old hill-forters, in line with the many instances of **Ward** or **Watch Hill** in northern Scotland. Certainly this north-eastern area has many corrupted Gaelic names, like cairn and mount, and Gaelic dictionaries do have *taip* meaning a mass or lump, equally appropriate for a hill, but the suggestion seems inept, the hill not being especially prominent; it is far more likely to be a later Scots word for top. More romantically, legend has it that its 'house-giant' Jack o' Noth, having stolen the sweetheart of Jack o' Bennachie nearby, was flattened (together with his 'bidie-in'!) on his own hilltop by a huge boulder hurled by his cuckolded neighbour. Bennachie itself has a summit called the **Mither Tap.**

Interestingly, neither the Tap o' Noth, the Tops of Craigeazle, nor the Mither Tap are actual main summits in their own right but merely the highest points of a long ridge which bears the name of the hill proper, respectively Hill of Noth, of Craigeazle, and the Oxen Craig of Bennachie. This suggests that the 'top' idea is similar to that of the later *Munro's Tables* in which the highest points are the summits or proper "Munros", while other high points on shoulders are mere "tops" often by-passed by Munro-baggers.

Elsewhere in south-western Scotland are the Scots hill-names of **Tippet Hill, Tappetknowe** and **Tappet Hill,** from the adjective tappit (more usually applied to hens!) meaning crested, and the local name of **Tintock Tap** for Tinto Hill. **Welltrees Tappin** near Sanquhar contains the word tappin, a local Ayrshire word expressive for a top, but not as delightful as the alternative Scots word tappietourie (the 'tower' on top?), meaning a cairn on a hill-top! Back in the north-east are the **Tops of Fichell** (probably from Gaelic *fiacaill*, a tooth), the **Meikle Tap** (big top) on the Hill o' Fare, and the expressive **Tips of the Clunymore** above Dufftown.

tor, tore, torr
Derived directly from the Gaelic *tòrr*, this word seems to be used in the English sense of a rock standing proud on a hill, as on Dartmoor. The **Newton Tors** and **Easter Tor** hills above Kirknewton in the southern Borders have outcropping rocks near the summit.

This does not exhaust the Scots collection of hill-names. Among others you will find, in different localities, a boorachie (small hill), a scaup (small bare hill, scalp-like), the expressive snib (a short steep hill), a steel (steep bank), a tummock (a hillock – probably from the Gaelic *tolm*) and a type (a low conical hill in Dumfriesshire). Not such a muckle as the Highland Gaels, yet the Scots have a fine hairst of hill-names!

Chapter Eight

Popular Hills

This chapter deals with many well-known and popular hills on the Scottish mainland, not covered by the other chapters.

Ben Alder

This lies in the very heart of the Highlands, a great hunk of a mountain sending streams forth west to the Atlantic and north-east to the North Sea. Its name however is something of a mystery, perhaps because so central and high a mountain mass would have a very old, possibly a pre or early Gaelic name. It appeared on early maps of the 17th century as Bin Aildir and it had a local Gaelic name Beinn Allair, later **Beinn Eallar***, which was interpreted by Professor W.J. Watson as *beinn alldobhar* (or *ail dobhar*) meaning 'rock (and) water' or 'precipice (and) water'. This would certainly fit its corried slopes, and this 18th-century description of Prince Charlie's hideout at Cluny's Cage here:

> ". . . 'Twas situate on the face of a very rough high rockie mountain called Letternilichk which is still a part of Ben Alder, full of great stones and crevices . . ."

('Letternilichk' is probably *leitir nan leac*, slope of the stones.)

Taking the 17th-century form of the name as Aildir, another possibility might seem to lie in the Gaelic *ail* (a rock or cliff) or *aill* (a rough steep slope) and *dìreadh* (climbing or ascending): the 'mountain of the ascending rocky slope' would be a fine name for this massive hill, and it would be a cousin to **Beinn Dìreach*** in the north-west, the upright or ascending mountain. But the first syllable of *dìreadh* is long, and couldn't really be compressed into the short second syllable of Alder, so we must look back to *ail dobhar* for the meaning.

Ail is an archaic word, and *dobhair* (water), also an ancient word (unlike *dìreadh*), would be an apt companion for it: and the name of Morar in the west, deriving from *mòr-dhobhair* (big water – Loch Morar), shows how the

---

Beinn Eallar – bYn **yalar**
Beinn Dìreach – bYn **dyee**:roch

element *dhobhair* can be shortened in speech just as *ail-dhobhair* here became (*beinn*) *allair* to the local Gaels. The position of the two words suggests too that *ail* was probably an adjectival noun (the genitive case, meaning 'of rock'), again paralleling the structure of Morar (adjective *mòr* preceding noun *dobhair*); and so the name *ail-dhobhair* literally means 'water of rock', describing the rocky chasm carved out by the burn as it tumbled down the slopes. The present name, Ben Alder, is as "worn down" from its original form as the rocks of its stream bed!

Beinn Alligin*

The nearest word in Gaelic dictionaries to this name is *àilleagan,* a jew-l or a darling, and the usual translation is jewelled mountain or mountain of beauty. The name is richly deserved, if unusual. However the pronunciation of *àilleagan* normally has a 'y' sound after the 'l', and this may have led Professor W.J. Watson to say that it was named after the River Alligin at its foot, a name in turn perhaps deriving from *ail*, a rock, as in Ben Alder above. It could be *ail-lagan,* the little hollow of the rock; but if this is the meaning of the name, then it is more likely to refer to the mountain itself and its eastern corries, facing the huge Coire Mhic Nobuil, than to the River Alligin which is on the western 'backside' of the hill. Furthermore the mountain's second peak **Tom na Gruagaich*** is hill of the damsel, lending authority to the mountain's claim to its chivalrous compliment of a name. 'Jewel' is an unusual name in Scotland, but it keeps good cosmopolitan company – with Les Écrins in the French Alps, the 'jewels' or 'jewel box', and the famous Kanchenjunga in the Himalaya, the 'five treasures of the snow'.

Back in Scotland **Sgòr na h-Ulaidh*** above Glen Coe is from *ulaidh,* a treasure, for which there is no historical evidence, although it may refer to the way that the summit is completely hidden from the glen by its north shoulder; or more poetically *ulaidh* can be a darling – another treasured peak, perhaps. And over in the Mounth the mountain **Mayar*** is sometimes translated as *m'aighear,* my darling, for no obvious reason since its top is but a gentle rise in a wide rolling plateau. Gaelic names in this area are often in very corrupted form, and *magh àrd,* high plain, might be more suitable to the landscape at least.

Ben A'n

(Sometimes Ben A'an). When Sir Walter Scott wrote his epic poem *Lady of the Lake* he effectively created the Trossachs as a tourist attraction, and also brought this sharp little peak into the spotlight – but made a bad mistake with its name in the process, creating a "Ben" where none had stood before! A fine

---

Beinn Alligin – bYn **aal**eegin
Tom na Gruagaich – towm n*a* **groo**-*a*geech
Sgòr na h-Ulaidh – skor n*a* **hoo**lee   Mayar – **may***a*r

viewpoint from which to look down on Loch Katrine and the surrounding woods and hills, it probably gets more visitors than any other Scottish hill of its modest 1750 feet (533m) height, and in fact it is not really a separate hill at all but a pointed bump on the shoulder of **Meall Gainmheich*** (sandy hill). From below it is a striking sharp little peak, and Scott wrote of it:

". . . While on the north, through middle air,
Ben-an heaved high his forehead bare."

The map spelling of Ben A'n has the bracketed alternative of Binnein, indicating that it might originally be from **Am Binnean*** meaning the small pointed peak. (There is a hill called **Binnean nan Gobhar***, goats' peak, not far away across Loch Ard.) Walter Scott's "Ben-an" may also be the simple diminutive *beannan*, 'little mountain' . . . there's a **Beannan Beaga*** in the Monadh Liath (though this may be an O.S. misprint for *beanntan*), an **Am Beannan** above Loch Rannoch, and two **Bennan** hills in the Borders . . . and it is indeed the Trossachs' 'little mountain'.

Arkle
Along with neighbour Foinaven, Arkle comes high in the recognition stakes because of the Duchess of Westminster's two famous racehorses of the 1960s that bore their names. This sporting fame belies their remoteness in the north-west, beyond the pale of the Munros and outwith the main walking areas. They are also in territory where the Norse and Gaelic tongues intermix with Ben Stack and Ben More, Lochinver and Laxford.

Suggestions that have been made for the name include *ark-fjall* or *àirc fjall* (Norse or Gaelic-Norse for ark mountain), and *àiridh-fjall*, mountain of the high pasture. One strength of the 'ark' suggestion is that the 'fj' of *fjall* would fall silent after 'c' or 'k', to produce a name like Arkle. One weakness of the 'pasture' name is the topography, for this is a gaint Moby Dick of a mountain with a mass of whitish-grey quartzite spilling off its surfacing ridge. There is a Old Norse word *orc*, whale, used by the Vikings to name the Orkney isles: could Arkle have been their 'whale rock'?

Arthur's Seat
The legend of King Arthur and his Knights took all Britain by storm in the 12th century, and places were named in their honour all over the land. In Scotland there's Arthur's Cairn in the north-east, a possible link in Ben Arthur in the west and Benarty in Fife, an Arthur's Seat on Hart Fell in the Borders, as well as this Edinburgh landmark of the same name. This sleeping

---

Meall Gainmheich – myowl gan*a*veech
Am Binnean – *a*m **bee**nyan
Binnean nan Gobhar – beenyan n*a*n **gow**-*a*r
Beannan Beaga – byen*a*n **bay**k*a*

volcano looks from many angles like a resting lion, but it got its noble name many centuries before Scots explorers brought back news and images of the "king" of the animals. For in the 12th century Giraldus Cambrensis in his medieval Latin wrote of *Cathedra Arturii* (Arthur's Throne) here, and in the 16th century it appeared in records as Arthurissete (a contemporary spelling of the modern name). Some books have suggested an origin in *àirde nan saighead* (height of the arrows) or the unlikely *àrd tìr suidhe* (seat on high land), or the even more imporbable *àirde Thor* (Thor's Height, after the Norse war god), but the Gaelic word *àirde*, a height, common in the west of Scotland, doesn't occur anywhere else in the Lothian area.

The main summit, Arthur's Seat, is surrounded by later names in Gaelic, Scots and English. The Gaels named Dunsappie Loch and Rock (*dùn sèapach*, crouching hill-fort). This may have been their name for the whole hill, but the lion has flicked the challenge to its authority aside, for Dunsappie is a small side-hill. The Scots gave names like **Whinney Hill** (whin or gorse hill) to one long rib and **The Lang Rig** to another, **Haggis Knowe** (where St. Anthony's Chapel stands). **The Dasses** (ledges), and the splendid name of the northern gully known as **The Guttit Haddie** (gutted haddock). This last was scoured out by a downpour in the early 18th century, and was also known as the **Speldrin** (a dried, split haddie). The local people also referred to the whole hill as Craigenemarf (Creag nam Marbh, dead men's crag) perhaps in confusion with **Hangman's Rock** down by Duddingston Loch, or just plain The Crag.

Englishman the Earl of Salisbury, who came up with Edward III in 1355, has the **Salisbury Crags** named after him. Nearby the basalt columns of Samson's Ribs commemorate the Biblical character who certainly never came here any more than Arthur himself did. But the power of the legend carried his name to the very summit!

Baosbheinn*

A little-traversed but highly-acclaimed Torridon peak, usually translated as wizard's peak, from *baobh* meaning a wicked person, a witch, a fury, and – occasionally – a wizard (*fiosaiche* is a more usual word for wizard). A *baobh* can also be a she-spirit, haunting rivers, dark cousin of that other ubiquitous Gaelic creature the water-horse that rose from lochs (like Loch Avon) to spirit humans to their watery grave – such creatures occur in names in several Highland places such as Loch na Beiste a few miles north. Interestingly, the loch at Baosbheinn's foot is Loch na h-Oidhche, the loch of night or darkness – a common name usually meaning that fish rise (to be caught) at night, but here with an interesting double meaning!

Baosbheinn – **boe:shvYn**

Alternatively, *baos* (pronounced boe:s) means madness or lust – the latter, perhaps for the 'damsel' (Tom na Gruagaich) on the 'darling peak' of neighbour Beinn Alligin!

Bennachie

Such is the fondness with which this hill is regarded in the north-east that it has its own 'Swiss Guard' of hill-lovers, the Bailies of Bennachie. Founded in 1970, they look after its care and conservation. The hill's pointed top is familiar from many viewpoints, sitting on a wedge of high ground in the Buchan lowlands, advance runner for the distant Cairngorms. More poetically, local bard Charles Murray wrote of it:

> ". . . Ben Nevis looms, the laird of a',
> But Bennachie! Faith, yon's the hill
> Rugs at the hairt where you're awa'"

The granite tor that protrudes from its plateau, the famous **Mither Tap**, is the goal of most walkers although the true summit is the **Oxen Craig**. This Scots name the Mither Tap (mother top) directs us to the Gaelic original of **Beinn na Cìche*** meaning mountain of the nipple or breast, *cìoch* (genitive *cìche*) being widely used in the Highlands for granite tors of this shape. One article on the hill says boldly that "the Gael, coming within view of this peak, was instinctively compelled to exclaim Beinn-na-ciche!" In 1170 the hill was written as Benychie, and in the 14th century as Benechkey.

Professor Watson's interpretation of the name as *beannachadh* meaning blessed (hill) seems fanciful by comparison with the anatomical meaning, but his is only one of many wild surmisings over the years. It has been translated as meaning the mountain of springs and also of the Tap, of rain, or sight, of the dog, of Ché (a pagan god), of God (*dia*), and even as the 'bend-up-high' hill! This last may have begun with a 19th-century English traveller who decided that Benahee (as spoken) was really the 'ben up high' (in the sky?) mountain! Subsequently a local minister spread the idea that it was 'bend up high' because its shape resembled someone bending over to touch their toes! Certainly for a minister in last century's more prurient times, any name would be preferable to 'the mountain of the breast' although that is exactly what it is.

Boar of Badenoch

Hogging the western skyline at Drumochter Pass together with his mate **The Sow of Atholl** the Boar's name is based on the Gaelic original **An Torc** (the boar) and it stood in the Badenoch estates. From the north (i.e., in Badenoch) its huge convex ridge is indeed of hog's-back shape. (In southern Scotland similarly-shaped hills are known as 'soo's backs'.)

Beinn na Cìche – bYn n*a* **kee:**cha

In 1773 one map showed it as Bin Torc and it is supposed to be haunted by the spectre of a boar, a native species that was hunted to extinction – perhaps here – over 500 years ago. The Sow of Atholl is however the product of a marriage of convenience, name-wise, for her maiden name was **Meall an Dòbhraichean***, hill of the watercress; she marked the northern limit of Atholl lands, on the south side of the pass.

Broad Law

The second highest hill in the Borders at 2754 feet (840m), this is one of a line of laws (a Scots name for a hill) linking **Cairn Law** to **Dollar Law** and **Notman Law**. 'Broad' could apply to the shape of many Border hills, with gently rounded summits providing spacious rooftops above the steep valley walls, and on this hill it provides the platform for a large but unlovely radio beacon on top.

Bynack More

The peaks of the eastern Cairngorms are often crowned with huge granite tors with a local name, barns, probably a translation of the local name Saibhlean Bheinneig: there's a hill called Cairn of Barns not far away. The **Barns of Bynack More** lie just below the summit, and may well be the root of the name. Originally it was called Am Beidhneag, suggesting an origin in *binneag**, a chimney pot or a house roof-ridge. Chimney pots, like the Barns here, are often set just beneath the topmost ridge of the roof. The 'More' part of the name is the Gaelic *mhòr*, big (and there's a 'wee' Bynack Beag nearby). One Gaelic scholar suggests that the name is from *beinneag*, little mountain, in which case Bynack More would be the big little mountain! *Beinneach* – mountainous – might fit the hill and the pronunciation better.

Other writers say it is from *beannag* meaning a cap, or handkerchief or headband (there are 'headwear' peaks elsewhere like **Sgùrr na Boineid***, or **Bonnyfleeces** hill in nearby Angus, from *boineid fleasg*, bonnet crown.) A Gaelic dictionary gives *beannag* (pronounced **bya**nak) as meaning 'a corner, a skirt, or a pointed coif (headwear), worn as a sign of marriage by women'. Certainly when you look up at the mountain from the path in Strath Nethy it does appear to rise to a fine point, unusual in the rounded Cairngorms. But both the headgear similes lack the power of the 'chimney pot' image that strikes the eye from the north.

Cairnpapple

Four thousand years ago this top in the Bathgate Hills was home and castle to a group of Beaker Folk. They looked out at other tops, islands of security in a

---

Meall an Dobhraichean – myowl *an* **doh**:reech*an*
binneag – **beenyak**   Sgùrr na Boineid – skoor n*a* **bonid**[y]

sea of watchfulness, like nearby Cockleroy and **Torphichen** (raven's hill). Four hundred years ago the local people were calling it by its present name, and it was written as Kernepapple in 1619. In 1919 its height of just over 1000 feet (300m) gave to West Lothian the honour of having "the lowest highest point" of any of the old Scottish counties. Today it is an ancient monument with a subterranean hill-fort, sheathed in glass and metal from the elements but overlooked by a large radio beacon.

The name may be Scots, cairn of the pap (or nipple), from its shape, with the small pimple of the fort right on the top: from the lowlands to the east and south it has a clear twin-peaked shape. Or from the Scots 'papple', to bubble up or boil, for the hill sits amid a bumpy landscape like the frozen bubbles of a volcanic crater. There are however several nearby Gaelic names – Torphichen, Ballencrieff Farm and Knock Hill (from *cnoc*, a knoll): the Gaelic word *pabail*, priest's village, is found in Lewis, and at Papple Village in East Lothian . . . and there *was* a medieval abbey nearby at Torphichen, so 'hill of the priest' fits nicely.

On its northern slopes is Cathlawhill, a farm whose name means hill of the battle – as do Borders hills like **Cademuir Hill** and **Cadelaw,** from the Gaelic *cath* or Brittonic *cad.*

Cairnsmore of Carsphairn

In the south-west Borders not far from Loch Doon, this hill's name means the big hill (*càrn mòr*) above the valley (carse) of the alder trees (*feàrna*).

Cairnwell

The skiers' mountain at the head of Glen Shee, and sharing with Cairngorm the 'distinction' of being a Munro easily completed from a chairlift. The name is believed to come from **Càrn Bhalg,*** literally the cairn of the bags, referring to the pouchy peatbanks on the slopes.

Canisp

Unlike its neighbour Suilven, Canisp is rarely asked to pose in the many photos taken from Lochinver, lacking as it does the allure of a dramatic shape. However its shape may have meant more to the Norse, for the Rev J.B. Johnston suggested it was from Old Norse *kenna ups* supposedly meaning well-known house roof. This is a bit unlikely as the neighbouring peaks mainly have Gaelic names and the Norse rarely went in for figurative description in names.

An earlier SMC *Northern Highlands* guidebook points out that there are whitish quartzite cliffs spilling down its north face and suggests that its name may come from an old Gaelic word *can* meaning white. It is found in words

---

Càrn Bhalg – kaarn **valag**

like *canaichean*, bog-cotton, the bobbing white tufts in the moors. If this is correct it would take its place with the many examples of Geal Chàrn, Sgùrr Bàn, and Fionn Bheinn dotted over the Highlands, all 'white hills'.

Clachnaben

Lying on the eastern shoulders of the Mounth, where the gentle swell of the hills lose their wave-power before dying out on the plains by the North Sea, Clachnaben is a landmark because of the huge granite tor on top. In Gaelic it is *clach na beinne*, stone of the mountain, and its prominence is clear from Hamish Brown's estimates of a 300 pace circumference and a 100 feet (30 m) height.

The Cobbler (Ben Arthur)

This lovely and much-climbed mountain has two names, Ben Arthur and The Cobbler. Several hills have two names, one referring to the whole mountain, the other to a summit upon it. This is the case here too, The Cobbler being the central peak of three, but one that has spread to refer to the whole mountain almost displacing the older name Ben Arthur or Beinn Artair. Like a popular person with a formal title and a nickname, the frequent use of the latter makes use of the former impossibly stiff-necked, and only maps and guides ever draw our attention to the official mode of address. Ironically this formal name with its 'Ben' would appear to be more Gaelic than the English nickname, but in fact the truth is the reverse, that the latter is a translation from Gaelic while the former may well commemorate an early British king.

The suggested origins of Ben Arthur include *beinn artaich* (stony mountain), *art mòr* (or Old Welsh *arth mawr*) meaning big bear, and even a Latin root in *arare*, to plough, supposedly from Arrochar village below it! These 'star-gazing' names (with their great bear and the plough!) are of little value compared to the more obvious root in the name *Artair*, Arthur. There are several Scottish hills named after the legendary British King, including two called Arthur's Seat, and nearby Aghaidh Artair (Arthur's face), and there's no reason why this crown-shaped hill should not join them. It is said of King Arthur that when the Romans left Britain and 'the heathens invaded, he tried to defend it from Cornwall to the Clyde: this mountain, at the head of sea-Loch Long, would mark the northern marches with the men of the north. Or, it could be from another Arthur, a 'local boy made good', a son of the 6th-century King Aedan of Dalriada.

The Cobbler's name is more straightforward. One suggestion is that it is from *gobhlach*, forked, from its shape. There *is* a mountain called **Beinn Gobhlach** near Ullapool with a serrated summit ridge (reminiscent of a factory roof), but its pronunciation **goa:lach** is not much of a basis for the word cobbler. A 1928 book asserted that 'Ben Gobhlach' was the local Gaelic at that time, but earlier evidence suggests that The Cobbler is in fact a simple English translation of an

The Cobbler

old local Gaelic name, for as John Stoddart wrote in 1800, in his book *Local Scenery and Manners in Scotland:*

> "This terrific rock forms the bare summit of a huge mountain, and its nodding top so far overhangs the base as to assume the appearance of a cobbler sitting at work, from whence the country people call it *'an greasaiche crom'*, the crooked shoemaker"

An early contributor to the *SMC Journal* had an interesting theory for how the shape was identified and named. Writing in 1901, William Inglis Clark noted that in the eastern Alps peaks whose summits 'terminate in perpendicular pinnacles' are sometimes named *'Schuster'* (cobbler) and that a prime example was the Dreischusterspitze (three cobblers' peak) in the Tirol. He speculates:

> "Is it possible therefore that the name may have originated by some traveller returning from these Dolomitic regions and seeing a fancied resemblance in our Scottish "Dolomites"?

Fancy indeed, that Gaelic-speakers would take on board an English-speaking traveller's description of a remote corner of the Alps! As for the Dreischusterspitze, the only Scottish peak it remotely resembles might be the pinnacle ridge of the Cuillins' Sgùrr nan Gillean. The author's enquiries at the local Italian tourist office were met by the explanation that it was named because 'it was first climbed by three local cobblers', although this was not confirmed in print (and may be cobblers in another sense!). So The Cobbler's name origin need not be sought abroad: the answer is the simple one, that Gaelic culture with its wide range of names for the hills, and its powers of imagination, came up with an excellent image.

Although to a modern eye, looking for a cobbler (a trade almost vanished from our towns) on the mountain is a bit like scanning the clouds for pictures, another *SMC Journal* writer of early this century was able to point straight at the central peak:

> ". . . on account of the very striking resemblance of the topmost blocks, when seen from Arrochar, to a little cowled figure sitting with his knees gathered up, like a cobbler bending over his work. He faces north, and over against him sits the ponderous and altogether disproportionate figure of his wife . . . like an old woman in a mutch (a night-cap), stooping with age."

It's a measure of how 20th-century eyes have lost the ability to 'see' the hill-shapes that the three peaks have had the names The Cobbler, The Last, and Jean transposed over the years, as this table shows.

YEAR	AUTHOR	SOUTH PEAK	CENTRE PEAK	NORTH PEAK
1899	SMCJ	Jean, his Lass OR his Last (by mountaineers)	Cobbler	Wife
1964	Poucher	Jean, his wife	Cobbler	His Last
1988	Brown	Jean	His Last	The Cobbler

Certainly Stoddart's 1800 quote could point to the north peak which is clearly overhanging, but it more probably and correctly points to the centre peak, which is the true summit. There is a tradition that the new chief of the Clan Campbell, the Duke of Argyll, had to prove himself by climbing to the top of the 'Cobbler's Cowl' (hood), which was the summit stone, and the keyhole on this rock which generations of walkers have wriggled through to get onto the top was known as Argyll's Eyeglass. (The North Peak is known to climbers as the Ram's Head from its shape).

But standing by the shores of Loch Long, now that you know to look at the *centre* peak, you should see the cobbler hunched over his last. (Elsewhere in Scotland is **Creag a'Ghreusaiche**[†] (cobbler's crag) near Aviemore, but this is a mere outcrop barely even proud of a hill-slope and probably commemorates a local cobbler in his croft nearby.)

Cockleroy

Looking down on the ancient and royal burgh of Linlithgow and its well-preserved mediaeval palace, this hilltop was the site of a hill-fort centuries before the settlement below. The royal connection in the town has led to suggestions that its name meant the cock, or top, of the king (*le roi*), but if so it would be the only French name among Scots hills. More likely is the Gaelic *cochull ruadh,* red cowl, hood or cap, the colour coming from the hues of its lavas. (In the Highlands there's a Munro called **Beinn a'Chochuill** near Dalmally.) On Pont's mid-17th century map it was shown as Coclereuf, and on General Roy's map a century later it was Cocklerewhill – both Gallic in sound, perhaps, but Gaelic in origin!

Looking north from Cockleroy the Firth of Forth can be seen over the tops of the **Erngath Hills**. These hills' name is from *àirde na gaoith,* height of the wind (or *earann na gaoith,* portion), rather a grand title for ground that rises to all of 250 feet (75m). Known in the 14th and 15th centuries as Arnegayth or Ardyngaith, and in more recent times as the Irongath Hills, the name is more often used by Bo'ness than Linlithgow folk.

Conival

Conival is a Munro tucked aberth the bigger summit of Ben More Assynt, and seems to be one of a name clan. There are at least four instances of this name in the north-west, as well as Little and Meikle Conval Hills in the north-east, and cousins Conachro, Cona Glen, Conachair and several Conachraigs strung across Scotland from St. Kilda to the Grampians.

Conival has been translated as *konna fjall,* or lady's peak: certainly *fjall* often became *-val* in the names of the Hebrides (as in Skye's Healaval), but rarely on the mainland. Professor Watson, searching Gaelic, suggests early Celtic *cunos* meaning high or *con* meaning dog. More likely, and appropriate, would be the Celtic prefix *con* meaning together or with, and *mheall* (a hill, pronounced val), for Conival and the Cona' Mhealls are all basically shoulders of lower tops of bigger peaks, and the name has the sense of a 'joined-on' hill. Three of them – Conival itself, **Cona Mheall** in the Ben More Coigach group, and Cona Mheall of Beinn Dearg – all lie within sight of each other, and *cona mheall* may have been a local dialect word for just such a hill. Further south, **Sròn Chona Choirein** is the nose of the joining of the corries. Near Loch Arkaig is another top **Streap Còmhlaidh,** a few feet lower than the Streap and linked to it by a narrow saddle, expressing the same 'adjoining' idea, in 'together with Streap'.

Corserine

In Scots the word corse is a common version of cross, a case of metathesis in the jargon of linguistics (where words' letters get mixed round). Corserine Hill in Galloway is the crossing of the rinns (or ridges), indicating transverse ridges.

---

cochull ruadh – kochul **roo**-ugh   Cona' Mheall – **konu** vy*a*l
Beinn a'Chochuill – byn *a* **cho**chee*l*ʸ
Streap Comhlaidh – strehp **caw**l*Y*
Sròn Chona Choirein – strawn chon*a* **cho**rin*ʸ*

Ben Cruachan

Often known simply as **Cruachan**[*], in the 14th century it was recorded as Crechanben, an attempt at the Gaelic name Cruachan Beinne. A *cruachan* is a conical hill, often one standing atop a broader mountain mass (as *cruachan beinne*, 'heap on the mountain' suggests), and this meaning describes the main peak's shape perfectly. Indeed the main ridge has two main summit cones, and the lower of these is **Stob Diamh**[*], (properly *Stob Daimh*) peak of the stag, and an outlying top is **Beinn a' Bhùiridh**[*], peak of the roaring (of the autumn stag rut). The other summits are **Stob Dearg**[*] (red top, also known as the Taynuilt peak from the village to the west), **Meall Cuanail**[*] (hill of the flocks), **Drochaid Ghlas**[*] (the grey bridge), **Stob Garbh**[*] (the rough top) and **Sròn an Isean**[*] (properly *isein*, promontory of the chick).

Cùl Beag[*] and Cùl Mòr[*]

Beag is little, *mòr* is big. But *cùl* means 'back of . . . (anything)'. So the names of these two fine bodyguards to Stac Pollaidh literally mean "big back of " and "little back of ". Back of what? Are they the 'backdrop' to the grander Ben Mor Coigach, or to lower but nearer and more spectacular Stac Pollaidh? There's another pair of Cùl Mòr and Cùl Beag in Easter Ross, very distinctive hills, backing a fertile strath: while **Culardoch** hill near Braemar is simply back of the high place.

Beinn Dorain

Beinn Dorain is a striking mountain towering over Bridge of Orchy. Its slope rises from the railway, steepening towards the summit in a crescendo of concavity. Streams scour out multiple parallel gullies on its face as they skid down. Its main claim to fame in Highland culture lies in the 18th-century poet Duncan Ban MacIntyre's celebration of the mountain in his epic work *Moladh Beinn Dòbhrain*.

A century earlier, Walter MacFarlane's manuscripts had referred to it as Bin Dowran. There are two usual candidates for its name; most often canvassed is *dòbhran* (pronounced **doa**:ran) meaning otter – creatures often feature in Gaelic hill-names and this would be a strong contender, and there is a **Beinn Dobhrain**, otter mountain, near Helmsdale. Or else it could be mountain of the streamlets from *dobhar* which would fit its gullied sides. Ben Alder across Rannoch Moor also contains *dobhar* (*beinn ail-dobhar*) and this connection, together with these striking streams, makes this meaning more

---

Cruachan – kroo*a*chan	Stob Diamh – (properly Stob Daimh) – stob dev
Beinn a'Bhùiridh – bYn *a* voo:ree	Stob Dearg – stob **dyer**ak
Meall Cuanail – myowl **koo**-aneel^y	Drochaid Ghlas – drocha*d*^y **ghlas**
Stob Garbh – stob **garav**	Sròn an Isean – strawn *an* eeshan
Cùl Beag – kool **bayk**	Cùl Mòr – kool **moa:r**

likely. (The two candidates are related, for the otter can be known as *dobhar-chù*, water-dog.)

There's also *dòrainn* meaning pain or anguish – certainly what some walkers experience on its relentless slopes! Just such a meaning is referred to in an old Gaelic song, which has (in translation) the line "There's aye keening on Ben Dorain." A commentary on the song, written by an expert in the 1940s, says that the mountain was known for making sounds at night – continuous murmurs like a child or creature in pain ('keening' in Scots) – when a wind got up before bad weather. Perhaps it was caused by the wind soughing over the many gullies, a huge natural chanter – the mountain of pain indeed.

Beinn Eighe*

This means probably the file mountain from *eighe*, or possibly the ice mountain from *eigh*. It's difficult to see why it should be called ice mountain, for it's not much higher and therefore colder than other peaks. Perhaps the whitish grey screes of quartzite give it a glacial appearance to merit the name, for as Principal Shairp wrote of it last century, it is "a magnificent alp blanched bare and bald and white". The file metaphor is more appropriate for its long narrow ridge in contrast to the broader shoulders of neighbour Liathach. The tops along the ridge run from **Creag Dubh** (black cliff) in the east, over **Spidean Coire nan Clach*** (peak of the stony corrie), **A'Chòinneach Mhòr*** (the big moss, which slopes away north from this top), **Ruadh-stac Mòr*** (big red stack atop the mighty sandstone pillars of the corrie) and **Sàil Mhòr*** (big heel, which rounds it off).

Foinaven*

Famous, like its neighbour Arkle, for its eponymous racehorse, Foinaven is a long raw bone of whitish quartzite rock sticking out of the green and brown peat moors of the north-west. A harsh beauty certainly, but barely deserving of the name of wart mountain, the translation of the Gaelic *foinne-bheinn*, on account of its having "three protuberances" (as the Rev. J B Johnston referred to them). The colour of its massive screes might suggest that it is a corrupted *fionn bheinn*, pronounced fion ven and meaning white mountain, and indeed several guidebooks' indexes have mis-spelt it Fionaven as if in Freudian error. However, although the colour name *fionn* is common in the north-west, there is little evidence for such an origin, as the local pronunciation, usually the most reliable guide, is indeed *foinne-bheinn*.

Beinn Eighe – bYn **ay-***a*
Spidean Coire nan Clach – speedyan kor*a* n*a*n **klach**
A'Chòinneach Mhòr – *a* chawnyoch **voa:r**
Ruadh-stac Mòr – roo-ugh stachk **moa:r**
Sàil Mhòr – saal **voa:r**   Foinaven – fony*a*vin

Fuar Tholl*

This simply means the 'cold hole' or 'cold hollow'. Hamish Brown in his book *Climbing the Corbetts* says:

> "There is some lack of clarity as to which corrie of this grand hill is responsible for the name but my money would go on that grim, cliff-held eastern hollow which is *the* feature of the peak seen from Glen Carron."

The word *toll* is found also in the names of **Tolmount** (hollow mountain), a Munro in the Grampians, and **Toll Creagach*** (rocky hollow) above Glen Affric.

Garbh Bheinn*

There are four peaks of this name, three within 15 miles of Ben Nevis, and of these the best-known is Garbh Bheinn of Ardgour, a rugged peak best seen against a sunset sky looking west from the Ballachulish bridge. Popular with rock-climbers when higher peaks are wreathed in clouds, it simply means rough mountain. In the western areas of high rainfall like this, the downpours give the hills little chance to develop a greensward to smooth over their rocky bones, and hence the name.

Beinn a'Ghlo*

This is a single mountain mass, with three separate peaks of Munro status lying within it, visible and striking for miles around above the broad strath at Blair Atholl. In 1769 Thomas Pennant on his *Tour of Scotland*, described it thus:

> ". . . the great hill of Ben y Glo, whose base is 35 miles in circumference and whose summit towers far above the others."

The great height that Pennant refers to (of 3671 foot, 1129m) and its tendency to catch the clouds will explain the name from an old Gaelic word *glo* meaning veil or hood, and stretched by imagination to suggest a veiled or cloud-capped summit. There was a witch who lived on its summit, with the power to control the weather in order to force humans to meet her demands – so the name may have roots in legend as well as geography. (In the local Gaelic its name is Beinn a'Ghlotha, or Na Beinnichean Glotha.)

The constituent trio of peaks are **Càrn nan Gabhar*** (hill of goats), **Càrn Liath*** (grey hill) and **Bràigh Coire Chruinn-Bhalgain*** (height of the corrie of round blisters).

Fuar Tholl – **foo**-ur howl   Toll Creagach – towl **kregoch**
Garbh Bheinn – **garav** vYn   Beinn a'Ghlo – bYn *a* **ghlaw**
Càrn nan Gobhar – kaarn n*a*n **gow*a*r**   Càrn Liath – kaarn **lyee**-u
Bràigh Coire Chruinn-Bhalgain – brY kora **chrY**n val*a*geen^y

The hill was and is sometimes spelt Ben y Glo, using a local Perthshire variant of a', as in Craig y Barns, Ben y Vrackie or Ben y Hone (Ben Chonzie), all sometimes hyphenated. But the letter 'y' is not part of the Gaelic alphabet, and it suggests that the first mapping which 'recorded' these spellings was done by an O.S. surveyor with origins or training in Wales where 'y' is the common equivalent of the Gaelic a'; Englishman Thomas Pennant may have based his spelling on the sound of the local pronunciation.

Hart Fell
Rising steeply but smoothly above Moffat, this innocuous-seeming hill apparently conceals a rich vein of Arthurian legend. According to author Nikolai Tolstoy, author of *A Quest for Merlin*, this hill was the site of the Arthurian figure Fergus' "Black Mountain" and at one point was the home of Merlin the magician himself. The hart, noble beast and prince of the animal kingdom, was the creature into which Merlin could magic himself on occasion . . . hence the hill's name. Today the more obvious memorial of this legendary wizardry is the hill's shoulder named **Arthur's Seat**.

Ben Hope
This is Scotland's most northerly Munro, from which on a clear day you can see the Orkneys beyond the ragged seaboard and the raging Pentland Firth, named by the Vikings after the Picts who lay to their south in 'Sutherland'. So the mountain's name is appropriately one of the very few on the mainland with an Old Norse name, from *hóp* meaning a bay. As an atlas shows it lies nipped between two long sea-lochs that break deep into the land, Loch Eriboll and the Kyle of Tongue, and with the resulting peninsula slit by its own Loch Hope. (The Norse *hóp* was adopted by Gaelic as *òb*, as in Oban.)

Ben Klibreck
Ben Hope lies about 12 miles (20km) from Ben Klibreck as the raven flies, but many Munro-baggers use a car to net this northerly two in one day. And the connection between them lies deeper in that they are probably the only two Munros with Norse names. For while Klibreck could be from the Gaelic *cliath bhreac*, the speckled slope or cliff, the letter 'k' gives it a Norse twang, and it lies in a chain of Sutherland hills with Norse names. It is probably Norse *clete brekka* or *klif brekka* meaning cliff slope (*klif* is pronounced klee as in Cleveland), and there is indeed a steep slope seamed by outcrops on its western flanks. Both Gaelic and Norse meanings are at least plausible – which is more than can be said for one guidebook's "mountain of the fish"! – and at least the name of the main summit is quite clear, for **Meall nan Con** * is the hill of the dogs in Gaelic.

Meall nan Con – myowl nan kon

The mountain's position in an area of Norse hill names surely clinches the argument. Just to the south is **Ben Armine** (from *àrmunn*, a hero or steward), and nearer the coast is **Beinn Hòrn** (possibly a horn): west is **Maovally** (*mjo-fjall*, narrow hill); and in the area are **Scaraben** (*skora-bheinn*, incised mountain), **Creag Scalabsdale** (*skalli*, bald-headed) and **Col-bheinn** (from *kollr*, a summit) all based on Norse.

Ben Ledi

Throughout the year the car park at the foot of Ben Ledi is packed, and the path to the top crawls with walkers, attracted by its fine shape and the views it commands over the Central Lowlands. This is not new, for in 1794 the local contributor to the *Old Statistical Account* wrote:

> "By reason of the altitude of Ben Ledi and of its beautiful conical figure, the people of the adjacent country to a great distance, assembled annually on its top, about the time of the summer solstice, during the Druidical priesthood, to worship the Deity. This assembly seems to have been a provincial or synodical meeting, wherein all the congregations within the bounds wished to get as near to Heaven as they could to pay their homage to the God of Heaven."

Two possible origins of the name arise from this. One – currently featured on the local tourist information boards – is that it is the Mountain of God (*beinn le dia*) which would certainly fit the history just related; *le* is a preposition meaning with or in the company of and *dia* is prounounced **dyee-a**. (Incidentally the iron cross near the summit has nothing to do with this meaning, for it was erected in 1987 to commemorate a policeman killed on a mountain rescue elsewhere). However the local pronunciation of a century ago recorded by Dwelly as (Beinn) Lidi or Lididh, with the stress on the first syllable, indicates that '*le dia*' (stressed on the second syllable) is nonsense. Besides, the "mountain *with* God" (*beinn le dia*) is a curious use of a proposition, and the "mountain of God" which would have made more sense, would probably have used the genitive formulation of '*beinn dhè*' . . . which it hasn't!

The other and more probable meaning is from *leitir* or *leathad*, a slope, from the way its long southern ridge climbs continuously all the way from the valley floor leading the eye up to the summit. W C MacKenzie hinted at this 'slope' meaning when he used the old-fashioned word "declivitous" for the hill, and there is a similar name in **Beinn Leòid*** in Sutherland, hill of the slope (or, of breadth) and in the first part of **Laidwinley** hill in Angus (from *leothaid*, genitive of *leathad*).

Curiously enough, the only word in the old tongues of Scotland that compares exactly in form and sound to the present name is *ledi*, an Old Norse word used in Shetland to mean a viewpoint, which would be highly

---

Beinn Leòid – bYn **lyawa**t^y

appropriate. But as there are no other Norse names within the bounds of Ledi's horizon, it cannot be accepted.

Religion had at least one sad outcome on the hill. Lochan nan Corp on its northern flanks is the lochan of the corpses, where a funeral party en route over the hill to St. Bride's Chapel was crossing the frozen loch when its ice gave way to swallow the body and the bearers.

(God, or gods, are rarely mentioned in hill-names, but **Loudon Hill** in Strathclyde may come, according to Professor W. J. Watson, from the pre-Christian god Lugus, the name then being *lugdunon*.)

Ben Lomond

Ben Lomond*

Like Ben Ledi, Ben Lomond is a landmark on the southern edge of the Highlands, visible from many Lowland spots. This gives credence to the idea that it comes from the Britonnic *llumon* or Gaelic *laom* meaning a beacon or blaze or light, giving the hill an ancient telecommunications function. The Gaelic *luimean* or *luimeanach*, a bare hill, is also very appropriate – indeed this word may have direct descent from *llumon* – as it rises near-naked above a heavily-wooded base.

Much more recent is the name of a shoulder of the hill above Loch Lomond, for **Ptarmigan** is the name of the archetypal bird of the high

---

Ben Lomond – (Gaelic, Beinn Laomuinn) – bYn **loem**Yn^y

mountains, and this is a name that was shown as far back as Roy's map of the 1750s. (The English suffix, 'pt-' was spurious, an attempt to give it classical Greek connotations; the Gaels call it *tàrmachan*).

Ben Loyal*

Sometimes praised, in guidebooks at least, as "The Queen of Scotland's Peaks", this epithet lends apparent support to a royal connection with the English-sounding 'loyal'. But reality is less deferential than the name, as we will see! Ben Loyal's striking feature is its range of castellated tops, with Gaelic names – indeed one is called **An Caisteal*** (the castle) – including **Sgor a'Bhatain*** (boat, or little stick, peak) and **Sgor a'Chlèiridh*** (cleric's peak). But Ben Loyal itself is more difficult to understand, sounding English as it does. Professor Watson (who took into account the local pronunciation) wrote that it was Beinn Laghail (legal mountain) from the Old Norse *laga fjall:* he was criticising another Gaelic scholar Alexander MacBain who has said it was from *leidh fjall* (levy fell) or *lauta fjall* (leafy fell) – for woodland, unusual in Sutherland although not in nearby Tongue, clings to its western slopes. The existence of a Gaelic version (*laghail*) of a Norse name (*laga fjall*) is not unusual in Gaeldom. An 1897 "poet" in the SMC Journal, unwittingly reversed the tendency in a series of rhyming couplets on hill-name pronunciation, when he wrote of this hill:

> ". . . Then for sport that is raoghal
> He hies to Beinn Laoghal"

Laga fjall (law mountain) is, as Watson suggested, the most likely origin, because there is a Norse tradition, strong in Iceland and with parallels in Scotland, in which hills were used for people to gather on to hear legal proclamations. Traditionally the chiefs built an altar to the god Thor on a hill-top, and after prayers would hear complaints, settle disputes and issue edicts. There are also two **Layaval** hills in the Uists, and since both they and the Sutherland part of the mainland are old Norse areas, the case for legal mountain surely rests.

This judgement has legal echoes throughout Scotland's hills. A few miles south is **Ben Klibreck** whose constituent word *brekka* was in Iceland often used for a hill for public meetings and legal proclamations. A few miles east above Scrabster is a hillspot called **Thingswa**, from the Norse *thing-svath*, the assembly slope where the local 'community council' gathered. Further south in Gaeldom **Tom a'Mhòid*** on Speyside is knoll of the justice court where the local clan chief sat in judgement. A *mod* is a meeting of significance (as well

---

Ben Loyal – (properly, Beinn Laghail) – bYn **loegh**al
An Caisteal – *a*n **kasht**yal   Sgòr a'Bhatain – skor *a* **vaht**Yn[y]
Sgòr a'Chlèiridh – skor *a* **chlay**:ree   Tom a'Mhòid – towm *a* **vawd**[y]

as a court), as in the Gaelic Mòd: and from this word comes the name of the **Moot Hill** near Scone where King Nechtan of the Picts met and decided to follow Rome, not Iona, in the matter of Easter dates.

Tom na Croich* near Blair Atholl is knoll of the gallows where an estate worker paid the penalty for murdering a colleague on the slopes of Ben a'Ghlo. (There are of course several instances of **Gallows Hill** in Scotland, indicating a traditional location for execution.) In the Lowlands the name of **Castlehill** (there are at least fifty of them) is said to indicate a site of ancient justice. They are usually low hills (perhaps so as not to exhaust portly magistrates!), such as the low hill near Carluke – nearby, maybe coincidentally, is the hill and village of Law. Another **Castle Hill,** above Campbeltown, is where the all-powerful Clan Donald had a fortress, making their laws and holding their Parliament independent of the Scots Crown. And in Skye above Glen Boreraig is the flat-topped grassy knoll of **Dùn Kearstach,*** justice hill (from *ceartas*).

Also in Skye near Duntulm was a hill originally called **Cnoc an Eireacht,** knoll of assembly, which Pennant on his 1772 tour wrote about:

> "*Cnock an eirid* (sic), the hill of pleas: such eminences are frequently near the houses of all the great men, for on these, with the assistance of their friends, they determined all the differences between the people."

So the tradition of hills as legal arenas has a long history in Scotland. That most of the hill-names referring to it are low is because of ease of access, Ben Loyal being the apparent exception.

Ben Lui*

Usually pronounced **loo-ey**, this might lend strong credence to *luaidhe*, lead (the mineral) for there are old lead mines on the flanks of **Beinn a'Chùirn*** and **Meall Odhar*** not three miles away, whose heavy metal poisons make barren the hillside above Tyndrum even today long after the mines ceased. (And 'lead mountain' would have a cousin in **Beinn Iaruinn***, iron mountain, 20 miles (30 km) north.) But the Tyndrum mine was first opened in 1739, and surely the local people would have given a hill as striking as Ben Lui a name of its own long before the 18th century. There is another hill (not far away, above Glen Lyon) called **Beinn Luaidhe***, where lead mining *did* take place, but it is a lesser top of the 'leftover' variety that were named much later.

Tom na Croich – towm na **kroych**
Dùn Kearstach – toon **kyar**stoch (properly, Dùn a'Cheartais: doon *a* **chyarsh**taysh)
Ben Lui – (Gealic, Beinn Laoigh) – Byn loo:ee
Beinn a'Chùirn – bYn *a* **choo:rn** Meall Odhar – myowl **oa-**ar
Beinn Iaruinn – bYn ee-arYn^y Beinn Luaidhe – bYn **loo-**aya

Another Gaelic word producing a similar sound is *laogh* meaning calf or fawn (and Beinn Laoigh is the form we find used by local Gaelic speakers) and there is a strong Gaelic tradition of giving the hills names of animals (neighbouring **Beinn Oss*** may be elk mountain). The resemblance of the mountain's gently two-horned summit to the head of a young calf, and the protuberance on the northern ridge called Cìochan (nipples of) Beinn Laoigh, almost certainly indicate that it is mountain of the calf. However one animal can be definitely ruled out, for although James Hogg "The Ettrick Shepherd," passing by in the early 1800s, managed to spell it Ben Leo, there were never lions here!

Creag Meagaidh*

This massive hill above Loch Laggan is usually translated as 'bogland rock' or 'the crag at the bog', from *creag* and an old Celtic word *mig* (over in the Angus hills **Meg Sweerie** is from the same word). Near the summit is an enigmatic pile of stone called Mad Meg's Cairn, but it seems unlikely that she is connected with the name.

The two other summits in the massif are **Càrn Liath*** (Grey cairn) and **Stob Poite Coire Àrdair***, peak of the pot of the high corrie, pot being a nice description of this long deep corrie.

Merrick

This is the highest hill in the south-west at 2764 feet (814m) and is often climbed from the tourist spot of Glen Trool at its foot. It is, in consequence of its height, number one in the Donald Tables, as well as being number seven in the Corbett Tables (both Munro-type lists of hills). Enough of this name-dropping!

Most names in this part of Galloway are of early Gaelic origin, the area having been colonised from Ireland, and the hills are no exception. The Merrick (Maerack Hill in Pont's 17th-century map) comes from *meurach* meaning pronged, branched or fingered (from *meur* a finger). Sheriff Nicolson of Skye, a Gaelic scholar, said it meant idiomatically 'the highest knuckle of the hand' and that its five branching ridges with deep glens in between were like a huge hand. Later writers called it – rather unfairly – the 'Awful Hand', and sometimes the group of hills are actually called the Awful Hand range. More recently Hamish Brown developed its original simple meaning to that of 'the branched finger'. The five ridges of the hill are Merrick itself, **Bennan** (*little mountain*), **Benyellary** (*beinn na h-iolaire*, eagle mountain), **Tarfessock** (*tòr fàsach*, grassy hill) and **Kirriereoch** (*coire riabhach*, specked corrie).

Beinn Oss – bYn **os**
Creag Meagaidh – krayk **megee**
Càrn Liath – kaarn **lyee**-u
Stob Poite Coire Àrdair – stop **potsh**a kora **aard**ar

A'Mhaighdean*

Almost recognisable to an English speaker, it means the maiden. This is Scotland's Jungfrau, lower than its Swiss namesake but just as beautiful as it soars above the remote blue lochans of the Letterewe Forest. While it is one of a hill family including several hills called **Am Bodach*** or **A'Chailleach*** (old man and lady), this hill like its family seems to have been named with no-one in particular in mind. Across the glen to the south is a top called **Martha's Peak,** named after a herdgirl who fell to her death here, but this bigger peak seems to be the 'Unknown Maiden'!

A maiden in both Gaelic and Scots cultures is also the last sheaf of corn cut in the harvest, and the outline of the peak seen from the west might suggest a bound stook in a field for its steep southern slope finishes in a near-vertical cliff.

Indeed this is the most likely origin of the name for there were many Highland traditions associated with the cutting of this last stook, 'A'Mhaighdean' as it was known, especially after a good harvest. Sometimes it was dressed up like a young girl before being cut or made into a corn dolly. (A bad harvest sometimes saw it clad in old woman's clothes and called A'Chailleach, the possible origin of *that* hill-name.)

Morven

There are two hills called Morven in Scotland. One, near Helmsdale, is especially striking from the road north, but the highest Morven (literally big mountain, *mòr-bheinn*), is on the eastern edge of the Cairngorms and dominates the views around Aboyne. In 1769 Thomas Pennant on his tour of Scotland wrote:

> "One of the great mountains to the West [of Donside] is styled the hill of Morven, is of a stupendous height, and on the side next to Cromar almost perpendicular . . . The other great mountains appear to sink to a common size, and even Laghin y Gair [Lochnagar] abates of its grandeur."

Certainly it's a Mòr Bheinn after that praise! It's even older names were Morvine, Morevene and Mons de Morving. It is intriguing to speculate why some 'big mountains' are Mòr Bheinn while others are Beinn Mhòr (or the anglicised Ben More). The Ben Mores are the highest hills with three Munros in Mull, Perthshire and Assynt – the spelling is due to the linguistic incompetence of the early O.S. surveyors. Most of the Beinn Mhòr names surviving as such on the O.S. maps are lower peaks – as low as 600 feet (182m) on North Uist, and 635 feet (193 m) in Easdale – although one reaches up to 2433 feet (741m) near Dunoon, and are more generally in the west and on the islands. The Morven hills lie in the intermediate height range

---

A'Mhaighdean – *a* **vY**tyan   Am Bodach – *am* **bo**toch
A'Chailleach – *a* **chal**yoch

between 2000 and 3000 feet (600m to 900m), but their significance probably does not lie in their height, nor in their location in the eastern Highlands. The word *mòr-bheinn* is a poetic Gaelic expression for the more usual *beinn mhòr*, used in names like Mull's soubriquet of Muile nam Mòr-bheann, Mull of the big mountains. It seems odd that these two should have an archaic, poetic Gaelic name, surrounded as they are by 'foreign names': Morven near Helmsdale has Norse name neighbours like **Scaraben** and even an English **Small Mount** top beside it; while Morven above Donside stands above corrupted Gaelic names like **Mona Gowan** (probably *monadh gobhain*, forked mountain-land) and Peter's Hill.

In the east, not far from Morven, are Mormond Hill (*mòr-monadh*) and a **Morrone** hill (*mòr-shròn*, big nose or promontory) above Braemar, sometimes known as Morven in books, although not in local parlance. Besides, the hill is hardly a '*mòr bheinn*', being an outrider of the much higher hills to its south.

Beinn Narnain

The Cobbler's 'left-hand mountain', and often ignored beside its lower but more dramatic neighbour, Beinn Narnain's name seems at first sight as enigmatic as C.S. Lewis mythical land of Narnia; most books say of it "origin unknown". The only similar name in Scotland is Nairn, a town on the river of the same name, which is said to come from an ancient European word for water, with cognates rivers Nar and Naro in the Mediterranean lands. But Nairn is one hundred miles from Beinn Narnain and a connection seems unlikely. However in an 1895 volume of the *Scottish Mountaineering Club Journal*, there is a reference to its old name Ben Varnan, and this may help us solve the mystery. For 'v' is usually the Gaelic pronunciation of 'bh', and a *beinn bharnan* would resemble *bheàrnan*, the notches or gaps, pointing at the rock fissures around its eastern Spearhead arête cliffs.

Quinag*

The local people in Assynt pronounce this mountain 'koonyak' confirming the name's Gaelic name of *cuinneag*, a milking pail or stoup. The Highlands are scattered with such domestic items as if some *cailleach* had strewn the household implements around after an argument with her *bodach:* on Speyside there's a cup (**Meall Cuaich***), in the Cairngorms a table (**Beinn a' Bhùird***), on Arran a comb (**Cìr Mhòr***), above Glen Shiel a basket and a knife (**A'Chràlaig*** and **Sgùrr na Sgìne***) together with **Sgùrr Mhùrlagain*** (wool-

---

Quinag – A'Chuinneag – *a* **choon**yak   Meall Cuaich – myowl **koo**-Ych

Beinn a'Bhùird – bYn *a* **voo:rsht**   Cìr Mhòr – kee:r **voa:r**

A'Chralaig – *a* **chra**leek   Sgùrr na Sgìne – skoor n*a* **skee:**ny*a*

Sgùrr Mhùrlagain – skoor **voo:r**lagYn^y

basket) and **An Sgruaboch*** (*sguabach*, a broom) . . . perhaps they were all flung out of her creel (**Beinn a'Chlèibh**)* as she stormed out past the doorpost (**Sgùrr an Ursainn***) past the big barn (**Sabhal Mòr***) to the cowshed (**Am Bàthach**)* to collect off the pulleys (**Mullach an Rathain***) this *cuinneag*, milk-pail. Many of these hills have a shape which fits their name – the upturned bowl of Meall Cuaich, the flat top of Beinn a'Bhùird – and in the case of Quinag a former SMC guidebook says of its **Spidean Còinnich*** (mossy peak) summit:

> ". . . the southern peak which stands out boldly like a water-spout. This peak gives the mountain its name Cuinneag in Gaelic as a narrow-mouthed water bucket."

It might be more accurate to say that it resembles the handle or lug of a traditional milk pail. Not far away in Easter Ross is **Càrn Chuinneag,*** another of the same, showing how the peak's shape struck a chord in the Gaelic countryside – the peak's shape is a more likely meaning than the alternative that it comes from the shape of some pail-like hollows in rocks somewhere on its slopes.

Beinn Resipol*

Pronounced **resh**apol, this rugged hill in Sunart has a farm at its southern foot with the same name, and Hamish Brown has suggested that it means the mountain of the horse farmstead, from the Norse *hross bolstadr*. This would be unusual in that hardly any large Scottish hills are named after farms at their base (one of the few exceptions being **Beinn Achaladair,** the farm by the hard water, near Rannoch). An alternative origin can be found below the steep north slopes of the hill where a bay-like inlet of Loch Shiel is called the "River" Polloch, from the Gaelic *poll* meaning a pit or pool: could the hill be *hreysi poll*, the cairn above the pool?

Ben Rinnes*

Ben Rinnes in the far north-east recalls the names of those lower hills in the south-west, the Rhinns of Kells, and the **Rhinns of Islay.** From the Old Irish *rind* meaning a headland, the word *rinn* in Gaelic means a sharp point. Now while Ben Rinnes is a great rounded whaleback of a hill, it is made distinctive by the outcropping granite tors known as the Scurrans near the summit, and they are probably the reason for the mountain's name. Cruach Àrdrain in the southern Highlands probably also contains the word *rinn*.

An Sgruaboch – *a*n **skroo**-*a*boch	Beinn a'Chlèibh – bYn *a* **chlay:v**
Sgùrr nan Ursainn – skoor n*a*n **oors**Yn^y	Sabhal Mòr – soal **moa:**r
Am Bàthach – *a*m **baa**hoch	Mullach an Rathain – mooloch *a*n **rahan**^y
Spidean Còinnich – speetyan **kawn**yeech	Càrn Chuinneag – kaarn **choon**yak
Beinn Resipol – bYn **resh**apol	Ben Rinnes – bYn **reen**yaysh

128

Rois-bheinn

In the far west, Rois-bheinn lies within sight of Beinn Resipol, and like it has been linked to horses as mountain of horses (*hross bheinn*). Horsy names were quite important to the Vikings as names like **Roishal** (Harris), **Hestaval** (a Lewis hill) and Roisnish (from *ness*, headland) show. A Gaelic alternative of **An Fhrosbeinn*** from *frois bheinn* (mountain of showers) has been suggested but while showery would be an understatement for the wild wet weather that regular soaks this area, *frois* usually means a shower of grain, not rain. Alternatively the Gaelic *ros*, meaning a headland, is a common element in placenames, though not usually in hills, and Rois-bheinn certainly does stand, headland-like, farthest west in its group of hills, up against the seaboard.

Schiehallion*

Schiehallion is often featured in calendar photos taken from the birch-fringed shores of Loch Rannoch in douce Perthshire, from where it appears as a shapely cone. The regularity of its shape, the result of weathering of its homogenous quartzite rock, attracted the Astronomer-Royal Maskeleyne here in the 18th century to conduct experiments on the earth's mass. And its shape gives credence to one of the two suggested meanings for its name, that of *sine chailinn*, breast of the maiden. But in Gaelic the usual word for a breast is *cìoch*, found all over the Highlands, and besides, the mountain's cone 'disappears' when viewed from most other angles; Schiehallion from the Glen Coe hills is said to have "an unusual truncated appearance."

The more likely meaning of the name is *sìth* (or *sìdh*) *chailleann**, the fairy hill of the Caledonians. *Sìth* is found in names like Glenshee or the **Shee of Ardtalnaig** a few miles away, and *sìthean* (fairy hills) are found all over Scotland. Furthermore Perthshire was the ancient heartland of the Caledonian tribes, known to the Romans – Dunkeld and Rohallion, both lying within twenty miles are respectively the hillfort (*dùn*) and fort (*rath*) of the Caledonians. In 1642 the spelling of the mountain's name as Schachalzean (the 'z' representing an old Scots letter pronounced 'y'), and the Schichallion form of the name prevalent well into the 20th century, stress the *chailleann* part of the names. And fairy hill of the Caledonians is certainly a fine name for this very individual Munro.

Seana Bhràighe*†

This means simply old height. But why 'old'? Not from its rocks since they are schists rather than the ancient gneisses found elsewhere in the north-west. Perhaps it is old in the sense of familiar . . . or 'wrinkled' with its furrowed ledges! There are several names in the Highlands with *sean*, and they are

---

An Fhrosbeinn – *an* **ros**v**Yn**   Schiehallion – shee**hal**y*an*
Sìth Chailleann – shee: **chal**-y*an*   Seana Bhràighe – **shen***a* vrY

scattered mainly along the western seaboard from Cape Wrath to Kintyre, and through the Hebrides – places called (in translation) old fort, old hill, old cliff, old heap and old knoll. Over in the Grampians **Càrn Aosda**[*] is the aged mountain (locally pronounced kaarn **oesh,** and probably from *aoise*). In the modern world the adjective old often has negative associations, but that certainly does not apply to Seana Bhràighe, with a dramatic drop plunging from its summit down to the far moors of Ross-shire.

Shalloch on Minnoch
Hamish Brown says that this hill means the heel of the Minnoch ridge, presumably from *sàil* or *sàileag* (heel or little heel). But on this lonely sprawling hill, near the Merrick, is a separate lower top called Shalloch, and with a southern ridge called Rig of the Shalloch. This is not the usual position of a *sàil* in hills, for they usually round off a ridge with a long steep drop down to the glen. Shalloch is possibly from the Gaelic *sealg* (pronounced **shellag**) meaning a hunt, and indeed just across the shallow valley to the west lies a hill called **Eldrick,** from *iolairig*, a deer trap; and a few miles away is **Mullwharchar** from *meall na h-adhairce*, hill of the huntsman's horn (or *adharcach*, horn-shaped). On the other hand, Shalloch bears a resemblance to *teallach*, a forge or hearth, of which there are other Gaelic examples farther north; and nearer to home are the Minnigaff Hills above Newton Stewart, whose name means hills of the smith. Minnoch may well come from *meadhonach*, middle, or more likely from the old Gaelic word for a hill mass, *monadh*.

Slioch[*]
Slioch is described in *The Munros* guidebook as "one of the great sights of the northern Highlands, well seen and much photographed from the A832 road." Protruding up from behind a long low ridge above Loch Maree, the main body of the mountain thrusts itself up by means of sandstone buttresses, matching the usual translation of the Gaelic *sleagh*, a spear. And within the two eastern arms of its summit ridge lies Coire na Sleaghaich, corrie of the spear.

However in the 1830s *New Statistical Account* the local Poolewe minister, the Reverend Donald MacRae, wrote that "The principal mountain of the range is Slioch or Sliabhach." This latter word is the adjectival form of *sliabh*, the early Gaelic word for mountain, mainly confined in Scotland to the south-west, where it had been imported by Irish Celts. Loch Maree at Slioch's feet is however named after a 7th-century Irish missionary Saint Maelrubha, and so it is possible that Slioch's name is also a relic of 'the old country' as Ireland was known. On the other hand, in the Wester Ross dialect *sliabhach* can refer

Càrn Aosda – kaarn **oe:st***a*
Slioch – **shlee***ch*

Slioch

simply to mountain grass, and early this century the locals called it An Sleaghach, meaning the spear-like mountain – or, less attractively, the place of the gully or rift, from a root *sleg*, and perhaps referring to the deep Glen Bianasdail beside it. (A 1750 map by Dorret, wildly inaccurate in location – it put Slioch on the shores of Loch Torridon! – probably reflected the local pronunciation of *sleagh* when he put 'Mount Sliach'.)

Obviously a simple meaning 'mountain' (from *sliabh*) does not have the charm and striking imagery of 'the spear'; and a spear would also be able to claim international company, for the Zulu name for the South African Drakensberg range is Ekhalamba, meaning barrier of spears. Nearer home, there's a hill above Loch Linnhe called **An Sleaghach***, the spear-like mountain.

Ben Starav

Rising straight up out of Loch Etive, this fine mountain's name gives few clues away. Is it from *starbhanach* (pronounced **starv**anach) meaning a well-built fellow, or from *starra*, a block of rock . . . or more probably, from *starabhan* (pronounced **stara**van) meaning a rustling noise? After all, only a few miles away is **Meall a'Bhùiridh***, hill of the roaring.

An Sleaghach – *a*n **shlye**ghoch
Meall a'Bhùiridh – myowl *a* **voo**:ree

Stùc a'Chròin[*]

A local Victorian minister, the Reverend MacGregor of Balquhidder, believed that Stùc a'Chròin's name meant the hill of moaning, or a 'lesser hill jutting out as it were from a greater one'. (The word *stùic* can mean a projecting hill.) The 'greater one' in this case will be Ben Vorlich, all of 10 metres higher, and divided from it by a deep, mile-wide pass. Certainly this gap is hidden from Balquhidder to the west, but from most other points it presents the clear image of two fiercely independent peaks, and from many spots in the Central Lowlands Stùc a'Chròin appears as an equal but independent twin . . . certainly not a 'lesser jutting-out' one. Another Reverend, the placenames' expert J.B. Johnston, thought that *chròin* came from *crann*, tree or plough, (though it is difficult to see why), or from an old Irish word *cron* meaning a round hollow. The commonest modern explanation is *cron* meaning harm or danger. (There's another hill called **Beinn a'Chròin**[*] a few miles west at the far end of Loch Voil.) But this word *cron*, also meaning hurt, has a short 'o' sound whilst the mountain name has a long 'o'. And the key to its meaning may therefore lie in a spelling recorded a century ago as Stuc a'Chroan, which would probably be from *cròthan*, a sheepfold. After all, it stands at the northern head of the deep crag-ringed Gleann a'*Chròin* which would act as a natural sheepfold, and one of the tops above it is **Meall na Caora,** hill of the sheep.

Suilven[*]

Contemporary photos of this striking hill are normally taken from Lochinver. From this seaward view, over a foreground of rolling moorlands, the mountain rises up with the suddenness of a surfacing submarine, an effect enhanced by telephoto lenses. And contemporary wisdom about the name, drawing upon its dramatic appearance, attributes it to the Viking sailors and their Norse *sul-r*, a pillar. Some say it was originally *sul-r fjall*, others *sul-r bheinn* (pronounced ven), and certainly the main summit of **Caisteal Liath**[*], grey castle, sits well on top of this 'pillar'. Now while 'pillar mountain' is evocative, and strikes a chord in English ears used to Lakeland's Pillar Rock, there are some difficulties with Norse names on the Scottish mainland: in the Hebrides Norse hill-names usually end in -val (from *fjall*), although it's probable that the locals Gaelicised -*val* to -*bheinn;* and the Vikings went in for simple description of hills rather than fanciful examples.

Is it a completely Gaelic name? One writer suggested *soillse-bheinn*, light mountain, indicating that communications bonfires may have been lit on it, but there's no archaeological evidence for this. The Rev. Johnston's

---

Stùc a'Chroin – stoo:chk *a* **chroan** (probably **chro-***an*[y], from chrothain)
Beinn a'Chroin – bYn *a* **chroan**
Suilven – **soo:l**avin
Caisteal Liath – kastyal **lyee**-u

Suilven

suggestion of *sùil-bheinn*, eye mountain (from its shape, he said – had he ever seen it?), is even wider of the mark. There is an alternative local Gaelic name of A'Bheinn Bhuidhe, the yellow mountain, hardly an eye-catching title!

But the 'pillar' must give way in imagery although not in name to the 18th-century traveller Thomas Pennant who called it the 'Sugar Loaf mountain', which is spot on for the view of it from the Lochinver, where we began!

An Teallach[*]

An Teallach is a sandstone-spired spectacular in Wester Ross: standing clear of other peaks, its pinnacled ridge can be seen from many points in the north-west. It is a collective name for a mountain of several separate tops with rather ordinary names like **Bidein a'Ghlas Thuill**[*] (peak of the grey-green hollow), **Sàil Liath**[*] (grey heel – from its quartzite screes), **Sgùrr Fiona**[*] (white peak, from *fionn* – or wine peak, from *fion*) and **Corrag Bhuidhe**[*] (yellow finger) – all these colours contrast with the maroonish-red of its main rocks. Another dizzy pinnacle called **Lord Berkeley's Seat,** spectacularly overhangs the cliffs, and got its name from the eponymous gentleman who, for a bet, sat on it with feet dangling over the edge – whatever he won that day in cash terms was but a trifle to the value of having a peak named after him for posterity!

An Teallach – *a*n **ty**aloch   Bidean a'Ghlas Thuill – beedyan *a* **ghlas** hil[y]
Sgùrr Fiona – skoor **fee***a*na   Corrag Bhuidhe – korak **vooy***a*
Sàil Liath – saal **lyee**-u

No actual summit on the hill is called An Teallach, this name applying rather to the whole mountain. In Gaelic *teallach* is usually a smith's forge, or possibly a hearth, a fireplace, or even the large flat stone that backs the fireplace in a croft. In the past it has also signified an anvil or furnace. Now perhaps the shape of the precipitous cliffs backing the main eastern corrie gave locals the picture of a hearth. Or perhaps it is a more literal meaning, for there *is* a building at the northern foot of the mountain the Old Smiddy, now a climbing club hut known as the Clarkson Hut (in memory of a climber killed on Ben Nevis), but still recognisable with bellows and forge. Perhaps this smithy was built here because the extensive woodlands of the nearby strath were a rare commodity in a mainly barren landscape. The smithy may have given the local people the idea for the name for the huge mountain beyond. And there may be a deeper significance, for the ancient Celts ranked the metal-working smith second only to the Gods themselves.

Beinn Teallach*, a newly-created 'life Munro' near Roy Bridge, has no dramatic shape nor industrial history to account for its name which may come from the shape of its craggy eastern slopes resembling a fireplace or hearth of a rather unspectacular kind.

Tinto

Tinto Hill stands a little clear of the main northern wave of the Border Hills. Being clear of the pack, and high enough to be registered as a Donald (ie – above 2000 feet, 610 m) and possessed of a gentle conical shape, it is a fine landmark far into industrial Lanarkshire and rural Midlothian. This prominence led, centuries ago, to its use as a beacon hill, and the name is probably from the Gaelic *teinnteach*, fiery. It was possibly a Roman signal station, for a Roman road runs over its shoulder, or a Druidic fire site, which tradition locates on the huge cairn on its summit. The tale of its ancient use could easily have been kept alive by word of mouth for centuries, passed on like a runner's torch from generation to generation, until Gaelic speakers gave the hill its present name. In an old book on the Pentland Hills, author Will Grant speculates that it comes from two Pictish words *teine* and *tom*, respectively a fire and a hill, but the words are in fact Gaelic not Pictish, and the Gaelic alternative of *teinnteach* meaning fiery seems to fit the modern name better. In the 14th century it was known as Kaerne de Tintou (cairn of Tinto) and as Tintock. The local name, still used, of Tintock Tap, is further evidence for *teinnteach*: however the suggestion that the pinkish colour of its summit felsite rock, or the deep purples of its northern screes, could be the origin of 'fiery' is rather fanciful.

The huge sprawling mound of stones on top (known as The Dimple) certainly suggests ancient use – the boulders shielding the ecosystem from

Beinn Teallach – bYn **tya**loch

scorching! The eastern shoulder and top of the hill is called **Scaut Hill** on the map, ostensibly from the Scots word scawt meaning scabbed: could it be a slight corruption of Scaud Hill, which would mean scorch hill, or indeed the 'glimmering of light'? (There are several examples of Scawd Hill or Law in the Borders). The top, **The Dimple**, could be a euphemism for nipple, for just south of the top is the Pap Craig, literally the breast crag, its mammary profile being especially obvious from the east.

Traprain Law

This East Lothian hill has seen a lot of history, having been occupied on top from late Stone Age times to Roman times. Once a hill-fort of the Votadini tribe, it was apparently known as Dunpender, meaning the hill-fort of the spear shafts (*dun peledyr* in Brittonic). In the 14th and 15th centuries it appeared in documents as Dumpeldar (1368) and Dunpender Law (1455). The name Traprain is of Brittonic origin from *tref*, a farm or simply a place, and *pren*, wood or a tree. The name was extant in the 14th century, and although it's not clear why or exactly when it replaced the more genuine hill-name Dunpender, it was probably transferred from a nearby farm within whose bounds it fell.

Ben Vane

There are several Ben Vane hills on Scotland's maps, in Fife, Argyll and Perthshire, the 'vane' being an anglicised pronunciation of *mheadhoin*, middle or central in Gaelic: **Beinn Mheadhoin*** (spelt properly!) a high peak in the Cairngorms, is sounded this way. Ben Vane in Fife is between the Lomonds and the Cleish Hills, Ben Vane in Argyll between Beinn Ìme and Ben Vorlich, and Benvane in the Trossachs is piggy-in-the-middle between Ben Ledi and Beinn an t-Sìthein. (There is no apparent geological or language reason to accept the alternative local suggestion that the latter is from *beinn bhàn* meaning white, and indeed it has dark cliffs when seen from the south.) Ben Vane in Fife is a shoulder of **Benarty Hill** (possibly from *artaich*, stony – it is seamed with small cliffs – or after King Arthur), and this Ben Vane is sometimes called locally 'The Footstool of The Sleeping Giant' of Benarty.

Ben Venue

Towering above the heart of the Trossachs and Loch Katrine, this means small mountain, for *beinn mheanbh** is pronounced in Gaelic very like the anglicised 'venue'. It might be large in its own immediate neighbourhood (2393 feet, 729m, and "the dominating height above Loch Katrine"), but is the smaller cousin of other Trossachs peaks like Ben Ledi, and dwarfed by hills of the Ben More (big mountain) group a few miles north. From the

Beinn Mheadhoin – bYn **vee**-oyn^y
A'Bheinn Mheanbh – *a* vYn **ven**av

Stirling area, looking along the line of the Highland edge, it is distinctive as one of three – Ben Ledi, Ben Venue and Ben Lomond – but is clearly the smallest. A recent author, Ralph Storer, has suggested mountain of the caves as its meaning. A cave in Gaelic is *uamh* (pronounced oo-av), and *uamhach* (oo-uvoch) is 'abounding in caves', and there are indeed caves on the hill at Coire na Uruisge (corrie of the spate – sometimes translated as Goblin's Cave), but the sounds 'wavuch' and 'venue' are not very alike. (For comparison, far to the west are two hills called **Beinn na h-Uamha*** and **Braigh nan Uamhachan***, both cave mountains, quite uncorrupted in name.)

Another suggestion for this name is milk mountain, *beinn a'bhainne* (pronounced **vanny***a*), which would fit the name's sound reasonably, and has cognates a few miles west in **Beinn Ìme*** (butter mountain) and The Cobbler's white-foaming Buttermilk Burn . . . but why would it be called milk mountain (in the days before EEC food surpluses)? Perhaps because, as the old edition of the SMC's guidebook to *The Southern Highlands* says of the hill:

"It shows a bold front to the Trossachs, rocky and deeply shadowed most of the year, and after rain is seamed by waterfalls."

These waterfalls fit well with the name of the Coire na Uruisge, for Highland burns in spate foam milky-white. However local pronunciations of the name, collected last century, suggest that it is indeed *beinn mheanbh*, the small mountain.

Vinegar Hill

This whimsical name for a remote hill east of Drumochter is, according to place-name writer Alexander MacKenzie, a corruption of the Gaelic *a' mhìnchoiseachd**, meaning the easy-walking one. It stands above one of the north-south Mounth passes, well-used by travellers on foot before the road and rail takeover of Drumochter.

Ben Vorlich

Which one? So the walker is often asked – the one above Loch Earn, or the Loch Lomond one? – for they lie in sight of each other and are both Munros. There are more suggested explanations than there are hills, though. Given that 'mh' in Gaelic is pronounced 'v' in English, the suggestions have included Beinn Mhòr Loch (mountain of the big loch), Beinn Mhòr-Luig (mountain of the big corrie or hollow, which is close to the local pronunciation early this century, and as with many hills fits the shape of its scooped-out corries).

Beinn na h-Uamha – bYn n*a* **hoo**-*av*a
Bràigh nan Uamhachan – brY n*an* **oo**-*av*och*a*n
Beinn Ìme – bYn **ee:**m*a*
A'Mhìnchoiseachd – *a* **vee:**nchoshochk

There is also the possibility of the mountain of the bay, Beinn Mhuir'lag, (literally mountain of the sack-shaped sea inlets), and Beinn Mhòr-Leacach (big stony mountain). All of these fit the scenery, though none has the beauty of the suggested origin of the Perthshire (Loch Earn) one from *mùrlach* meaning kingfisher. There are many other 'bird' peaks in the Highlands, and this suggestion fits well with Pont's 1650 mapping of 'Binvouirlyg' and the 1794 spelling Benvurlich. However, before the twitchers arrive, it should be noted that the kingfisher is a bird favouring slow-moving rivers (not tumbling Highland burns) and is a very rare sight in the mountains, having bred rarely and even then only in the west.

So the truth is probably more prosaic, lying in the geographical explanations. Of these, the mountain of the "sack-shaped inlets", (or in a word "bays") is most likely. Both mountains have a farm at the foot called Ardvorlich, the height above the bay (on the loch), although it has to be said that the one at the foot of the Ben Vorlich on Loch Lomond is a more distinct bay than the Loch Earn-side one.

At the west end of Loch Arkaig is a mountain with a similar name, **Sgùrr Mhùrlagain,** probably a northern cousin of the Vorlichs.

Chapter Nine

Island Hill-names

Scotland has 787 islands, restricting the count to those of size big enough to ". . . afford sufficient vegetation to support one or more sheep or which is inhabited by man." This count excludes sea-washed skerries, large or small such as the all-rock Rockall. Most of the true islands are grouped into the Shetlands and Orkneys, the Inner and Outer Hebridean archipelagoes, and the Clyde Firth islands. Many of these have mountains or hills of note. Some, like Skye's Cuillins or Arran's Goat Fell, famed far into the mainland. This chapter visits the higher hills of these and other sizeable islands.

Norse was at one point the ruling language in many of these islands, especially in the north and north-west. The suffix -ey or -ay in many of their names (Islay, etc) is from the Norse word for an island. As a seafaring people the Vikings used hills primarily as landmarks, and consequently most of their names are simple descriptions of their function (like Ward Hill, from Old Norse *vardhe* meaning guard or watch hill) or shape. Adjectives meaning rough, stony, flat or high recur, and not for them are the human or animal associations of the later Gaels. The words *bjerg* (a precipice) and *cleit* (a rock or cliff) are quite common, but are overshadowed by the main Norse word for mountain, *fjall*. The word *fjall* became *field* in Shetland and Foula, *fiold* in Orkney, and as it sea-frogged round Cape Wrath and down through the Hebrides it became the suffix -*val* (as in Rum's Askival) or sometimes -*shal* (as in Lewis' Cleitshal). By the time it reached the mainland at Cumbria it had become *fell*, a word now thoroughly absorbed into the English language.

Arran

The granite knot of Arran's higher hills is a landmark in the Firth of Clyde and from much of south-western Scotland, and on a clear day its profile can be seen from forty miles (60 km) inland. Viewed from the Ayrshire coast the mountain profile is known as **"The Sleeping Warrior"** for it is said to resemble a warrior's effigy reposing full-length on his bier.

This knot of its northern peaks is largely Gaelic-named. Although the glens of north Arran have Norse names – Glen Rosa, Sannox and Iorsa – the heights are firmly Celtic. **A'Chìr** and **Cìr Mhòr** are the comb and the big comb (with

A'Chìr – *a* **chee**:r
Cìr Mhòr – kee:r **voa**:r

their rocky teeth), **Caisteal Abhail** is probably castle of the fork (*caisteal a'ghabhail*), with its granite battlements – or just possibly the melodramatic death's castle, from *abhail;* **Am Binnean** is simply the pinnacle, and **Suidhe Fhearghais** is Fergus' seat: Fergus was a ruler of Arran, Bute and Kintyre as viceroy for the Irish conquerors, the first 'King of the Scots'. He was a definite historical figure, circa 500 AD, whereas the Fingalians who are named in hills like **Dùn Fhionn** (fort of the Fingalians) near Lamlash, were legendary.

The softer contours of the outlying hills enfold **Beinn Nuis** (*beinn an uis*, hill of the fawn), **Beinn a'Chliabhain** (hill of the little cradle), **Beinn Tarsuinn** (transverse hill) and shapely **Cìoch na h-Òighe** (the maiden's breast).

But among all these Gaelic peaks the highest hill in Arran stands as the odd mountain out, for **Goat Fell** (2,868 feet, 874m, correctly Goatfell) is apparently an English name. On the surface this name could be taken at face value, for goats and hills are associated in the popular mind. Indeed among the many novice walkers whose holiday itinerary includes this hill – in the patronising words of an earlier SMC guidebook "The ascent of Goat Fell is a popular amusement among summer visitors to Brodick . . ." – there must be many who feel that their achievement merits them mountain goat status! And there are other 'goat mountains' elsewhere in the Gaelic Highlands, such as Stob Ghabhar.

But although 'Goat Fell' is *apparently* English, unlike any other important Arran place-name, it is more probably of Old Norse origin. One of the earliest references we have to the mountain is in 1628 when a writer enthuses:

> ". . . a larger prospect in the world no mountain can show . . . (than that from) . . . **Goatfieldhill**."

This version of the name has the addition of the superfluous word 'hill', but more importantly the 'field' element of the name is probably from the original Norse *fjall* (a mountain), and the source too of *fell* in the Lakes and Galloway. Several thousand longship lengths away in the Shetlands, *field* is the standard derivation from *fjall*. The name Goatfieldhill has a close similarity to the first-recorded mapping of Arran's hill as **Keadefell Hill,** on Timothy Pont's map of 1650. The Gaelic version of the name is Gaoda-bheinn (pronounced **goed***a*-vYn), which suggests that the Gaels took the probable Norse original of Geitar-fjall (or its form Geitar-field, and meaning goat fell –

Caisteal Abhail – kashtyal ava*l*ʸ   Am Binnean – *a*m beenyan

Suidhe Fhearghais – sooy*a* e*r*aghaysh   Dùn Fhionn – doon eenʸ

Beinn Nuis – (properly Beinn an Uis) – bYn *a*n oosh

Beinn a'Chliabhain – bYn *a* chlee*a*vYnʸ

Beinn Tarsuinn – bYn tarsh Ynʸ   Cìoch na h-Òighe – kee:ch n*a* hawy*a*

or more precisely nanny-goat fell!), and changed only the suffix, replacing -*fjall* with *-bheinn*, in the way they often did in north-west Scotland. The first element *geitar* was reshaped, over the passing of the centuries, into the similar-sounding *gaoda* (and there's an old Gaelic word *gadhran* meaning goats); but it probably co-existed with the older Norse name, and since English-speakers are more familiar with Norse than Gaelic name-elements, they easily translated *geitar* into the similar-sounding and identical-meaning word goat. But why did the Norsemen name only *this* one hill on the island? Probably because, as seafarers, it was a mountain critical for their navigation in the Firth of Clyde which it dominates, and the other hills were inconsequential to them. Doubtless too their early wanderings and lootings in the adjacent Norse-named island glens had alerted them to the numerous wild goats watching them from the hill's skylines.

The Vikings were not the only warriors around: on the north coast of Arran at **An Scriadan*** meaning The Scree, huge blocks of sandstone crashed down nearly 300 years ago with a tumult that was heard in Bute. The Sleeping Warrior had stirred a little in his sleep.

Barra
Barra in the Outer Hebrides is scattered with Norse names. Among them is the highest point **Hèaval*** (in Gaelic Hèabhal, 1260 feet, 384m). The suffix '-val' is from the old Norse *fjall*, while the prefix may come from *hav*, the sea, or more simply and likely *hei*, a mound, particularly as it is pronounced **hay**:uval. Another summit **Ben Tangaval** (Beinn Tangabhal) is 'peak of the tongue peak', the Ben being a superfluous addition. Highland mountains elsewhere take their name from a tongue shape, such as Meall na Teanga. (See the chapter on The Body of the Land.)

Just off Barra lies Mingulay. It has a **MacPhee's Hill,** said to be named after a rent collector landed there to collect Chief MacNeill's dues and then abandoned by his colleagues when they realised that the plague had struck among the islanders. It was fully a year before they judged it safe to return to collect him, and no doubt he spent much of this time on this hill scanning the horizon for the boat's return, like a Hebridean Robinson Crusoe!

Benbecula
The highest point **Rueval** (408 feet, 124m) means either red hill (from *roe*), or rough, scabrous hill.

Bute
This is probably the only Scottish island of any size whose highest hill bears a completely English name – **Windy Hill** (913 feet, 278m) – although this is possibly a translation from the Gaelic, *beinn na gaoithe*. Nearby the hill Torran

An Scriadan – *an* **skree**a*tan*   Hèaval – **hay**:aval

Turach, meaning the turreted hillock, indicates that Gaelic was the old language of the island. Above Rothesay Bay the hill **Kames** is said by some locals to be from the Gaelic *camus*, a bay – perhaps it was once Meall a'Chamuis, hill of the bay. There's probably no connection with the Scots word *kame* for the low twisting hills of glacial sand found in lowland areas, common in names like Aberdeen's Kaimhill and Kaimes in Edinburgh.

Canna

Canna in the Small Isles peaks at 693 feet (211m) on **Càrn a'Ghaill***, cairn of the stranger from *gall*, the Gaelic word for the Norsemen, for Canna would be about the southern limit of their main settlements. It also has a **Compass Hill**, so-named in English because the iron in its dolerite rock attracts ship's compasses, and **Sliabh Mheadonach*** (middle hill) whose first name-element indicates early settlement from Ireland.

Coll

Coll's high point of **Beinn Hògh*** (340 feet, 103m) resembles in name the Norse word for a burial mound, *haugr*, often corrupted to *heog* or *ho*. (**The Hoe** hill on Barra's Pabbay island is from the same word, and in present-day Norway *haug* means simply a summit.) Another burial hill on the island is **Cnoc a'Chrochaire***, the hangman's knoll, and it marks the exact spot where four men were hanged in 1596 for betraying island chief Neil Mòr to the invading Duarts. Their bones were found interred on the hilltop three centuries later.

Colonsay

Càrn an Eòin* at 470 feet (143m) is cairn of the bird. An old book on the placenames of Argyll translates it as John (Eòin)'s little cairn, but while birds are common in Gaelic hill-names, personal names are rare. Besides there is some interesting circumstantial evidence in naturalist Fraser-Darling's *The Highlands and Islands*, a natural history published in the 1960s which tells us:

> "In gazing on these woods now (which were planted by an improving landowner) and noting Colonsay's wealth of small birds, we should remember the effort entailed in establishing these conditions"

So the 'hill of the bird' is most fitting.

Càrn a'Ghaill – kaarn *a* **ghYl**ʸ
Sliabh Mheadonach – shlee-uv **vee**anoch
Beinn Hogh – bYn **haw**   Cnoc a'Chrochaire – krochk *a* **chro**charya
Càrn an Eòin – kaarn *an* **yaw:een**ʸ

Eigg

The conventional explanations of her name are a hollow, or a nick, both translating from Gaelic, *lag* and *eag* respectively. Both are quite inadequate to describe her most outstanding feature, the single giant rock molar of the **Sgùrr of Eigg** soaring up to 1292 feet (393m) almost from the sea. The peak, known variously as An Sgùrr (the rocky peak), the Scuir and the Scurr (it was Scur' Eigg on an 1825 estate map), is obviously linked by name to the many *sgùrr* mountains in Skye and on the mainland, and it is possible that this is the original from which they all took their generic name. For there was a Norse word *sguvr* meaning a cliff, which may well have been the basis of the later Gaelic *sgùrr*, which was to push east inland from the Viking's western islands. Apart from An Sgùrr, and a couple of low *beinn* hills, Eigg's hill-names are dominated by diminutives – appropriately since they lie in the Small Isles! – and signified by the suffix *-an:* packed into its eight square miles are a *càrnan*, a *beannan*, a *bidean*, a *cruachan*, a *corragan*, and a *dùnan*.

An Sgurr, Eigg

Fair Isle

Fair Isle's highest hill is **Ward Hill** (712 feet, 217m). This is from the Old Norse *vardhe* meaning guard place, from where a watch could be kept in case of attack. The highest hills of Orkney and Hoy are also Ward Hills, and there are others in the Shetlands and in Caithness. There former Viking islands' Ward Hills are very functional names compared to their Gaelic cousins on the mainland, for unlike them the hills of the Northern Isles don't have colours or creatures in their names.

Foula

On the jacket of a book about Foula called *Island West of the Sun* is a photo of the whole island taken from a boat approaching from Shetland, as the first Vikings probably saw it. In it the hills of Foula dominate the island, and reflect the very pattern of the ocean, with waves of high ground swelling up from the west to break steeply down on the trough before the next rise.

Not surprisingly the names of these hills are Norse, changed little from the days when the longships skimmed the waves, except that *fjall* (a hill) has become *field*, as in Shetland. Above the longships' former beaching place is **Hamnafield** (harbour hill). Other field names include **Bodlafield** and **Codlafield,** respectively from *bollotr* (rounded hill) and *koddi* (small rounded hill, literally pillow), and **Nebifield** and **Tounafield,** from *nebb* (nose) and *tuva* (mound). The highest hill is **The Sneug** at 1373 feet (418m) from the Old Norse *knjukr*, a steep conical mountain. The Norse *gnúpr*, a peak, is found in **The Noup**: while the hill **Soberlie** is a compound of three words – *saudhr*, *bol* and *hlít* – respectively sheep, hill and resting place. The only hill without direct Norse ancestry has that fine northern Scots word for wee, in the **Peerie Hill** (although it too comes originally from Norse).

Gigha

Gigha's 339 feet (103m) **Creag Bhàn*** is simply white cliff, from the pale epidiorite rock that is exposed on the hill's top. And **Dùn Chiofaich*** was the hill where Celtic chief Kifi fought Diarmaid over his wife, and was hurled from it to his death.

Harris

Harris is the hilly end of the Vikings' Long Isle, its mountains sharing the accommodation with Lewis' peat bogs. Although its name has been attributed to the Old Norse word *herudh*, a portion or land division, it seems more likely to come from Old Norse *hoerri*, the higher (parts) – the hilly areas of Rum and Islay are also called Na Hearadh in Gaelic. And although it was an important part of the Vikings' southern empires, Harris was also a centre of the Gaelic-speaking Lordship of the Isles, remaining a relative bastion of the language even today. So in its lonely hills are names Norse, names Gaelic, and names with parts from both languages like the double-barrelled children of the aristrocracy. Names like Stulaval, Husival Mòr and Beinn Dubh stake out this three-party spectrum.

In a moment we will look at more examples, but first the question, why should some be Norse, others Gaelic, and still others hybrid? One theory put forward by Alexander MacBain in his *Placenames, Highlands and Islands of Scotland* is that the Gaels, while applying Gaelic names to the spots

---

Creag Bhàn – krayk **vaan**   Dùn Chiofaich – doon **chifeech**

immediately surrounding their coastal settlements, kept the older Norse names inland for the landmarks encountered during the summer movement to the hill pastures. However, in Harris settlements like Rodel have Norse names, as do the high peaks. A more likely explanation for the mixture is that when the Gaels took over they retained the Norse names for both villages and hills, using Gaelic for their own new hamlets and for "filling in" the gaps in the hills left by the Norsemen: most of the Gaelic names in Harris proper refer to the corries, noses, passes and shoulders rather than the peaks. Some of the Gaelic hill-names incorporate the Norse word -val as a suffix, from fjall, a peak.

The 'pure' Norse names include **Ullaval*** (Ulli's or Ulfr's peak – he being the landowner), **Husival Mòr*** (big house peak), **Stulaval*** (probably from stol, a shieling hut), **Uisgnaval*** (oxen peak) and **Gillaval*** (gully peak). **Oreval*** has been translated as moorfowl mountain from orri – the bird now commonly known as a grouse – but in Orkney many old Norse names beginning with or signify 'of water'. On the other hand Orri is a common Norse nickname – based on the bird name – and he, like Ulli, could have been a landowner. These names are all very spare of description. This fits with mountain names in Norway, home of the Norse, where peaks are named ". . . in relation to nearby valleys, farms, etc . . . locations which were more important . . . than the uninviting peaks."

Hybrid Norse-Gaelic names include **Mullach** (summit) **an Langa***, possibly from the long Langadale valley below – but much more likely the mullach (summit) of An Langa (the long peak) – indicates that the Gaelic speakers came later than the Norse and incorporated their names into their own, rather than trying to 'paint over' them. **Clett Àrd*** combines Norse klettr (rock) and Gaelic àrd (high) and **Gillaval Glas** is the grey gully peak. The Gaelic adjectives for big and small, mòr and beag, are found as appendages in the likes of **Tirga Mòr*** and **Husival Beag**.

Pure Gaelic names are rare in Harris proper, though common just across the border in Park, Lewis. The long summit ridge of the island's highest hill running south from Mullach an Langa to Clisham includes **Mulla fo-thuath*** and **Mulla fo-dheas***, literally north and south summit: such geographic directions are very unusual in Gaelic names. Also unusual in Gaelic use are nearby **Sgoth Ìosal*†** and **Sgoth Àrd*†** – literally the low and high steep

---

Ullaval – **ool**aval   Husival Mòr – hoosh*a*val **moa:r**

Stulaval – **stool**aval   Uisgnaval – **ooshgn**aval

Gillaval – **geely**aval   Oreval – or*a*val

Mullach an Langa – mooloch *a*n **lang***a*

Tirga Mòr – tyeerg*a* **moa:r**   Clett Àrd – (properly, Cleit Àrd) – klaytsh **aard**

Mulla fo-thuath – mool*a* fo **hoo-***a*   Mulla fo-dheas – mool*a* fo **yes**

Sgoth Ìosal – sko **ee:sh***a*l   Sgoth Àrd – sko **aard**

hills (from *sgoth,* steep rock or high hill) – **Mullach an Ruisg*** (peeled summit, referring to the peat turfs that 'peel' easily off it), and **Màs Garbh***, rocky bottom. Just over the border in Lewis is **Rapaire***, dividing hill, from Norse *hreppa . . .* although it could conceivably be from the Norse *reip,* a rope (made from heather).

But what of Harris' highest hill **Clisham***, at 2622 feet (799m)? Being the highest, it surely should be a Norse name in tune with its high neighbours. Or could it be another hybrid based on Gaelic words like *cliath,* a slope? Since Norse is more likely, a possible explanation could involve starting with *klif* meaning a cliff or rocky area, pronounced klee as in Sutherland's Ben Klibreck or Barra's Ben Cliad. The ending could well be from *hamarr,* a rocky outcrop or hillside. *An* or "The" Clisham, as it is locally known, could then simply be rocky cliff, which is a fairly accurate description of its geography.

Hoy

Since 1966 when the BBC carried live coverage of the second ascent of the **Old Man of Hoy,** this famous sea stack has become the instantly recognisable symbol of Hoy, indeed of Orkney itself. Yet overshadowing the Old Man rises St. John's Head, a cliff over twice the Old Man's height at 1100 feet (335m). The endless lines of Atlantic breakers that thump ashore at its feet are paralleled in the lines of sandstone strata that climb skywards up the cliff, with tiny wheeling specks of white to give it perspective. So for the Vikings who discovered Hoy some time before the BBC, the island was simply *ha-ey* or high island. Among the shoals of the Orkney Islands Hoy looms humped like a whale.

Its highest point is neither the Old Man – a common if sexist term for a Scottish sea stack – nor the cliff, but **Ward Hill** further inland, at 1572 feet (479m). Its name comes from the Norse *vardhe* meaning a cairn, ward, guard or watch, where lookouts were probably posted in times of trouble. Standing where it does with a splendid view over the sheltered anchorage of Scapa Flow, sea-heart of the Orkneys, and with a clear view to the south over the Pentland Firth where lived their Pictish enemies, its situation fully merits its name.

Other Hoy heights include The **Cuilags** (behind St. John's Head), the **Knap of Trowieglen** (from the Norse *gnípa,* a peak) and **Withi Gill** (from Norse *hvítr,* white, and *gil,* a gully).

Iona

The many thousands of pilgrims who visit this lovely island, a splash of white sand and green grass in a turquoise sea, take away abiding memories of it. But

---

Mullach an Ruisg – mooloch *a* **roo:shk**   Ràpaire – **raa**par*ya*
Màs Garbh – maas **garav**   Clisham – **klee**sham

it is unlikely that these would include the name of the island's highest hill, for it only rises to 333 feet (101m). However, its name, simply **An Dùn** (or sometimes **Dùn Ì***, (the fort of Iona) suggests a past importance, for *dùn* is a generic Gaelic name indicating the site of a prehistoric fort, on a hilltop used as a defensive site. At one point in Scotland's history there were nearly 1,500 such hill-forts in use.

The usual association between Iona, home of St. Columba, and peace, was made at a later date. Prior to Columba there was supposedly a colony of Druids here, and the Druidic sun circle symbol which they worshipped is incorporated into the Celtic cross in front of the Abbey. However, **Cnoc Druidean*** is the knoll of starlings (not the Druids!), while Christianity is reflected in the Hill of the Angels, where Columba supposedly met the heavenly visitors, and the hill whose name Hill of the Back to Ireland (translated from the Gaelic Càrn Cùl ri Èirinn) refers to the saint's determination to turn his back on his homeland until he'd converted the Scots to Christianity. **Tòrr an Aba***, the small hillock beside the Abbey, is the knoll of the abbot, where Columba is said to have had his cell. The island's other named hill **Druim an Aoineidh***, means the ridge of the steep rocky brae, a name of prosaic geography beside the romantic history of its neighbours!

Islay

Overshadowed in mountain terms by its neighbour Jura and its Paps, Islay is chiefly known for its whisky industry, and in recent years for its peat bogs, fought over by distillers and conservationists. Its rolling landscape does however rise to 1612 feet (491m) in **Beinn a'Bheigier***. This name is rather obscure, the Gaelic dictionary giving no exact equivalent; it has been suggested that it comes from the name of a nearby river, although this still begs the question of its meaning. Other possibilities are three rather uncomplimentary words, *baghaire,* a fool, *bagaire,* a glutton or fat man, and *baigear,* a beggar. But the true explanation is to be found in Blaeu's 17th-century map on which it is Ben Vicar, for Beinn Bheigier is properly *Beinn a'Bhiocair,* the Vicar's mountain – possibly the same vicar who owned Bail' a'Bhiocair (Ballyvicar) nearby.

Jura

Like a rock band's players the higher hills of this island are best-known by their group name, and only the keenest fan could name the individuals. The famous **Paps of Jura,** the three distinctive swellings above the horizontal sea-lines, are a landmark from many summits of the south and west Highlands.

Dùn Ì – doon **ee:**   Cnoc Druidean – krochk **droot**y*an*
Druim an Aoineidh – drim *an* **oe:**nee   Torr an Aba – tor *an* ab*a*
Beinn a'Bheigier – (probably Beinn a'Bhoicair) – bYn *a* vikar[y]

The name was originally a sailors' description, likening them to paps, the old Scots word for breasts. According to Martin Martin's 1703 book *A Description of the Western Isles:*

> "There are four hills of approximately equal height, of which the two highest are well known to seafaring men by the name of the Paps of Jurah."

In fact there are only *three* sizeable hills of roughly equal height – the next highest being 800 feet (240m) lower – and *all* three of them are now collectively known as The Paps, in spite of the obvious anatomical absurdity of such a number!

What of their individual names? The highest, and most central peak, is **Beinn an Òir**, hill of gold. In the absence of legends connecting this with some treasure trove, it most likely gets this name from the amount of Fool's Gold (iron pyrites) found both here and on Islay. The name is old-established, for on Blaeu's 17th-century map it appears as Bin na Noir. Another scar on the hill is **Sgrìob na Cailleach**, the witch's scrape, where she is said to have gashed the hill with her broomstick in an aerial hit-and-run.

To its west, above the narrows of the Sound of Islay, lies **Beinn a'Chaolais** (*chaolois* on the map), peak at the narrows. To the east is **Beinn Siantaidh**, consecrated or holy peak, locally A'Bheinn Sheunta: this after all is not far from Iona and the seaborne missionary invasions from Ireland. There is another holy peak, **Ben Hiant** in Ardnamurchan.

St. Kilda

The highest point of these savage ocean-whipped rocks is **Conachair**. It has been interpreted as 'the coming together of the hills', but Gaelic dictionaries tells us that a *conachair* is "a sick person who neither gets better nor worse"! Alternatively it means simply 'uproar', an apt description of the continual racket as ocean, winds and gannets wheel around this defiant rock. However, it is most likely to be the 'place of folds', from *con-* and *crà*. This explanation would fit with its land-locked cousin, **Creag Chonochair** in Glen Spean.

Lewis

Lewis' highest peak is not **Beinn Mhòr**, big mountain, at 1874 feet (571m), but the slightly higher **Mealisval**, also known as Mealasbhal. The *–val* ending is the standard outer isles' form of *fjall*, the old Norse for hill or mountain. And while there is also a Norse word *meal* meaning a sandbank, or *melr*,

---

Beinn an Òir – bYn *an* **aw-eer**[y]   Sgrìob na Cailleach – skree:p n*a* **kalyeech**
Beinn a'Chaolais – bYn *a* **choe:leesh**
Beinn Siantaidh (properly A'Bheinn Sheunta) – *a* vYn **haynt***a*
Conachair – **konachayr**[y]   Beinn Mhòr – bYn **voa:r**
Mealisval – **myal***a***sval**

grassy, the Gaelic *meall*, a hill, is the more likely candidate for the first part, producing the meaning 'lumpy hill hill'. Similarly the mountain **Keàrnaval*** or **Càrnaval** a few miles away is certainly Càrn-fjall, also a tautological 'rocky hill hill'.

In the Park district around Beinn Mhòr, Gaelic rules the tops. There is **Càrn Bàn*** (white cairn), **Sìdhean an Airgid*** (fairy hill of silver), **Monadh Mòr*** (big mountain) and **Crionaig*** (from *grionaig*, green grazing land). Also in southern Lewis, near the boundary with Harris (where Norse names dominate the hills), are **Tahaval** and **Cracaval** (from *kráku*, a crow), as well as Gaelic names like **Beinn a'Bhoth*** (bothy mountain). And although the rest of Lewis to the north was firmly under Norse control for many years they must have paid scant regard to the lowly hills that struggle like shapeless prehistoric animals from out of the blanket peat bogs that cover Lewis. It was left to the later Gaels to name them, chief among them being **Beinn Mholach***, rough or hairy hill.

Mull

Ben More, in Gaelic Beinn Mhòr, (3169 feet, 965m) is sometimes cursed by lazier Munro-baggers for it is the only 3000-footer outside of Skye requiring a ferry trip. Others held it in more affection. An anonymous Gaelic poet wrote:

> ". . . Straths grass-tawny, stepping waterfalls,
> And mighty Ben More of the eagles,
> Set high over all"

Waterfalls do step over the staircased layers of lava that form the island's base; and eagles, nesting on crags like nearby **Creag na h-Iolaire** have long soared above the hills.

The name Ben More simply means big mountain, from its relative size on the island, and in contrast to the neighbouring **Beinn Fhada***, long mountain. A subsidiary summit is called **A'Chioch***, the breast, for it tapers smoothly to a point, without the main peak's shoulders.

The island is known in Gaelic as **Muile nam Mòr-bheann**, Mull of the big mountains, and there are many other sizeable hills on it. **Dùn dà Gaoithe*** is fort of two winds or maybe windy fort, **Cruachan Dearg*** red heap, **Ben Buie***, yellow peak, and **Beinn nan Gabhar** peak of the goats.

Kearnaval – kyaarn*a*val	Càrn Bàn – kaarn **baan**
Sìdhean an Airgid – shee:-an *a*n er*a*git	
Monadh Mòr – mon*a*gh **moa:r**	Crionaig – **krinak**
Beinn a'Bhoth – bYn *a* **vo**	Beinn Mholach – bYn **voloch**
Beinn Fhada – bYn at*a*	A'Chìoch – *a* **chee:ch**
Dùn dà Gaoithe – doon **da:goey***a*	Cruachan Dearg – kroo*a*chan **dyerek**
Ben Buie – bYn **vooy***a*	

Orkney

The 'mainland' of Orkney, sometimes known as Pomona, offers little challenge in height to its offshore island Hoy, whose **Ward Hill** rises to 1577 feet (480m). Yet the main isle's highest hill at 881 feet (268m) is of identical name, one which it shares with others on Shetland, Foula and the mainland. From the Norse *vardhe*, it means a guard or lookout hill, and like Hoy's Ward Hill it stands above Scapa Flow, the great sea anchorage between these two watchful island hills.

Most Orkney names of farms and villages are of Norse origin, which makes the relative absence of Norse names on the hills rather odd. Apart from Ward Hill itself and **Vestra Field** (from *vestr fjall*, west hill) in the north-west, the remaining eminences usually end in the English 'hill', as in **Starling Hill, Wideford Hill** and **Hill of Miffia** (mid-fell), indicating a later naming by Scots-speaking immigrants. For the Vikings, to whom the Orkney hills were as molehills after Norway's mountains, would barely have rated them except for the highest, as watchtowers. The modern use for Orkney's hills, for TV masts and the prototype windpower generator on **Burgar Hill** (from *bjerg*, a precipice), make them distinctive to our eyes, while to the Norsemen one Ward Hill was enough for the whole island.

Raasay

Raasay the roe-deer island rises to 1455 feet (443m) in **Dùn Caan***. A flat-topped hill, it had the doubtful distinction of being Highland-danced upon by Boswell in the course of his journey at the heels of the great Dr Johnson. Boswell recorded that the summit was a landmark to sailors who knew it as **"Raasay's Cap"** (probably because the clouds collected on it to form a bonnet). While the word *dùn* signifies a hill-fort, the only history Boswell afforded us was his report of the local legend of the entrapment near the top of a maiden-eating sea-horse. Of more relevance to the hill's name is the personal name of a 7th-century Celtic prince, Cana Mac Gartnain. His first name is close, too, to the proper Gaelic name for the hill, **Dùn Cana,** and it may well have been his fort.

Rousay

Rousay lies close to Orkney's northern shore. In these islands the Norse *fjall*, peak, has become *fiold*. **Kierfea Hill** is *kyr fiold*, cow hill. The highest point of **Blotchnie Field** (821 feet, 250m) is more elusive: *blot* can mean blood, or a sacrifice. Rousay is one of the oldest inhabited sites in Europe, with remains dating back nearly six thousand years to 3,700 BC, and although there is no archaeological evidence of slaughter here, there is a legend of Pictish resistance to the Viking invaders on this island alone, that must have ended at sword-point.

Dùn Caan (properly Dùn Cana) – doon **kan**a

Rum

Rum's highest range, like Skye's, is called the **Cuillin,** although it is not clear whether one name imitated the other or whether they were both named independently. (The chapter on hill ranges discusses the name Cuillin, concluding that it is probably from the Norse *kiolen,* a rocky mountain range.) But unlike Skye's Cuillin the Rum Cuillin's individual peaks' names are apparently largely of Old Norse rather than Gaelic origin, probably because on Rum the individual peaks are quite distinct from each other, with large drops in between. Askival and Allival, Trollaval and Barkeval, Ainshval and Orval, trip off the tongue like characters entering Edvard Grieg's *Hall of the Mountain King.* What does each have to say for itself?

The *-val* suffix is the Hebridean form of *fjall,* a peak. **Askival** the foremost at 2663 feet (811m) is probably from *askr* meaning ashwood but used figuratively for a spear, a name apt both for its pointed form and for the minds of the warrior-namers. (One writer has suggested the name is from *hoska,* dangerous, but to a seafaring race, daily facing a watery fate and who had no reason to venture up mountains, the characterisation would be quite inept.) And in Sutherland the same word *askr* is the root of the hill-name **Asc-na Grèine**[*] (spear of the sun), from the same pointed shape.

Allival (sometimes **Hallival**) is probably from the Norse *hallr,* a slope or ledge. (Other suggestions have included *hali,* a wild beast's den, and another writer goes for *all,* an eel, from the sinuous shape of the ridge, but this is fanciful, implying either an aerial vision or the use of maps.) The prime candidate for the origin of Allival must be the ledge mountain, very accurate because, as the old SMC Guidebook puts it;

> ". . . The conspicuous *escarpments* (my emphasis) which run nearly round the summit of Allival, except on the south, are of allivalite, a pale variety of gabbro . . ."

Allival thus joins Marsco of Skye (home of marscoite granite) and Cairn Gorm as one of the few peaks to have rocks named after them. And over at the western tip of this diamond-shaped island, **Bloodstone Hill** also has a name connected with minerals. Standing poised above plunging screes and cliffs, it used to be quarried for the bloodstones or carnelians on its north side, and the beach far below is stained with them. Bloodstone is a green rock, spotted with the red mineral jasper, and was used to make jewellery.

Trollaval is sometimes shown on maps as Trallval, but the former is surely the happier sounding. The trolls, goblins or giants of Norse legend, were skilled metal workers living in the mountains, occasionally sallying forth to steal from humans. Dwarves in some legends, giants in others, craggy peaks

---

Asc-na Grèine – ask n*a* **gray:ny***a*

like Trollaval could surely accommodate all sizes. Now, high on this mountain are the burrows of the shearwater, a bird whose night-time shrieks and mutterings may have suggested the subterranean sounds of trolls to the Vikings. The birds' habit of flying unseen in and out of its nesting area under cover of darkness would add to the mystery of the noises. (Further north but still in Viking territory another shearwater breeding area on the Faroes bears the name Trollkarp.)

Barkeval is from *bjarg*, a precipice, for its southern slopes are particularly broken up by cliffs. **Ainshval** is from *àss*, a rocky ridge, **Orval** is probably the water peak (or possibly Orri's peak, as on Harris' Oreval) and **Ruinisval** from *hruna*, a heap of rocks.

As on Harris and Skye the lower peaks and passes have become the crumbs picked up by Gaelic to name, as in **Meall Breac*** and **Mullach Mòr*** (speckled hill and the big summit) to the north. One commercial map of these islands carries alternative 'Gaelic' names for the main peaks: for Allival there is Ailbe Meall (from *ailbh*, rock, and *meall*, hill); for Askival there is Aisge Meall (*aisgeir*, rocky mountain hill); Ais Meall (hill hill) for Ainshval and Tràill Meall (drudge hill) for Trollaval, complete the list of optional names. But these placenames just do not ring true. They are out of line with the dominant Norse pattern of the northern Hebrides, with the pronunciation of the names, and their Gaelic "meanings" are tenuous.

Scarp
Lying off Harris' west coast, its peak **Sròn Romul** (1011 feet, 308m) combines the Gaelic *sròn*, a nose or headland, with Romul, a Norse personal name, for the Vikings quite often left their own first names on a place.

Seil
Seil island is famed chiefly for the hump-backed bridge that leads onto it from the mainland, over a sea-channel as wide as a small river, and given away only by the tresses of seaweed: it is known as the Bridge over the Atlantic. This tendency to exaggeration is complemented by its hill **Meall a'Chaise***, struggling to reach all of 481 feet (146m), and meaning hill of steepness.

Shetland
Shetland's hills are a tale of 'wards and all', for scattered across the island group are names like Ward of Scousburgh, Ward of Bressay and several plain **Ward Hills**. They derive from the Norse *vardhe* meaning guard or watch. One pair of these hills, originally called Vordeld, with ruins of watchtowers on top, are commonly called the **Vord Hills** or – laments Danish writer Jakobsen – as

---

Meall Breac – myowl **brechk**   Meall a'Chàise – myowl *a* **chaash**a

Mullach Mòr – mooloch **moa:r**

the "Wart of . . ." by 'the younger generation'. On these seafaring islands the need for a high vantage point to spy the fishing boats in time of storm, or the enemy in time of trouble, would have been essential, and hence the many Ward Hills here, as in Orkney and Fair Isle. In the Shetlands there are over thirty such hills, appearing in various guises such as Ward or Vord or Virda.

However, the highest point in these isles is not a ward hill but **Ronas Hill** (1475 feet, 449m), perhaps from *hraun* meaning rocky, or *roni*, a rocky place. Although it also had watchtowers on top like the ward hills, what makes it distinctive is the collection of large pink granite boulders on top, so another possible origin of its name is from *ro nes*, red headland. In its role as a landmark it can be seen by the fishing boats thirty miles out over the Bank Haaf, with Ronas Hill "sitting like a kishie (peat basket) upo da water".

The use of the English word 'hill' (in Ronas Hill and Ward Hill) in this Norse heartland may seem peculiar, and there are many other eminences called 'Hill of . . .' as in **Hill of Deepdale** or **Hill of Fitch**. Evidence suggests that these generally lower hills were named later, in the 16th century, by Scots incomers, filling in the 'gaps' left by the Norse names which focussed only on the highest ground. Another apparently English name, *field*, is not what it seems but in fact the Shetland version of the Norse *fjall*, a peak: **Scalla Field**, the skull or bald-headed fell, is a nice description of this wind-scoured pate, **Hoo Field** is high fell, and **Hamari Field** is from *hamarr*, a rocky outcrop.

Other Norse hill-words are found in the **Beorgs of Skelberry** (from *bjerg*, a precipice or hill), **Lamb Hoga** and **The Heog** (from *heog*, a hillock or burial mound), and **The Neap** on Unst (from *gnìpa*, a peak). **The Compass** Hill near Sumburgh airport has nothing to do with air navigation, but is a corrupted form of *kumbr*, a ridge or mound: **Hoo Kame** and **The Kames** are more faithful to the original.

On an island which lived by the sea and for whose seamen landmarks were vital, the southern headland **The Ords**, rising 930 feet (283m), would be significant. Its name comes from Norse *uro*, a heap of stone, and it may be related to the Gaelic òrd meaning a steep rounded hill.

Skye
Although this island is a centre of Gaelic art and culture, the placenames of its major features, and certainly its hill-names, are dominated by Norse.

In the hills and mountains Norse names stake out the highest ground, marking out the landmarks for the seafarers. The fingers of the northern peninsulas are tipped by **Ben Volovaig** (*voll-r vík*, field bay), **Ben Halistra** (from *hallr*, a slope) and **Reieval** (smooth fell), while the western peninsulas have **Bens Skriag, Scaalan** (skull), **Arnaval** (eagle fell) and **Idrigill,** meaning outer gully . . . **Ben Edra** or Eadarra in Trotternish originally had the same meaning (outer mountain) in Old Norse, being the outer of a threesome including Beinn Mheadhonach, middle hill. In being assimilated into Gaelic it changed its form (from *edra* to *eadarra*) and its meaning from outer to 'in-between' – demonstrating the arbitrary nature of such geographical names as outer, middle or back of! The east coast hills like a chain of beacons see the Norse fires flicker in **The Stòrr** (from *staur*, a stake – one Gaelic alternative Am Fiacaill Stòrach is the buck tooth), **Ben Tianavaig** (from *tindar*, a peak, and *vík*, a bay for it stands above Portree Bay, **Ben Lee** (slope, from *hlìdh* . . . the Gaelic is Beinn Lì), **Glàmaig** (gorge mountain), **Marsco** (seagull rock), **Blàven*** (blue mountain) and **Beinn Aslak.**

In the south the **Cuillin** range (as examined fully in the chapter on hill ranges) is from the Norse *kiolen*, high rocky mountains. Nearby on the Strathaird peninsula are **Bens Meabost** and **Cleat** (from *klettr*, a rock or cliff). Even in the heart of the island **Ben Uigshader** (bay of the township), **Ben Aketil** (from Ketil, a Viking king) and **Hòrneval** (horned peak – or eagle peak from *orn*), and **Roineval*** (rough fell) are Norse. Gaelic hill-names were given later, after the Norse power waned, and were applied to the island's lower hills, and to the *individual* hills of the Cuillin.

In the Cuillin there are many high Gaelic-named peaks. This may seem odd when all the other high ground is Norse. But the explanation is surely that the Vikings treated the Cuillin or Kiolen as one single mountain for their landmark purposes, stretching as it does in one long high ridge away from the sea. The Gaels named many of Skye's lower or subsidiary peaks as they moved onto the higher ground for hunting or herding, and their names are descriptive of the hill or its function: **Sgùrr na Banachdich***, sometimes translated (from *banachdaich*) as literally the smallpox peak due to the pockmarked rock appearance, but it is more likely the milkmaid's peak from the days when the cattle were summered in the corries – and the local name Sgùrr na Banaraich confirms this. Names like **Sgùrr Dearg***, **Sgùrr Dubh Mhòr*** and **Sgùrr Dubh na Dà Bheinn*** (red, dark and dark two-peaked peaks) and **Bruach na Frìthe*** (slope of the wild mountainous land or deer-forest) paint an accurate picture of the land.

Sgùrr na Strì* is the hill of strife; it is said that heirs to the local clan chieftainships, of Macleod and MacKinnon, were taken there to have pointed out to them the importance of maintaining good "fences" or boundaries with their neighbours in order to avoid trouble and strife. There was a cruel tradition where clan boundaries were marked by the ceremonial building of cairns, followed by the severe thrashing of a young boy from each clan so that they would grow up remembering exactly where the border was! Perhaps

---

Blàven – (properly, Blàbheinn) – **blaav**Yn   Roineval – **rawn**y*a*val
Sgùrr na Banachdich – skoor n*a* **banachteech**
Sgùrr Dearg – skoor **dyer***a*k   Sgùrr Dubh Mòr – skoor doo **moa:r**
Sgùrr Dubh nà Dà Bheinn – skoor doo n*a* **daa vYn**
Sgurr na Strì – skoor n*a* **stree:**   Bruach na Frìthe – broo-uch n*a* **free:ha**

Sgùrr a'Ghreadaidh*, peak of the thrashing or whipping, refers to this too. Another simpler and less colourful explanation for them is that the 'strife' and 'thrashing' is that of conflicting and buffeting winds.

However even the Gaels had little use for the high rocky wastes of the ridge itself, and so many of the ostensibly Gaelic names are barely a century old, given by the early Victorian mountaineers who first trod these tops, to distinguish between what would appear as minor peaks from a distance. (These are described in the chapter on Mountain Characters under the paragraph heading 'Climbers'.) These explorers also gave names like **Sròn na Cìche*** (after the Cioch buttress discovered by Collie), the **Inaccessible Pinnacle** ('with an infinite drop on one side, and an even longer one on the other') and **Knight's Peak** after a St. Andrew's University Professor.

However, the English name of the pair of hills in west Skye called **Macleod's Tables,** is not so recent; it co-exists with their Old Norse/Gaelic names of **Healaval Mhòr*** and **Healaval Bheag,** the big and little flagstone fells. The first element of these latter names is from Old Norse *hellyr*, a flagstone (or possibly *hyalli*, a ridge of terraces), and the second elements are the Gaelic *mòr* and *beag* (big and little) which came later. Their flat or ('flagstone') tops, reflect the layer cake of basaltic rock flows that built them. (*Beag*, meaning small, is actually higher than *Mòr*, meaning big, but *Mòr* has the larger plateau area on top.) Legend has it that God angrily sliced off their previously-pointed peaks after a local chieftain had tried to eject Columba from the isle for preaching a sermon. Another version tells of God creating a flat bed and table for Columba after this rejection. (Some say that their name means holy fell, from the Norse *helgi*, from this divine intervention, but the Vikings' names were largely prosaic, so this is unlikely.)

The name **MacLeod's Tables** comes from a much more recent tale of the 16th century. The story goes that when King James V entertained clan chief MacLeod in Edinburgh, the chief boasted that he had a finer table in Skye. (Another version, casting MacLeod in a more seemly light, has him being provoked beyond endurance by a boastful southern lord into a wager on the topic.) Either way when the King (or Sassenach lord) was staying some time later at Dunvegan Castle, he was taken at nightfall to the broad flat top of Healaval Bheag where a banquet was laid out on the springy turf. "This," said the chief, "is my table, larger and finer than yours". Indicating the hundreds of his clan bearing torches around the feast he added ". . . And these are my candlesticks". It is recorded that the weather was fine – the Milky Way being indicated as "my splendid ceiling" – but not whether the Skye midges were also banqueting: simply that MacLeod's Tables is the name that comes down to us for these two flat-topped hills. (The Gaelic is Bòrd Mòr 'ic Leòid).

Sgùrr a'Ghreadaidh – skoor *a* ghredee   Sròn na Cìche – strawn n*a* **kee:**ch*a*
Healaval Mhòr – **he**laval **voa:**r

Far away across Scotland, but Skye-bound at the time, another royal figure, Bonnie Prince Charlie, while crossing the Corrieyarick Pass, also dined at a piece of level ground, leaving the name **Prince Charlie's Dining Table** to outlast the crumbs. And, back on Skye, there is yet another table, **The Table** at the heart of the fantastic cliffs of the **Quiraing**[*] rocks. From a distance it is inconspicuous, a mere rise in the long backbone of the Trotternish peninsula, presenting slumped cliffs to the east coast. On closer inspection and penetration walkers can discover a veritable grotto of fantastic pinnacles and nooks, with names like **The Needle, The Prison** and **The Table.** Quiraing itself is probably the pillared enclosure (from *cuith raing*), and one placename writer Alexander Forbes gave a Norse origin in *kvi-rand*, or *quoy-rand* (the direct ancestor of the two Gaelic words *cuith raing*). The 'pillar' probably refers to The Needle itself.

The Quiraing

Further down the east coast of Skye are two hills called **Beinn na Caillich**[*], peak of the old woman in Gaelic. It is held in legend that on the summit of the one above Broadford, under "an artificial cairn of the most enormous size" (Thomas Pennant), lie the remains of a Scandinavian princess, looking out to her beloved Norway. Beneath her is supposed to be a pot of gold. Thomas Pennant goes on to recount the local story that she was a giantess who used the summit as a launch pad for her fusillade of rock missiles at the isles of Raasay

---

Quiraing – **kweer**Yng   Beinn na Caillich – b**Y**n n*a* **kalyeech**

and Scalpay. Some writers connect this hill with the Norse princess who, it is said, stretched a chain across the narrows at Kyleakin to force boats to pay her taxes. However, this will be the other Beinn na Caillich nearer Kyleakin, which also has a legend of a gold-underlaid summit-buried crone, this one a giantess of the Fingalians. Burying Norse princesses on hilltops was obviously a local pastime: **Sròn Bhiornaig*** in north Skye marks the high grave of a princess whose ghost faces eternally out towards her native Norway. Her name (sometimes spelt Bhiorail) apparently derives from the Old Norse *bjorn,* bear – not very lady-like! The adjacent summit **Meall na Suireanach,** hill of the maiden or nymph, is probably related and definitely more flattering!

Our stravaig around Skye's Norse and Gaelic hills could end with a consideration of one of the Cuillins' finest peaks, **Sgùrr nan Gillean***, a saw-toothed array of rock spires, known as Pinnacle Ridge, leading to a sharp point, highlight of the view from Sligachan. Apparently a Gaelic name, meaning peak of the young men, it has been suggested that it is a hybrid of Gaelic *sgùrr* with the Norse *gil,* a ghyll or gully: the word occurs elsewhere in Skye, as in Idrigill. For a peak described by the modern Gaelic poet Sorley McLean, as – "The forbidding great *Sgùrr* of danger, The *Sgùrr* of Skye above them all" – it is perhaps appropriate that it has both Norse and Gaelic origins.

Sgurr nan Gillean

Tiree
In this "the land of corn", the peak of **Ben Hynish*** (460 feet, 140m) is from *hà-nes,* the high ness or headland.

Sròn Bhiornaig – strawn **virn**ak   Sgùrr nan Gillean – skoor nan **geely**an
Ben Hynish – bYn **hY**neesh

Uist (North and South)

The hills of South Uist are almost twice as high as North Uist, and can be seen clearly across the Minch from the mainland near Mallaig on a clear day, pale blue through the gap between the Cuillin of Rum and Skye. The highest point is **Beinn Mhòr*** (2034 feet, 620m), big mountain in Gaelic: however, to Uist people the hill is always **Gèideabhal,** possibly derived from *sgèite,* referring to the sparseness of grass on its slopes. Alternatively this name is a Gaelicisation of an Old Norse name Keitval or Geadeval, from *geitar fjall,* goat mountain, for it appeared on a 17th-century map as Keadefeald.

North Uist also has a Beinn Mhòr, but it is only half the height of **Eaval*,** the north's highest at 1138 feet (347m). Eaval's name is probably from *ey fjall,* island fell, since it is almost completely encircled by Loch Obsidary at its foot and the Minch, and lies in a moor studded with innumerable tiny lochs. It is thus literally an 'island-like mountain'; on Timothy Pont's 1654 map it was spelt Bin Aefelt, the 'ae' element sounding like 'ey'. Nearby **Marrival** is the mare fell, while **North** and **South Lee** hills are from *hlìdh,* a gentle slope.

Returning to South Uist we find Stulaval (probably shieling fell from *stol),* **Easaval*** (possibly from Norse *esia* referring to volcanic stone – there is an Icelandic mountain called Esja), and **Hecla,** named as Bin Heck La on Pont's map! There's another Hecla in the Hebrides (on Mingulay) and a more famous one in Iceland, a smoking volcano that on occasion erupts in incandescent rage. From this it has been suggested that the name means cowled or hooded, as if by a cloak, from the plume of smoke or cloud that often drapes its head. Such fancy does not square with Norse name practice in the Hebrides, and the alternative meaning of serrated or comb-like is probably more accurate if less romantic.

Beinn Mhòr – bYn **voa:r**   Eaval – **ay**aval   Easaval – esaval

Chapter Ten

The Natural World

Introduction

All over Scotland there are hill-names dedicated to the natural world. Birds of the air, and beasts of the field and hillside, mix with flora and serpents, weather and rocks, in words English, Scots, Gaelic and Norse. The Gaelic areas have the lion's share of these, with nearly a quarter of the Munros and many of the lower hills having nature-based names.

Nature has always occupied a core part of Gaelic culture, and so in the Highlands and Islands' hill-names wild birds and animals, deer and cattle predominate, while by contrast in the Borders hills the domesticated sheep grazes the tops both literally and in names. This difference is to be expected. The lower and gentler southern hills were long ago tamed by the shepherd's crook, while in the sterner Highland environment the hunting of wild animals and birds went hand-in-hand with the rearing of the hardy 'black' cattle to eke a living from the land. The incoming Sassenach landowners, and the anglicised descendants of clan chiefs, brought in the hated sheep which drove the people off their ancestral land. As a Gaelic poet wrote 200 years ago:

"An iad na caoirich cheann-riabhach,
Rinn aimhreit feadh an t-saoghail"

("Was it the grizzly-faced sheep
That turned the world upside-down?")

Later these landlords turned the wide open spaces into Killing Grounds for gilded guns to bag stags and shoot 'vermin' (including, at that time, eagles). Both these developments were quite foreign to Gaelic culture, for while they hunted creatures for food, they lived in balance, with them: slaughter for its own sake was unnatural. Donnchadh Bàn Mac an t-Saoir (Duncan Ban MacIntyre), arguably the greatest Gaelic poet, and himself a hunter, expressed this view of nature two hundred years ago in his poem *Cead Deireannach nam Beann* ("Final Farewell to the Hills"):

"'S aobhach a'ghreigh uallach
Nuair ghluaiseadh iad gu farumach
'S na h-èildean air an fhuaran
Bu chuannar na laoigh bhallach ann
Na maoisleichean 's na ruadh-bhuic
Na coilich dhubh is ruadha
'S e'n ceòl bu bhinne chualas
Nuair chluinnt' am fuaim 's a'chamhanaich"

('Joyful was the proud flock,
Strutting, full of spirit,
When the hinds were at the spring
How graceful were the speckled fawns
The does, the red roe-bucks,
The blackcocks and the red grouse,
No sweeter music was ever heard
Than their calls, heard at sunrise.)

Another famous Scottish literary figure, Sir Walter Scott, who overlapped Donnchadh Bàn in lifespan, took a quite different approach to nature, romanticising its beauty, without the real appreciation of it that comes from the struggle to make a living from it that Donnchadh Bàn knew. It was no accident that Scott the romantic dwelt in the heart of the southern Borders, where nature had been largely tamed by man and his sheep: romanticism about nature was not appropriate in the wild Highlands.

Berries

The hill on Hoy in the Orkneys called **The Berry** is probably a direct descendant of the Old Norse *berg*, a hill. In southern Scotland there are several straightforward **Berry Hills,** as well as a **Goldenberry Hill** in the Renfrew Heights and a **Nutberry Hill** in the Borders – both exotic fruits, the one being a Cape gooseberry (not known in the Borders!) – and the other not known even to botany! This is probably because they are corruptions of *berg;* **Bizzyberry Hill** near Biggar has an ancient fort on top.

In the Highlands there *are* true berry hills, like **Meall nan Subh*** (hill of the berries, or raspberries) near Loch Lyon. There's a ridge of blackberries in **Druim Ruighe nan Smeur*** on Deeside, whilst **Meall nan Oighreagan*** near Cannich is hill of cloudberries. Cloudberries fruit more readily the further north they grow – in Scandinavia they're a common jam fruit – and it's not surprising to find other hills with this name, like **Beinn nan Oighreag*** above Glen Lochay. In the north-east **Everon Hill** is from a Scots word *averin,* this same berry.

Meall nan Subh – myowl n*a*n **soo**
Druim Ruighe nan Smeur – drim rooy*a* n*a*n **smayr**
Meall nan Oighreagan – myowl n*a*n **oe-eerakan**
Beinn nan Oighreag – bYn n*a*n **oe-eerak**

These berries would have been part of the autumn diet, and it is surprising to find no bilberry or blaeberry – in Gaelic *braoileag* – hill, for it grows plentifully. Many a walker of today has been caught purple-fingered in the evening sun, and it certainly was part of the Gael's diet – as well as a dyestuff and, apparently, a cure for dysentery; the Border hills manage a **Blaeberry Hill** in Eskdale. Buachaille Etive Mòr has the rock climb of **Crowberry Tower,** English-named after the shrub much favoured by ptarmigan, and growing on its ledges. In the far north-west lies **Beinn nan Cnàimhseag***, the mountain of bearberries. Berries are often associated with nuts, and although **Chnò Dearg*** above Loch Treig literally means red nut (*cnò dearg*), it is almost certainly a misprint for Cnoc Dearg (red hill). However **Sgurr a'Bhraonain*** near Loch Hourn is probably earth-nut (or pignut) peak, from a type of root-tuber.

Birds

Birds make little appearance in the names of the southern hills, apart from a couple of **Goose Hills,** but they are rarely absent from any Highland skyline. Birds were of course a source of food, as the name of **Beinn Eunaich*** near Dalmally (fowling mountain) indicates. A short crow's flight away lies **Meall nan Eun***, peak of the birds, while a migration away in Torridon **Beinn an Eoin*** is peak of the bird. Meall nan Eun has slabby sides useless for nesting or perching, but on the flatter grassy top on a wet August day I was surprised by the sheer number of small birds, pipits and wheatears, bobbing around on every available boulder and even on the summit cairn.

On Speyside is **Tom an Eòin***, knoll of the bird, and legend has it that whenever the stolen bell of Insh church, sited on it, was rung in its far-off home, it pealed 'Tom-an-Eòin' as a rebuke to its captors!

These bird peaks were probably so-named from the relative density of breeding birds on them. On the little isle of Colonsay, rich in birdlife due to the tree-planting efforts of an early improver, is **Càrn an Eòin***, and at over 2500 feet (750m) in the hills east of Glenshee the lonely **Loch nan Eun** echoes to the playground shrieks of the gulls who have bred there for decades, as at **Loch nan Stuirteag** (loch of the seagulls) near Cairn Toul. Elsewhere hillsides were simply B&B calls for the birds, where they rested or roosted: **Meall nan Spàrdan*** in the west means just that. **Marsco** on Skye was seagull mountain to the Norsemen, while **Meall nan Faoilean*** on Staffa is its Gaelic equivalent.

Beinn nan Cnàimhseag – bYn nan **krY:v**shak
Chnò Dearg – chnaw **dyer**ak (probably Cnoc Dearg – krochk **dyer**ek)
Sgùrr a'Bhraonain – skoor *a* **vroe:**nan^y   Beinn Eunaich – bYn **ee**aneech
Meall nan Eun – myowl nan **ee**-an   Beinn an Eòin – bYn an **yaween**^y
Tom an Eòin – towm *an* **yaween**^y   Càrn an Eòin – kaarn *an* **yaween**^y
Meall nan Spàrdan – myowl nan **spaar**dan
Meall nan Faoilean – myowl nan **foe:**lan

The two classic birds of the high tops are the grouse – exploding from the heather underfoot with motorbike staccato – and the ptarmigan, discreetly belching as it cranes snake-like over boulders at you. Yet while the ptarmigan (*tàrmachan* in Gaelic), habitant of the very highest plateaux, has rightly had the fine **Meall nan Tàrmachan***ridge above Loch Tay named after it, as well as the **Ptarmigan** shoulder of Ben Lomond (and another on a hill in Knoydart), the grouse appears to have been overlooked apart from a mere shoulder in Torridon called **Meallan na Circe-fraoich** (little hill of the grouse). Its Gaelic names are *cearc fhraoich* or *coileach ruadh*, literally heather hen and red cock, and unless the Fannaich's peak **An Coileachan***(little cock) counts, it has been forgotten in the honours. It was the Norse who gave it airspace in the three peaks named Oreval (moorfowl fell) on Harris and South Uist.

But surely the sweetest-sounding bird mountain is **Beinn Trilleachan***above Loch Etive. Better-known among southern visitors for its steep slabs where rock-climbers perch, its Gaelic meaning is the mountain of sandpipers, or oyster-catchers. The latter name is more likely, for the sheltered sea-loch Etive at its very foot would provide excellent feeding for this loud-trilling flashy bird. (Sandpipers prefer fresh water, and have an alternative form *drilleachan*.)

Another bird fond of the summits is the raven, distinctive both for its acrobatics and its eerie croaking in the mist, and it has crags named for it like **Creag an Fhithich***on Ben Lawers. The raven is the adopted bird of Clan Dougall, and it's interesting that in the clan's heartland around Oban, there's a **Creag an Fhithich** and a **Creag nam Fitheach** within a short distance. The Norse named **Krakkaval** on Lewis after the crow (probably the raven member of that family, since it was considered sacred in Scandinavia), and **Criffel** hill above Dumfries is from the same root. **Càrn a'Chlamhain***, cairn of the kite near Glen Tilt, is not to be confused with **Creag a'Chalamain***near Glenmore, dove's crag. The southern Cairngorms have bird-hills too: there is **Tom Bad na Speireige***(sparrowhawk), **Coire na Feadaige***(plover), the Munro **Càrn a'Gheòidh***(goose) and **Tom na Riabhaig***(lark) near Loch Callater.

Some birds are more timid than others, **Beinn Enaiglair***in Ross is said to be the hill of the timid or fearful birds from *eun eagal*, while **Bonxa Hill** in Shetland refers to the bonxies, local name for the skuas, the bovver boys of the bird world who attack other birds for food.

Meall nan Tàrmachan – myowl nan **taarmochan**	An Coileachan – *a*n kol*a*chan
Beinn Trilleachan – bYn **tree**lyochan	Creag an Fhithich – krayk *a*n **ee**-eech
Càrn a'Chlamhain – kaarn *a* chlaveen^y	Creag a'Chalamain – krayk *a* **chalamna**ʼ
Tom Bad na Speireige – towm bat n*a* **spayreek***a*	
Coire na Feadaige – kor*a* n*a* fedeeg*a*	Càrn a'Gheòidh – kaarn *a* yawee
Tom na Riabhaig – towm n*a* **ree**av*a*k	Beinn Enaiglair – bYn en*a*kl*a*r

Cattle
While bird and animal hunting may have provided food intermittently, the rearing of domesticated animals was the mainstay of the Highland economy. In particular the keeping of the so-called 'black' cattle (in reality as often brown, fawn, grey or dappled) for dairy produce, and later for sale to the Sassenachs for beef. This trade has faded away over the last 150 years, but has left its memorial in the hill and corrie names. **Druim nam Bò*** is ridge of the cattle: **Meall Greigh*** of Ben Lawers is herd hill and **Beinn a'Chuallaich*** above Rannoch Moor, on one of the great drove roads, is mountain of herding.

A calf or fawn in Gaelic is *laogh* – and also means, significantly, dear one. **Ben Lui*** is from this word. One well-hoofed drove route was the **Làirig an Laoigh*** in the Cairngorms, the pass of the calf, easier going for the beasts than the higher and stonier Làirig Ghrù a few miles west. In the north flank of Cairn Gorm itself is Coire Laoigh Mòr, which once echoed to their lowing, and above Loch Monar lies **Bidein a'Choire Sheasgaich***, referring to the farrow cattle (those kept temporarily without calf at udder or womb) that grazed in its corrie.

Cattle were liable to theft, to the extent that it was a young men's pastime to make raids on other clan's herds, and in the west there are three mountains called **Creach Bheinn***, hill of spoil or plunder. In Glencoe the famous **Lost Valley** – so-named because it is a glacial 'hanging valley' lost to view from the main glen – was where the MacDonalds hid away their still-hoofed hamburgers! At the eastern mouth of Glencoe stand **Buachaille Èite (Etive) Mòr*** and **Beag**, the big and little herdsmen of Etive; the old names were Stob Dearg and Stob Dubh (red and dark peaks), and perhaps the 'herdsman' was an ironic name given by the wary drovers edging their herds past here.

Dairying
In the earlier centuries when these cattle were kept for their milk and hides, transhumance was practised. While the men went fishing in the summer, and the women tended the crops, the young girls took the cattle to the high summer sheilings (*àirigh*) for summer pasturage, so there are names like **Beinn Àirigh Chàrr*** in Ross, mountain of the bogland sheiling – **Martha's Peak** on

---

Druim nam Bò – drim nam **boa:**   Meall Greigh – myowl **gray**
Beinn a'Chuallaich – bYn *a* **choo**aleech
Ben Lui – (Gaelic: Beinn Laoigh) – bYn **loe-ee**
Làirig an Laoigh – la:reek *a* **loe-ee**
Bidein a'Choire Sheasgaich – beedyin *a* chor*a* **hes**geech
Creach Bheinn – **krech**vYn
Buachaille Etive (Èite) Mòr/Beag – boo-ucheely*a* ay:ty*a* **moa:r/bayk**
Beinn Àirigh Chàrr – bYn aaree **chaar**

162

this hill commemorates a cowherd who slipped to her death. **Ben Ìme*** near
The Cobbler in Argyll is the butter mountain – a name long predating the
Common Market! – while on the other side of The Cobbler the Buttermilk
Burn churns its way down to Loch Long. **Beinn Smeorail** in the north is its
Norse counterpart. (Butter and cheese were of course made *on* the hill, at the
shieling pastures.) Speyside's **Craig a'Bhainne*** is the milk crag while
Rannoch's **Meall na Meòig*** is the whey hill. Small islands offshore were also
used for summer pasture, as Staffa's **Meall nan Gamhna*** (hill of the stirks)
indicates.

Although the cowherds had time to dally – **Caisteal Samhraidh*** (summer
castle) above Glen Lyon being probably a sunny belvedere to lie on –
milkmaids who tended the cattle in the shielings faced certain risks. Both
Martha's Peak and **Sgùrr Mhàiri*** (Mary's Peak) in the Red Cuillin
commemorate two who died in falls while on pastoral service. A more frequent
if less serious risk was that posed by the visits of young men to these lonely
spots, and Gaelic poetry is full of references to amorous encounters of the
shieling kind. As Donnchadh Bàn recalls in his *Final Farewell:*

> "Fhuair mi greis am àrach
> Air àirighnean a b'aithne dhomh
> Ri cluiche, 's mire, s' mànran
> 'S bhith 'n caoimhneas blàth nan caileagan"

("I spent a part of my youth, in the shielings I knew well . . . playing, frisking
and flirting, among the warm kindliness of the girls")

Could **Beinn Alligin***, possibly darling peak (from *àilleagan*) and **Beinn
Èibhinn***, delightful mountain, be named from such sweet memories?

Deer

If the eagle was king of the skies, the stag, long before painter Landseer, was
monarch of the mountain. **Beinn Damh*** in Torridon is one of many stag
mountains. **Sgùrr Èilde Mòr*** in the Mamores (properly Sgùrr na h-Eilde
Mòire) is for its female companion the hind, *eilid*, while **Beinn nan
Aigheanan*** has the same meaning (from *aighean*). Near Ben Nevis is **Sgùrr a'
Bhuic***, peak of the buck, the young deer, and there is **The Buck** near
Tomintoul. Near Cannich **Càrn na h-Earbaige Bige*** refers to the young roe,

---

Ben Ìme – bYn ee:ma   Craig a'Bhainne – krayk *a* vany*a*
Meall na Meòig – myowl n*a* myaweek
Meall nan Gamhna – myowl n*a*n gown*a*
Caisteal Samhraidh – kashtyal sowree   Sgùrr Mhàiri – skoor va:ree
Beinn Alligin – bYn aaleegin   Beinn Èibhinn – bYn ay:veenʸ
Beinn Damh – bYn dav   Sgùrr na h-Èilde Moire – skoor n*a* hay:ltya moa:ra
Beinn nan Aigheanan – bYn n*a*n Y*a*nan   Sgùrr a'Bhuic – skoor *a* vooeechk
Càrn na h-Earbaige Bige – kaarn n*a* hyer*a*bak*a* beek*a*

as does **Craignarb** hill in the east, and the roe's colour is apparent in **Meall nan Ruadhag**[*] (red roe) above Loch Ness.

Another *eilid*, **Meall na h-Èilde**[*] above Glengarry was, according to local naturalist Edward Ellice, so-called from its provision of good feeding and shelter from the westerly gales for the nursing hinds. Red deer are conservative animals, returning to their traditional calving areas time and again. Above Glen Coe the peak **Stob Coire Altruim**[*] is from *altrum*, nursing or rearing, and nearby runs the Làirig Èilde Mòr, big pass of the hind. **Am Biachdich**[*] and **Meall Tionail**[*] mountains are respectively the feeding place (from *biadhtach*) and hill of the gathering place – the latter is a common name, and may refer also to the gathering of cattle or sheep.

This Gaelic attention to natural detail is apparent too in peaks like **Meall a'Bhùiridh**[*] – of which there are two, one on either edge of Rannoch Moor – the hill of the roaring, from where the rutting autumn stags bellow soulfully through the lengthening black nights. The similar name **Ben Vuirich** near Killiecrankie is said to be so-called from the howling of wolves. Other 'noisy' peaks with probable similar meanings include the Quoichside duo of **Gàirich**[*] and **Gleouraich**[*], from *gàirich* and *gleadhraich* for prolonged shout and uproar.

Meall nan Ruadhag – myowl n*a* **roo***a*ghak

Meall na h-Èilde – myowl n*a* **hayl:**dy*a*   Stob Coire Altruim – stop kor*a* **altrim**

Am Biachdich – *a*m **bee-***a*chteech   Meall Tionail – myowl **tyi**nal

Meall a'Bhùiridh – myowl *a* **voo:**ree   Gàirich – **gaa**reech

Gleouraich – **gloe:**reech

Deer hunts and dogs

Beinn Chabair* probably means antler mountain (or just possibly hawk, from the obsolete *cabhar*) while Ben Wyvis' pointed **An Cabar*** is simply the antler (one of several in the area), as are the hills **Cròic-Bheinn*** and **Crock. Beinn Oss** near Tyndrum may be from *os*, a stream outlet – there is a lochan in its southern corrie – or more likely from *os*, an elk, an animal that was hunted to extinction in c.1300. No such fate attended the red deer, whose numbers are now believed to exceed the human population of the Highlands, in spite of hunting, for in the age before the high-velocity rifle, dogs and traps and simpler weapons were used to cull rather than slaughter the deer. Hunting was part of every man's yearly round. Strath na Seilge in Ross is from *sealg*, the hunt. **Meall nan Con*** is peak of the dog, whilst **Sgùrr nan Conbhairean*** above Glen Shiel is peak of the keepers of the (hunt) dogs; there are legends relating to the Fingalian hunting dogs being kept here. **Creag a'Leth-choin*** above Glenmore means lurcher's crag: a lurcher is a hunting dog, a formidable cross between a greyhound and collie. But on the occasion that led to this name several of the lurchers plunged to their deaths over the cliff while in foaming pursuit of a stag all the way from Ryvoan. The nearby **Lurchers' Gully** – over which ski promoters and conservationists have had dog-fights – is a translation of Coire a'Leth-choin. The nearby peak of **Càrn Eilrig*** is from an elrick (in Gaelic *iolairig*) which was a natural V-shaped notch in the hillside into which the deer were driven to be trapped and killed.

There's another fearsome if fantastic legend associated with hunting dogs on **Creag nan Caisean*** near Foss in Perthshire. It tells of a large party of hunters, ghillies and their dogs who paused to rest on its top. The ghillies encouraged two of the dogs to fight; the excitement of the fight sucked in the ghillies and then their masters and the other dogs, and the whole episode ended with the dogs, ghillies and hunters (who were brothers) tearing each other's throats out, leaving but one half-brother as survivor and witness to this bloody tableau. The word *caisean* in Gaelic means short-tempered person or quarrel, and the hill's name is a wild understatement *if* the legend is true!

Deer-killing was to be a double-edged sword for the Gaels. It provided them with an important source of food through the centuries, but when the 19th-century industrialist landlords discovered the joys of organised deer-hunting for their rich friends, they speeded up the clearances and evictions to create people-less, tree-less deserts called ironically deer forests, the empty quarters

---

An Cabar – **kap**ar   Beinn Chabair – bYn **chap**ayr^y

Cròic-bheinn – **kraw**eek vYn Meall nan Con – myowl nan **kon**

Sgùrr nan Conbhairean – skoor nan **kon**averan

Creag a'Leth-choin – krayk *a* **lye**chan^y

Càrn Eilrig – kaarn **ayl**areek

Creag nan Caisean – krayk nan **kash**an

that now dominate the high ground. **Bruch na Frìthe*** in the Cuillin is from *frìth* meaning both deer forest and, aptly, wilderness, and in the southern Highlands **Auchnafree Hill** is hill of the field (*achadh na frìthe*) of the deer forest.

Eagles

In Gaelic mythology the seagulls (*stuirteag*) were believed to be the spirits of the good on earth, their black caps being worn to expiate sins. But if they were Heaven's angels on earth, surely the Lord of the sky was the eagle, in Gaelic *iolair*. Yet curiously few summits bear the bird's name. Partly this reflects the fact that they nest lower down, in the pines or for security on remote crags, generally below 2500 feet (750m). Thus there are several instances of **Creag na h-Iolaire***, for instance at 1600 feet (500m) on Mull, and in Glen Shiel a shoulder called **Sgùrr Nid na h-Iolaire***, peak of the eagle's nest. In the Trossachs **Meall na h-Iolaire** barely reaches 2000 feet (600m). In the south west Borders, **Benyellary** is in fact Beinn na h-Iolaire. But whilst it nests lower down it hunts and soars high over the tops, and the Gaels did recognise the significance of the bird with a special alternative word *fìor-eun*, literally the "true" or "notable" bird: and above remote Glen Pean is a top

---

Bruch na Frìthe – broo*a*ch n*a* **free:**y*a*
Creag na h-Iolaire – krayk n*a* **hyoo**l*ara*
Sgùrr Nid na h-Iolaire – skoor nyeet n*a* **hyoo**l*ara*

called **Meall an Fhìr-eòin***. **Meall Horn** in the north may also be from this word, as *meall fhìr-eòin*. Yet the absence of its name from any of the high peaks on mainland Scotland seems to be an omission by the Gaels, when even the rather prosaic Norse found space for **Arnaval** (eagle fell) on both Skye and South Uist, maybe inspired by the white-tailed sea eagle of the Hebrides which also soared over their ancestral Norwegian fiords. (**Mount Eagle,** an unprepossessing tree-covered ridge in the Black Isle, is probably a corruption ("Gleneagles" style) of *monadh na h-eaglais,* hill of the church.)

Stob Gabhar

Goats

Far better suited than the sheep to the terrain (and to the people) was the goat, *gobhar,* whose name occurs throughout the Highlands, as in **Stob Ghabhar*** in the Black Mount or **Sgòr Gaibhre*** facing it across Rannoch Moor. **Coire na Minseag*** near Glen Lyon is the she-goat corrie. Edward Ellice, in his account of Glengarry, noting a **Goats' Crag** above Aberchilder says they were extensively kept for milking.

Like all economically valuable goods, they were subject to theft. A 16th-century raid by the rapacious MacDonalds on Glen Garry carried off 1,302 goats and 763 kids – in the circumstances, of these semi-wild creatures, a prodigious feat of counting let along thieving!

Meall an Fhìr-eoin – myowl *a*n **ee:**ra*n*[y]
Stob Ghabhar – stop **gow***a*r
Sgòr Gaibhre – skor **gY**r*a*
Coire na Minseag (properly Coire nam Minnseag) – kor*a* nam **meen**shak

Heather, peat and moor

Heather, *fraoch*, is commoner on the actual slopes than in names, and while there are a few hills called **Fraoch Bheinn*** in the west, there is only one Munro-high mountain with it, **Mullach Fraoch Choire***. This is probably because heather does not grow much above 3000 feet (900m) because it needs a six-month growing season free of snow cover, and so does not reach the summits. Partly too because the heather is so common as to be unremarkable. In southern Scotland some examples of the common name **Black Hill** refer to heather. Moors blanketed with bog are found stretching almost to the summits, especially in the eastern plateaux, as names like **Càrn Bhac*** (peat bank), **Bac nam Fòid*** (banks of peat, above Loch Hourn) and **A'Chòinneach*** (the moss) show. The two hills called **Sgùrr na Lapaich*** are peak of the bogland.

Ben Chonzie* (alias Ben y Hone) in Perthshire may be *beinn a'chomhainn*, mountain of narrowness, which is not an appropriate name for this broad hill. More probably it is a terrible anglicisation (often pronounced as it is spelt in English) of the gentle Gaelic *beinn na còinnich* (mossy mountain). And **Conic Hill** at the foot of Loch Lomond has little to do with its shape and everything to do with pidgin Gaelic, from the same word *còinneach*. **Waggle Hill** in the north-east is from the Scots word *waggle* meaning a quagmire, suggesting one's probable movements across its shoogly surface. Meanwhile in the heart of the Cairngorms the **Mòine Mòr*** (A'Mhòine Mhòr, big peat bog) is no idle warning!

Horses

Of some importance in the Highland economy was the horse, which ran free on the hills unlike today's corralled creatures. It is believed that the summit of **An Sgarsoch*** above Tarfside was where they were brought to a great annual horse market. (An Sgarsoch's name is usually given as meaning the place of sharp rocks, from its grey hairpiece of scree, unusual in these flat-topped hills). The horses' place in the name pantheon is in hills like **A'Mharconaich***, the horsy place above Drumochter, and **Sgùrr nan Each*** and the popular **Beinn Each** near Callander, both horses' mountains.

Around Kintail in Wester Ross is an intriguingly 'horsy place': here there are foals (in **Sgùrr an t-Searraich*** on the Five Sisters and **Beinn an**

Fraoch Bheinn – **froe:ch** vYn   Mullach Fraoch Choire – moolach **froe:ch** chor*a*

Càrn Bhac – kaarn **vachk**   Bac nam Fòid – bachk n*a*m **fawt**^{y}

A'Chòinneach – *a* **chawn**yoch   Sgùrr na Lapaich – skoor n*a* **lah**peech

Ben Chonzie (Beinn a'Choinnich) – bYn *a* **chawn**yeech

Mòine Mhòr – mawny*a* **voa:r**   An Sgarsoch – *a*n **skar**soch

A'Mharconaich – *a* **vark**aneech   Sgùrr nan Each – skoor n*a*n **yech**

Sgùrr an t-Searraich – skoor *a*n **tyar**eech

t-Searraich), a mare (in Sgùrr na Làire Brice*, as in Beinn Làir further north), another mare above Glenelg (in Beinn a'Chapuill*), a mane (A'Mhuing*), and Norse and Gaelic horses (in Rosdail near Glenelg and in Sgùrr Leac nan Each* on the Saddle). The Saddle itself (An Dìollaid* in Gaelic) is so-named from the yoke-shape of its 330 feet (1000m) summit slung between two peaked tops – like its English little cousin Saddleback, and its distant relative the Sattelhorn in the Swiss Bernese Oberland – and completes the equestrian connection in this area. The concentration in this western seaboard area may be due to the Norse influence, for the Norse word *hross* occurs throughout the Western Isles, as well as in placenames like Rosdail and Rois-bheinn. The Vikings did use horses, and may well have introduced new strains to the local people.

Elsewhere in the Highlands the word *dìollaid* has passed into general use for a saddle or wide pass between two hills. In contrast to the horses which gave their name to hills, Arkle and Foinaven are two hills which gave their name to two famous racehorses! In the Borders, Riding Hill in upper Tweeddale refers to the Common Riding, or marking out of local boundaries.

Insects

The southern hills are the home of two insect hills, Golloch Hill in the Ochils from the horny goloch or earwig (from the Gaelic *gobhlach*, forked), and Midge Hill near Camps Reservoir. It is curious then that in the Highlands where the true midge dines out (on people) there are no hills dedicated to its Gaelic name of *meanbhchuileag*, literally tiny fly – but then, even Donnchadh Bàn could not bring himself to mention it in his "Final Farewell"! The closest name is Meall Cuileige* above Glen Moriston, hill of the fly.

Landscape

The Gael had an eye too for the stiller, geologically-creeping aspect of nature, the shape of the land. (Other chapters deal with the wide variety of names for distinctive mountain shapes, and the plethora of colours picked out.)

Adjectives like *eagach* (notched – as in the Aonach Eagach*, running like a corrugated fence along Glencoe) and *cas* (steep – as in Coire Cas of Cairngorm), *fada* and *geàrr* (long and short as in Beinn Fhada* and Geàrr Aonach*), *garbh* and *leacach* (rough and slabby) are all accurate for their particular hills. *Garbh* (rough) is common (Meall Garbh* hills abound) while the word for

---

Sgùrr na Làire Brice – skoor n*a* laar*a* breechk*a*
Beinn a'Chapuill – bYn *a* chapal[y]   A'Mhuing – *a* vooeeng
Sgùrr Leac nan Each – skoor lyechk n*a*n yech   An Diollaid – *a*n dyee*a*lat
Meall Cuileige – myowl koolik*a*   Aonach Eagach – oe:noch egoch
Beinn Fhada – bYn at*a*   Geàrr Aonach – gyaar oe:noch
Meall Garbh – myowl gar*a*v

smooth appears in Speyside's **Càrn Sleamhuinn***, and fat or stout is found in the score of hills called **Meall Reamhar*** in the southern Highlands. A more unusual word for fat appears in **Meith Bheinn*** in South Monar. And in the same vein, **Duncryne Hill** overlooking Loch Lomond (*dùn cruinn*, rounded hill-fort) is usually known by the unflattering name "Dumpling Hill".

Mòr and *beag* (big and little) are widely used, usually to distinguish two proximate hills like **Aonach Mòr*** and **Aonach Beag**: sometimes the 'wee one', the *beag*, is actually higher than the bigger *mòr*, as in the two just named, but the *mòr* may well be bulkier, or nearer the local village and therefore higher-looking in the view. *Meadhon* (often pronounced as in the several Ben Vanes) means the middle or intermediate peak, so **Aonach Meadhoin*** above Glen Clunie is between the higher Sgùrr a'Bhealaich Deirg (red pass peak) and the lower Sgùrr an Fhuarail. **Ben Mannoch** in the east is from the same word, while **Beinn Stumanadh*** is the 'modest' hill alongside Ben Loyal. In the Borders **Drochil Hill** is the Scots-named dwarfish or dumpy hill.

Tarsuinn, transverse or oblique, is commonly used of hills whose axis runs counter to the grain of the land. Thus **Beinn Tarsuinn*** in the Letterewe forest, a west-east running hill, is set at right angles to the long north-south ridge running up to Beinn a'Chlaidheimh (sword). Another hill that ends a long ridge, but in this case is simply set apart from it, is perfectly described in its name **Cruach Innse***, literally the island heap, standing 'offshore' from the Grey Corries chain.

Finer details of the landscape are picked up in names like **Beinn Sgritheall*** (or Sgriol, maybe related to *sgrìodan*, scree – it pours its stone shoots down towards Loch Hourn), **Càrn na Caim*** above Drumochter (cairn of the curve) and **Carn of Claise** (cairn of the ditch or hollow). **Beinn nan Imirean*** is ridged mountain, **Meall na h-Aisre*** the defile hill, **Meall na Leitreach*** slope hill, and **Fireach*** is simply 'sloping'. Among other descriptions are the precise **Bràigh Coire Chruinn-Bhalgain***, height of the corrie of the rounded blisters, the imaginative **An Tunna*** in Arran, meaning the barrel, and the unexpected **Creag Gaineamhach***, sandy crag above Strathglass, perhaps from an outwash of glacial sands. The Cuillin's **Sgùrr nan Eag*** is peak of the

---

Càrn Sleamhuinn – kaarn **shly**eveen^y   Meall Reamhar – myowl rev*a*r
Meith Bheinn – **may** vYn   Aonach Mòr – oe:nach **moa**:r
Aonach Meadhoin – oenach **mee**-on^y   Beinn Stumanadh – bYn **stoo**man*a*gh
Beinn Tarsuinn – bYn **tars**Yn^y   Cruach Innse – kroo*a*ch **ee:**nsh*a*
Beinn Sgritheall – bYn **skree**h*a*l   Càrn na Caim – kaarn n*a* **kY**m
Meall na h-Aisre – myowl n*a* **hash**r*a* Meall na Leitreach – myowl n*a* **lyay**troch
Beinn nan Imirean – bYn n*a*n **yeem***a*ran
Bràigh Coire Chruinn-Bhalgain – **brY:** kor*a* **chrYn** – val*a*keen^y
Fireach – **fee**roch   An Tunna – *a*n **toon***a*
Creag Gaineamhach – krayk **gany**avoch   Sgùrr nan Eag – skoor n*a*n **ek**

notches, its rocky teeth-gaps. Other descriptions are almost superfluous, like the two mountains called **Sgùrr nan Coireachan**[*] in the west, for there can hardly be a Highland mountain (after millenia of ice-sheets) without a gouge of corries on its flanks. Others should not be taken too literally; **Càrn Ghluasaid**[*] is hill of movement, apparently from the slippage of its screes, while nearby **Aonach air Chrith,** ridge of trembling, causes you to shake in your boots!

Subjective feeling rather than objective description must account for **Càrn a'Choire Bhòidhich**[*†] on the White Mounth, cairn of the beautiful corrie, and Gleouraich's ridge called **Sròn na Breun Leitir**[*], the nose of the filthy or rotten slope. **Beinn Sgreamhaidh**[*] in Sutherland is loathsome hill. And what tale lies behind **Luinne Bheinn**[*] often translated as the angry peak, or sometimes as the hill of mirth or melody? Perhaps it is from *luinne* suggesting the swell of the sea, a fine description of its shape; when the adjective precedes the noun it indicates a poetic turn of phrase, and 'sea-swelling mountain' conjures up a lovely picture of this peak: as does **Moruisg,** big water!

Beinn Heasgarnich[*] near Glen Lyon is often translated as peaceful or sheltering mountain, from *seasgairneach*. Its main ridge runs north-south and would be a barrier to the strong westerly winds, for cattle sheltering in the glen of its main burn. It is interesting that, close by, are two hills **Sgiath Bhuidhe**[*] and **Sgiath Chùil**[*], *sgiath* being a wing, and expressing the 'sheltering' idea well in the crook of their wing-shaped north-south ridges. The mountain may be the source of a little mystery, for in an 1872 guidebook is listed, among Scotland's principal peaks, one Ben Feskineth at 3530 feet (1075m) in Perthshire. The peak has never since been heard of, but the height and county are identical to Heasgarnich's!

The Border hills convey little of the landscape bar the frequent references to subsidiary features like coomb (a corrie), cleuch (a gully), hope (a valley), and craig (a cliff). However, there are some more interesting names: **Steygail Hill** is from stey, steep, and gail, a crack; **Shankend** is the expressive name for a slope running from high to low ground, like the Gaelic *sròn;* and **Spango Hill** is apparently from *spangie* or *spanghue*, a Scots word for leaping frog-like up in the air. The Norse on the other hand in their naming of Hebridean hills did go in for topographical description. Peaks like **Breaclete** (broad rock), **Hartaval** (rocky fell), **The Hoe** (high), **Reieval and Roneval** (smooth and rough fells), and **Sletteval** (flat fell) occur in several places, for the Norse, however, were primarily seafarers naming peaks for maritime identification purposes.

Sgùrr nan Coireachan – skoor n*an* **kor***a*chan   Càrn Ghluasaid – kaarn **ghloo***a*sat
Càrn a'Choire Bhòidhich – **kaarn** *a* chor*aa*vawyeech
Sròn na Breun Leitir – strawn n*am* **brayn laytyeer**[y]
Beinn Sgreamhaidh – bYn **skrevee**   Luinne Bheinn – loony*a* vYn
Beinn Heasgarnich – bYn **heskarneech**   Sgiath Bhuidhe – skee*a* **vooee**
Sgiath Chùil – skee*a* **choo:l**

Sheep

Sheep were kept by the earlier Gaels, in small numbers. But the introduction of large-scale sheep farming by the 19th-century landlords was the means of impoverishing the people and evicting them from their ancestral lands. As Donnchadh Bàn laments in his *Final Farewell:*

> "'S a'bheinn is beag a shaoil mi
> Gun dèanadh ise caochladh
> O'n tha i nis fo chaoraibh
> 'S ann thug an saoghal car asam."
>
> (I hardly thought
> That the mountain would ever change,
> But now it is under sheep,
> The world has cheated me.)

The ecologist Fraser Darling has argued that, amongst its other sins, the sheep's grazing destroyed the rich natural vegetation of the hills, found now only on a few inaccessible ledges. Scarcely surprising then that not many hills bear the creature's name, in complete contrast to the hills of southern Scotland. The name is only borne by lesser hills like **Beinn nan Caorach*** by Loch Hourn and **Meallan nan Uan***, little hill of the lambs in Strath Conon. **Sòval**, a Lewis hill meaning sheep fell (from the Norse) represents the more ancient breed of sheep brought by the Vikings, a beast that did not trample livelihoods underhoof as the later Cheviots did on the mainland.

The wet boggy conditions of the west Highlands do not make it ideal terrain for the sheep, exposing them to the risks of footrot, ticks and the like: the peak **Spidean Mialach*** above Loch Quoich in the wettest part appears to mean literally lousy peak, perhaps from *mial-caorach*, the sheep-louse. In fact it was probably named long before sheep moved onto the hill, and comes from an obsolete meaning of *mial* for any animal, probably deer. Over time it changed its meaning to louse, and its name was therefore something of a puzzle and apparently the Glengarry people created a 'folk etymology' to the effect that it had come from *spidean neulach*, cloudy peak, and that their ancestors changed it to the similar-sounding *spidean mialach* to distinguish it from the many other 'cloudy' peaks in this the wet west! (Such 'jokey' explanations for name origins are common in the Lowlands, and often come to be believed by later generations).

Close to Spidean Mialach is **Beinn Mhialairigh*** from the same word *mial*, while **Sturdy Hill** in Angus may well be from Scots *sturdy* (Gaelic *stùird*), a sheep brain disease producing dizziness ('mad sheep disease'!). But it is significant that none of the highest peaks bear the sheep's name.

Beinn nan Caorach – bYn nɑn **koe:**roch
Meallan nan Uan – myalan nɑn **oo**-an
Spidean Mialach – speetyan **mee**aloch
Beinn Mhialairigh – bYn **vee**alɑree

There is only one hill in southern Scotland called simply **Sheep Hill; it is in** the Renfrew Heights. But there are several **Lamb Hills** or **Rigs** – and the Lammermuir Hills themselves may come from 'lamb' – as well as **Ewe Hills** and **Hog Hills**, a hog being a yearling sheep. The ubiquitous **Wether** (or sometimes **Wedder**) **Hills, Laws,** and **Dods,** of which there are at least a dozen, are named from a wether, a castrated ram: and hill-points **Wedder Lairs** in the Lammermuirs, as **Hoglayers** in the Lomonds of Fife, refer to the lairs or scoops where the wethers weather the storms. But unlike the magnificent Swiss peak the Wetterhorn (the 'weather peak') at the northern edge of the Bernese Oberland, our many Wether Hills have neither the height nor the position to indicate the outlook by catching the first of the cloud. **Bught Knowes** in Eskdale refers to a sheepfold, while the intriguing **Minny E'** hill near Sanquhar may indicate a place where lost lambs were rejoined with their mothers, a practice called *minnie*.

Shells
Several Highland peaks appear to be named from shells, surprisingly in view of their general distance from the sea. In fact the shell meanings suggested by several books are probably wrong by reason of location and interpretation. **Beinn a'Chreachain** has been translated as peak of the clamshell: but lying as it does at the head of Glen Lyon it would be a fish out of water so far from the sea, and probably a secondary meaning of *creachann*, the bare summit of a hill, is more apt – one guide describes its top as 'stony and dome-shaped'. **Am Faochagach** in the Deargs (another landlocked location) has been translated as the place of shells, but since the original O.S. spelling was Am Fraochagach, it is probably the heathery or berried place. Similary **Faochag** above Glen Shiel looks like *faochag*, a whelk, but since its original O.S. spelling was *fraochag*, it probably means heathery place.

The most plausible of the four 'shell' peaks might be the nearby **Sgùrr a'Mhaoraich**, apparently from *maorach*, a shellfish. Certainly it does stand near the head of sea-Loch Hourn, and its peaked and ribbed shape could resemble a shell: but its local name (and old O.S. name) is Sgùrr a'Mhorair, the peak of the landowner. A shoulder of this hill is **Bac nan Canaichean**, bank of bog-cotton, not a very maritime name, although **Meall Onfaidh** nearby is hill of the sea's fury.

Shrubs and Flowers
Flora in hill-names include the broom, as in Deeside's **Tom Bealaidh**

Beinn a'Chreachain – bYn *a* chrechYn^y Sgùrr a'Mhaoraich – skoor *a* **voe:reec**
Am Faochagach – *a*m **froe:**chakoch Faochag – **foe:**chak
Bac nan Canaichean – bachk n*a*n **kaneech**n

Sgùrr a'Mhaoraich – skoor *a* **voe:**reech
Meall Onfaidh – myowl **onf**Y Tom Bealaidh – tom **byalee**

(though surely not as well-known as Glasgow's Broomielaw!), the bramble (Glen Doll's **Dreish** from *dris*), and the holly (**Sgùrr a'Chuilinn*** above Glen Shiel). Flowers are rare, but there are hills with names like **Leac na Buidheag***, slab of the buttercup, and even thrift (the sea-pink) in **Sgùrr na Fearstaig***. This plant grows not only on sea coasts but also mountain tops, favouring very exposed habitats where other plants do not dare to spread, and that's why there's another **Sgùrr na Feartaig**, a few miles away. **Meall an t-Seamraig*** above Loch Lochy is the hill of the shamrock, while **Beinn Lurachan*** is garlic mountain. **An Geurachadh*** is the agrimony herb, **Cnoc Bad na Conaire*** willowherb knoll, **Meall Copagach*** docken hill, and **Creag Rainich*** ferny crag.

Plants in the southern hills include bent, a coarse grass, in the Ochils' **Bentie Knowe**, some **Peat Laws, Turf Laws** and **Broom Hill,** and two hills which seem to refer to crops: **Carrot Hill** in the Sidlaws and **Corn Law** in the Ochils (though the latter may be a corruption of *corum* meaning little round hill). **Rispie Hill** and **Rashy Hill** are covered in coarse grass and rushes, respectively.

Snakes

The adder was popular with no generation. Modern landowners sometimes fix 'Beware of adders' on gates to deter hillwalkers, the 20th-century equivalent of 'Here Be Monsters'. Perhaps it was an earlier landlord who named hills like **Meall Nathrach Mhòr*** (properly Meall na Nathrach Mòire) above Rannoch Moor, hill of the big adder – nasty-sounding, but a mere wriggle compared to the ominous **Beinn a'Bheithir*** at Ballachulish which might translate as mountain of the prodigiously large serpent!

Trees

Peeping like rotted molars from the gaping peat hags are bleached tree stumps, the remains of the great Caledonian Forest that covered the Highlands centuries ago before man and climate laid waste to it. Today, depending on exposure to the wind, the treeline reaches up only to about 2000 feet (600m). But several hill-names include trees, usually from plants growing on their lower slopes. The ancient Highland tree cover was mainly of pine, birch and oak, in Gaelic *giubhas, beith* and *darach*.

Sgùrr a'Chuilinn – skoor *a* **chol**een^y   Leac na Buidheag – lyechk n*a* **boo**yak
Sgùrr na Fearstaig – skoor n*a* **fyarsh**tik
Meall an t-Seamraig – myowl *a*n **tsham**arik
Beinn Lurachan – bYn **loo**roch*a*n   An Geurachadh – *a*n **gee**arach*a*gh
Cnoc Bad na Conaire – krochk bat n*a* **kon**ara
Meall Copagach – myowl **koh**pakoch   Creag Rainich – krayk **ran**yeech
Meall Nathrach Mhòr (properly Meall na Nathrach Mòire) – myowl n*a* naroch
    moa:r*a*   Beinn a'Bheithir – byn *a* **vay**heer^y

Beinn a' Chaorainn

The last-named of this trio, the oak, is probably the least hardy, preferring to huddle down in the river valleys of the milder west; it therefore appears rarely in hill-names, with exceptions like **Meall na Doire Darach*** above Kinlochleven. Within sight of this hill is **Sgòr an Iubhair*** in the Mamores, the peak of the yew tree, often associated with churchyards (and it can be clearly seen from the old graveyard in Glen Nevis) but a tree which grows wild in the milder west. Not far away, in Glen Coe **Stob Coire nam Beith*** represents one of the few birches in names, and another one is in **Barbay Hill**

Meall na Doire Darach – myowl na dor*a* **da**roch
Sgòr an Iubhair – skor *an* **yoo**-*a*r
Stob Coire nam Beith – stob kor*a* n*a*m **bay**

(*bar na beithe*) in the Cumbraes. But the birch, like the oak, grows in lower spots, and tends to huddle with its own kind: in contrast trees that grow both high, and as loners, get noticed more. So it is that the rowantree (or mountain ash), *caorann* to the Gaels, has a veritable copse of mountains named for it – the many instances of **Beinn a'Chaoruinn***, **Sàil Chaoruinn**, and **Creag Chaoruinn**. Sometimes planted as a lone tree by a crofter seeking protection against evil spirits, sometimes germinating in a rock crack (hence the Creag examples) from a bird's dropping, this rugged individualist contributes a striking splash of blood-red berries to the blues and golds of autumn, and a worthy name for a mountain. **Sgùrr a'Chaorachain*** in deepest Monar is peak of the rowan-berried place. It is also virtually the only tree of note in the southern hill-names, with **Rowantree Hills** in both the Renfrew Heights and the Lammermuirs.

The pine – not the modern narrow-shouldered regiments, but the beautiful free-branching Scots pine – is a hardy individual that can grow alone on a slope. In the Fannaichs the hill **Beinn Liath Mhòr a'Ghiubhais Lì*** is the big grey hill of the colourful pine, a name that speaks almost orientally of its beauty. The beautiful Glen Derry is encircled by a scattering of such lonesome pines riding shotgun high up on the slopes like outriders. Ironically for this lovely forest of ancient pines, Glen Derry – which gave its name to Derry Cairngorm above it – is named from *doire*, a thicket, usually of oak trees. The pine itself is named in the Cairngorms in Glen Geusachan – although the glen is now bare of trees – and in **Càrn a'Phris-Ghiubhais*** (cairn of the pine thicket), an outlier of the famed Rothiemurchus pines. The Scots pine is found more in this eastern part of the Highlands since it prefers sandy, drier soils. On the north side of Derry Cairngorm lies **Càrn Etchachan***, named from the corrie between; it is probably derived from *aiteann*, the juniper, whose wind-dwarfed shrubs green the stony corrie floor. South of Derry Cairngorm is **Coire Craobh an Òir**, corrie of the tree of gold, beneath which a crock of gold was supposedly buried. And near Glen Luibeg is **Preas nam Meirleach,** thicket of the robbers, where thieves lay in wait for the drovers passing through the Làirig Ghrù.

The destruction of the Scots pine forest is not all in the distant past. Above Loch Arkaig is **Druim a'Ghiùbhsaich***, ridge of the pine, whose northern slopes are still scarred by the charcoaled remains of a great Caledonian pine forest here, burnt down in the last war by commandos training at nearby Spean Bridge, the trees' bleached bones not yet covered by new plantation.

Beinn a'Chaoruinn – bYn a **choe:**rYn^y
Sgùrr a'Chaorachain – skoor *a* **choe:**rachYn^y
Beinn Liath Mhòr a'Ghiubhais Lì – bYn lyee-uy **voa:r** *a* yoo-*a*sh **hlee:**
Càrn a'Phris-Ghiubhais – kaarn *a* freesh **gyoo**eesh
Càrn Etchachan – kaarn **etsh**ach*a*n
Druim a'Ghiùbhsaich – drim *a* **yoo:**seech

Meall na Feàrna* near Callander is the alder hill, while **Fafernie** is *fèith na feàrna*, bog of the alder. **Spirebush Hill** in the Lammermuirs is from a *spire*, Scots for a small tapering tree (usually pine) used to grow paling wood.

Weather

The weather in its unpleasanter form manifests itself in the names of the westerly Ayrshire hills of **Windy Standard** and **Cloud Hill,** and **Misty Law** in Renfrew. Above Lauder **Scoured Rig** evokes a windswept top, while shelter beckons leeward of the intriguing **Windshield Hill** near Moffat. As for the hill shoulder above Megget Water called **Dead for Cauld** . . .

The weather dominates life more in the north. There, mountains can provide shelter from the westerly gales or funnel them down on you, as in a spring Cairngorm "roarer". They can rip open the clouds' rain-laden bellies, or break them up to let the sunshine through. So we find hills that are called misty (**Ben a'Ghlo***, from *glo*, a veil of mist, and **Beinn Cheathaich***) or wind (**Sgòr Gaoith***), wet (**Maoile Lunndaidh***), and cold (*fuar*, as in **Fuar Tholl*** by Glen Carron, and **Fourman Hill** in the north-east catching the bitter winds off the North Sea). **Cnoc Braonach*** by Lochinver is knoll of drizzle, and **Brat Bheinn*** on Jura is literally the veil or mantle mountain, perhaps from its cloud cover. **Cnoc na Fuarachad** on the Atlantic shore of Skye's Sleat peninsula is the coldness hillock.

Not all the weather names are gloomy, though, for there are several small hills called *grianan* – like the shoulder **An Grianan*** above Glen Lochay – meaning the sunny spot or hillock. And comfort might be sought in the names of **Caisteal Samhraidh*** over Glen Lyon, the summer castle, and **Beinn an Dòthaidh*** above Bridge of Orchy, literally mountain of scorching!

Wild Animals

The wild boar, which followd the elk (**Beinn Oss**) into extinction in about 1400, lives on in peaks like **An Torc***, The Boar of Atholl, which with its partner. The Sow of Atholl hogs the western skyline at Drumochter, and **Càrn an Tuirc** at Glenshee. The bear was exterminated by the 10th century, but according to the naturalist David Stephen was remembered in hill-names like **Ruigh na Beiste***. **Beinn Ulbhaidh*** above Strathoykel is the 'wolfy' mountain; the last wolf is supposed to have been killed in 1700 by MacKintosh of Moy in

---

Meall na Feàrna – myowl n*a* fyaarn*a*

Ben a'Ghlo – bYn *a* ghlaw   Beinn Cheathaich – bYn **cheheech**
Sgòr Gaoith – skor **goe-ee**   Maoile Lunndaidh – moel*a* **loond**ee
Fuar Tholl – **foo**-ur howl   Cnoc Braonach – krochk **broe:**noch
Brat Bheinn – **braht** vYn   An Grianan – *an* **gree***a*nan
Caisteal Samhraidh – kashtyal **sowree**   Beinn an Dòthaidh – bYn *an* **daw**hee
Ruigh na Bèiste – ree n*a* **bay:**shty*a*   An Torc – *an* **toohrk**
Beinn Ulbhaidh – bYn **ool***a*vee

Inverness-shire. Hunted too – but too wily to be exterminated – was the fox, *sionnach* or *madadh ruadh* (literally red dog). **Druim Shionnach*** above Glen Shiel and **Sgùrr a'Mhadaidh*** in the Cuillins are but two of several hills where pads the sly beast, and **Càrn na Saobhaidhe*** in the Monadh Liath is the cairn of the fox's den. Foxes nest in boulder-tumbles, so they are spoiled for choice in the Highlands, which is why there are several spots called **Creag a'Mhadaidh** (although these could possibly have been wolf lairs as well). The fox was not always seen as the villain of the countryside – this is the view of the later sheep-farmer – and to the Gael dispossessed by these bleating animal cuckoos, their predators might be smiled on. Donnachadh Bàn was moved in his *Song of Foxes* to cry:

> "Mo bheannachd aig na balgairean
> A chionn bhi sealg nan caorach"
>
> ("My blessing to the foxes
> Because they hunt the sheep")

Small wonder then that the fox's name appears quite often in hill-names. However, although *madadh* is also a dog, the name of **Dog Hillock** above Glen Clova is *not* a translation, for a 'dog hillock' is a north-east Scots name for a hill covered in long grass. In this Clova hill's case, it's in contrast to the nearby **Sandy Hillock**.

Druim Shionnach – drim **h**inoch   Sgùrr a'Mhadaidh – skoor *a* **v**atee
Càrn na Saobhaidhe – kaarn n*a* **soe:veey***a*

Cnap a'Dhòbrain in Glen Avon is otter hillock, **Càrn a'Gheàrraich** near Inverness and **Meall nam Maigheach** are both hare's hill and there are several wild cats in spots like **Beinn a'Chait** by Atholl and Lochan nan Cat on Ben Lawers. Wild cats are apparently as populous as foxes, preferring similar rock-strewn habitats – but being less bold they are very rarely seen, except by the sharp-eyed Gaels who gave these names. However **Cat Law** and the **Hill of Cat** in Angus are deceptive: the old name Carnecaithla (1458) might suggest cairn of the battle (from *cath*). And the **Cat's Back,** a low crouching hill by Strathpeffer, is a local name from its arched shape, and certainly *not* a translation of its Gaelic name Cnoc Farril (probably hill of watching, from *faire*).

In southern Scotland the hare is one of the few wild animals mentioned, in the **Hare Hills** and **Laws.** In Scots, however, a *hare stane* is a boundary stone or marker and the several **Hare Laws** or **Harlaws** are probably from this meaning.

Swansong

The wide range of nature names on the hills indicates a deep concern for the environment. The bitterness that the Gaelic people felt at the Clearances was not just at the loss of home and livelihood, but also at being torn from the natural world they had been so intricately a part of. This bitterness was expressed so clearly by Donnchadh Bàn, in his lament:

> "Mo shoraidh leis na frìthean
> O's mìorbhaileach na beannan iad,
> Le biolair uaine is fìor uisg,
> Deoch uasal, rìomhach, cheanalta:
> Na blàran a tha prìseil,
> 'S na fàsaichean tha lìonmhor,
> O's àit a leig mi dhiom iad,
> Gu bràth mo mhìle beannachd leò."

> (Farewell to the deer forests – they are marvellous mountains,
> With green watercress and pure spring water,
> A noble, beautiful, royal drink;
> To the moorland that is precious,
> And the many lonely places,
> This is my land that I have left,
> A thousand blessings be with them for ever)

Today's nature reserves and the general 'green' movement towards conservation may be fighting a rearguard action for wild life and wilderness in the Scottish countryside, but the rich heritage of nature names is part of this legacy that is worth studying and preserving.

Cnap a'Dhòbhrain – krahp *a* **ghoa**:rYn^y   Càrn a'Ghearraich – kaarn *a* **yareech**
Meall nam Maigheach – myowl n*a*m **mY**-och   Beinn a'Chait – bYn *a* **chetsh**

Chapter Eleven

Mountain Characters

Highland mountain-names often contain characters, people or professions, as mountains elsewhere do. One of the most famous peaks in the Swiss Alps in the Eiger, on whose black north face scores of mountaineers have perished. In translation it means, The Ogre, appropriately. It is part of a famous trio of peaks in the Bernese Oberland together with the Mönch (the monk) and the Jungfrau (the maiden) with the man of God separating the black rock of evil from the pristine white snows of innocence. Do they have Scottish namesakes?

Monks, Maidens and Ogres
In the Scottish Highlands we too have monks, **Beinn Mhanach*** near Tyndrum, and indeed a priest in **Càrn an t-Sagairt Mòr*** near Braemar. We have too a maiden in **A'Mhaighdean*** in the north-west, and indeed a pair of damsels in **Na Gruagaichean*** in the Mamores, with its two finely counterpoised tops. But we have no clear-cut Ogres in spite of the many dark and sinister figures haunting Highland legend, though there are several pretenders.

Prime among the candidates for the title must be **An Riabhachan*** above Glen Cannich, which can be translated straightforwardly as the brindled, greyish one, but in Gaelic An Riabhach Mòr can also mean The Devil, though it does seem a harsh name for this innocuously grassy hill. Grey rather than black is the colour Gaelic often associates with dark things, as in **Am Fear Mòr Liath*** (the Big Grey Man) of Ben Macdhui, the neck-bristling presence which has driven several lone climbers in mortal terror to flee the mountain, out along the **Làirig Ghrù*** (gloomy pass). **Sròn an Tachair*** above Kinloch Rannoch is the promontory of the ghost, and travellers were reputed to feel the hairs on their necks rising as a presence descended.

Beinn Mhanach – bYn vanoch
Càrn an t-Sagairt Mòr – kaarn *a*n tag*a*rsht **moa:r**
A'Mhaighdean – *a* v**Y**dyan
An Riabhachan – *a*n **ree**uvochan
Na Gruagaichean – n*a* **groo**ageechan
Am Fear Mòr Liath – *a*m fer moa:r **lyee**-u
Làirig Ghrù – laarik **ghroo:**
Sròn an Tàchair – strawn *a*n **taa**cheer[y]

Ben Nevis, Scotland's highest mountain, has been translated as the venomous or evil one, from an obsolete Gaelic word *neimheas*. For a mountain that has claimed the lives of many more people than the Eiger, snuffing them out on its northern cliffs, its lethally concave icy north-east shoulder, and on the treacherous southern slabs, the name might seem apt. The tabloid press certainly think so, and the headline "Killer Mountain" is dusted off each winter for the Ben's latest victims. But the name was given to the mountain long before 20th-century humans, climbers and tourists, came in swarms to cast themselves into this Venus Flytrap of the mountains, and in any case the name has other plausible meanings, discussed in the "Top Twenty" chapter.

Another mountain, without Nevis' statistically-deadly reputation, but sometimes translated into notoriety, is **Ben Wyvis*** north of Inverness. (Interestingly, Dorret's map of 1750, often very inaccurate, marks the name of Ben Nevis at the site of Ben Wyvis). Its name has been linked with the Gaelic *fuathais* meaning terror . . . or dismal and gloomy. Both meanings seems quite unreasonable for this long flat bulk of a hill, beached in Easter Ross like a giant whale stranded far from the main mountain schools. A now-obsolete meaning of *fuathais* is 'a great quantity', a closely related word to *uamhas* (pronounced **wa**vas) signifying a horrid deed or atrocity or equally – and here more likely – an enormous quantity. The word 'enormity' has the same double meaning in English. Professor W. J. Watson felt that majestic or awful (as in 'awe-full') was most appropriate to its massive isolated bulk, and perhaps awesome might be the best meaning.

Only **Ben Donich*** in the Arrochar Alps appears to be literally evil mountain, from *dona*, evil or vile, but we do not know why. Although Highland folktales are spirited by demons and water-sprites of various kinds, one of the few that seems to have left its mark on a hill-name is on **Beinn a'Bheithir*** above Ballachulish. Named after the Celtic goddess of winter and death (and with ministerial responsibility for wind and storm), it was believed to be the home of Cailleach Bheithir, who could be a nasty piece of interference in human lives, able, they said, to raise floods and move mountains; but when so inclined she could be a beautiful maiden with the gift of immortal youth. Her contradictory character is mirrored in the dictionary, where a *beithir* was a destructive demon of rather unspecific nature, a kind of indiscriminate vandal. Alternatively it can mean an electric storm, a bear, a thunderbolt, or again a very large serpent. Sea-serpents play an eye-widening role in Gaelic mythology, being responsible on occasion for destroying entire fleets. There's also a **Beinn an t-Seilich*** (from *seilch,* a water-monster rather like a giant snail) on the east shore of Loch Fyne. In any event not nice creatures to meet on a dark night.

Ben Wyvis – ben **wi**vis (locally bYn **wee**vis)   Ben Donich – ben **do**neech
Beinn a'Bheithir – bYn *a* **vay**heer[y]   Beinn an t-Seilich – bYn *an* **tshay**leech

Across Loch Leven from Beinn a'Bheithir, **An Gearanach*** (the complainer) and its neighbour **An Garbhanach*** (the rough one) sound more like a couple of hungover hikers than a dangerous duo. Another candidate for Highland demon king is Skye's **Am Basteir*** often translated as the executioner (from *bàsadair, bàs* means death), supposedly because the nearby Bhasteir Tooth has a resemblance to a headsman's axe. In fact Gaelic for this capital job is more usually *am crochadair* (did he shed crocodile tears at his work?), while Am Baisteir may mean the baptiser or baptist, and the tooth does resemble, even from a long way off, the cowled and stooped head of a monk or priest.

Beauty and the Beast
There are hills whose name appears to be highly complimentary, like **Beinn Alligin*** (darling peak?), **Beinn Èibhinn*** (delightful mountain), and **Càrn a'Choire Bhòidhich*†** (cairn of the beautiful corrie); but beauty appears to be outnumbered by beasts. The word *bèiste*, literally beast, appears in several names. The **Bealach na Bèiste*** (pass of the beast) near Belig in Skye is said to be the spot where a much-feared water horse (*each uisge*) was killed by a MacKinnon, cut down in its maiden-seizing prime. Whilst according to naturalist David Stephen the **Ruigh na Bèiste,** the slope of the beast, is named after the bear, exterminated in the Middle Ages.

The Devil
The devil himself was a stravaiging man, featuring in Gaelic in **Bod an Deamhain*** (the Devil's Penis, now politely translated as Devil's Point) in the Cairngorms, and in **Meall Diamhain*** in Assynt. In English or Scots he pops up in the **Devil's Kitchen** above Loch Callater, his now-straightened **Elbow** above Braemar, his **Cauldron** by Comrie, his **Beeftub** and **Barn Door** near Moffat, his **Putting Stane** in the Carsphairn Hills, his **Thrashing Floor** in Galloway, his **Bite** on Feughside, his **Burdens** in the Lomonds, his **Staircase** above Glencoe, and his **Ridge** in the Mamores. Hell, his centrally heated home – though it was supposed to be dark and cold in Gaelic lore – is *iutharn* (or *ifrionn*, from *i* + *fuar*, cold) in Gaelic, perhaps as in dark Loch Hourn – although **Beinn Iutharn Mhòr*** in the Grampians is more probably from *fiubharainn*, related to *faobhar*, meaning sharp edged or the ridge of a hill – like **Sgor Iutharn,** above Culra, also known as **Lancet Edge** from its shape. After all none of the "Devil's . . ." names were Gaelic originals, it being Sassenach fancy that named them.

Beinn Alligin – bYn aleegin
Càrn a'Choire Bhòidhich – kaarn *a* chor*a* **vawyeech**
Bealach na Bèiste – byaloch n*a* **bay:sht**y*a*
An Garbhanach – *a* gar*a*vanoch
Bod an Deamhain – bot *an* **dyeveen**ʸ
Beinn Iutharn Mhòr – bYn yoo*arn* **voa:r**

Beinn Èibhinn – bYn **ay:veen**
An Gearanach – *an* **gyar***a*noch
Am Basteir – *am* **bastyar**ʸ
Meall Diamhain – myowl **dyeeaveen**ʸ

Witches

In Gaelic and in Scots the word for an old woman can also mean a witch, implying a degree of overlap. In Scots the word is carlin, and there is a **Carlin's Cairn** in Galloway, and also the **Carlin's Loup,** a giant rock at Carlops which is by tradition the witches' Cape Canaveral, with a broomstick-like bush sprouting from the cliff face! In Gaelic the word is *cailleach*, appearing in the several hills called **A'Chailleach***. Some of these mountains perhaps commemorate the legendary Cailleach Bheur who wandered the hills, calling the deer hinds to her with her siren-like voice in order to milk them. But she was a 'wild old woman' rather than a dangerous witch.

The **Sgrìob na Cailleach*** or Hag's Scrape on Jura's Beinn an Òir is said to have been made during a flypast by the powerful Goddess of Storm, Beithir (see Beinn a'Bheithir). This tale echoes the legend attached to **The Whangie** cliff near Glasgow, said to have been split off its backing hill-slope by a flick of the devil's tail. The resultant 'window' between the hill and the cliff may be the origin of the name from *uinneag*, window.

There are two Munros called **A'Chailleach,** one in the Monadh Liath and one in the Fannaichs in Ross-shire, as well as other lesser examples. One, the **Ceum na Caillich*** nick on Arran's rocky ridge, is usually translated as the Carlin's Leap or Witch's Step, a libel by English-speakers on little old ladies everywhere and particularly those many who have crossed this gap with no problems! The sexism implicit in the minds of the men who equate old women with witches is revealed too in the hill-name of **Beadaig***, a petulant female, although as a Skye name it may have had a similar-sounding Norse original name.

Darby and Joan

Joan's Darby is the *cailleach's bodach* (old man), and one such pair face each other above Glen Einich in the Cairngorms. Legend has it that when no mortal is looking this **A'Chailleach** and **Am Bodach*** hurl boulders playfully at each other across the gulf – a second courtship, or perhaps a second childhood? Another two examples of Am Bodach, old man, frown over Glen Coe and in the Mamores. In a pre-industrial society where survival to a ripe old age was unusual, the old were respected, so it was natural to name a few peaks after them.

Commoners and Kings

In the hills of southern and central Scotland hill-names rarely bear the names of people other than the landowners and others of high station. This tendency

---

A'Chailleach – *a* **chalyoch**   Sgrìob na Cailleach – **skree:p** n*a* **kalyoch**
Ceum na Caillich – **kaym** n*a* **kalyeech**   Beadaig – **bet**a**k**
Am Bodach – *a*m **botoch**

to sycophancy is to be found in the several **Laird's Hills**, the two **Earl's Hills** and the **Earl's Seat**, the Ochil's **King's Seat** and the Lomonds' **Bishop Hill**. Representing the ordinary people there is only a **Hunter's Hill** in the Sidlaws, a **Thief's Hill** in the Kilpatricks and a **Priest Hill** in the Lammermuirs. In the Gaelic Highlands by contrast there are few high-status names, with but one large hill named after a king in **Càrn an Rìgh*** in the remote eastern Grampians. This may refer to King Malcolm Canmore who in the 11th century hunted at Braemar and resided at Blair Atholl, passing and re-passing Càrn an Rìgh half way between.

Sròn na Ban-rìgh* in Glenfeshie, promontory of the Queen, is the hill where Mary, Queen of Scots, sat to personally supervise the execution of her order to fire the woods below, a punishment for the Marquis of Huntly who – putting green before queen – had enquired after his trees' health before asking after hers. **Creag Rìgh Tharold*** is a low hill on Speyside named after King Harold, the Viking, defeated here – and perhaps buried on the hill. King Nechtan of the Picts was noted in the Pentlands' **Carnethy Hill** and in **Dunechtan Hill** but Gaelic has few hill-names for the 'high-heid-yins', and far more for ordinary people.

Craftsmen and Musicians

The best-known craftsman in the hills is surely **The Cobbler** at Arrochar, a direct translation of the old Gaelic name An Greasaiche Crom*, the crooked shoemaker, from the shape of the summit rock. There's a less well-known craftsman **The Tanner**, a translation of Beinn an t-Sudaire near Kirkcudbright sometimes horribly anglicised to Ben Tudor! **Beinn a'Chlachair***, stonemason's mountain, lies above the Laggan valley. It is an ironic name, for the peak is too many miles from valley and village to be practical for a mason's work. The droll significance of the name will be appreciated by any walker who has climbed it from the *bealach* on the east and stumbled along its ridge strewn with rocks angled this way and that, like the jumbled mass of ice floes that piles up downwind on a winter lochan.

In the Làirig Ghrù (another jumbled mass of rocks) one particularly large stone is the **Clach nan Tàillear***, the tailors' rock. Here three tailors saw out one New Year's Eve but failed to see in the New Year, scythed down by exposure as they struggled to fulfil a bet that they could dance a reel the same night both on Speyside and on Deeside. Not even the doctor in **Meall Lighiche*** above Glencoe could have helped them that night! Perhaps one of

---

Càrn an Rìgh – kaarn *a* ree: Sròn na Ban-righ – strawn n*a* **bowree**
Creag Rìgh Tharold – (properly Creag Rìgh Harailt) – krayk **ree har***a*ltsh
An Greasaiche Crom – an **greeu**sheech*a* **krowm**
Beinn a'Chlachair – bYn *a* **chla**cheer^y   Clach nan Tàillear – klach n*a*n **ta:l**yar
Meall Lighiche – myowl **lyee-eech***a*

the musicians at the dances was related to the **Càrn an Fhìdhleir** (the fiddler
– sometimes incorrectly Carn Ealar) on Tarfside, or **Uchd a'Chlàrsair** (the
harper). Perhaps too the lament for their sad deaths could be played on the
Feadan na Cìche (the chanter, on Sgùrr na Cìche), where the wind whistles
soulfully through the rock gaps on wild days.

Hunters and Hunted

Hunting was a natural activity in the hills, and has left an echo in names.
Thus we have **Sgùrr nan Conbhairean** above Loch Cluanie, peak of the
keepers of the hounds (probably Fingalian hunters), and **Creag an Leth
Choin** above Glenmore, the crag of the lurcher, a hunting dog (see the
"Natural World" chapter, under Deer Hunt).

Herdsmen and Shepherds

Cattle-herding (not to mention cattle-thieving) was an important part of the
Highland economy, before the black cattle and the humans were driven out by
'The Great Sheep' in the Clearances. Across Glenmore from Leth Choin we
find **Meall a'Bhuachaille** hill of the herdsman. More famous, at the junction
of Glens Coe and Etive we have **Buachaille Èite (Etive) Mòr** and **Beag**, big
and little herdsmen of Etive. They are sometimes translated as 'shepherd',
which may be true in the Biblical sense of watching over the glens. But given
Gaeldom's reaction to the hated Clearances that introduced sheep, – "Woe to
thee, O land, for the Great Sheep is coming." – shepherd seems less likely
than herdsman. The word for sheep, *caorach*, appears only in a few peaks like
Beinn nan Caorach near Glenelg, whereas words for cattle appear in several
names like Ben Lui (calf), **Làirig an Laoigh** (pass of the calf) in the
Cairngorms, and **Bidein a'Choire Sheasgaich** (fallow cattle). So 'herdsman'
is the more apt translation of the Glen Coe Buachailles. Indeed the
neighbouring glen **Coire Gabhail** (corrie of the booty, known as the Lost
Valley), a hanging valley high above and invisible from the main Glen Coe,
was so-named from the hiding there of cattle, legitimate or stolen, from other
raiding clans.

   On lower hills throughout Scotland the word *buachaille* often appears in
corrupted form in hills like **Tillybuckle** (Angus), **The Bochel, Barnbougle
Hill** and **Barnbauchle Hill**. On these lower hills, often in the Borders where
sheep-farming is long-established, *buachaille* almost certainly *is* the shepherd.

Càrn an Fhìdhleir – kaarn *an* **yee:l**ar   Uchd a'Chlàrsair – oochk *a* **chlaars**ar
Sgùrr nan Conbhairean – skoor n*an* **kon**averan
Feadan na Cìche – fetan n*a* **kee:**ch*a*
Meall a'Bhuachaille – myowl *a* **voo-uchee**ly*a*
Creag an Leth Choin – krayk *a* **lyechon**[y]
Buachaille Etive (Èite) Mòr – boo-uchee**ly***a* **ay:ty***a* **moa:r**
Beinn nan Caorach – bYn n*an* **koe:**roch   Làirig an Laoigh – laarik *a* **loe-ee**
Bidein a'Choire Sheasgaich – **beedyin** *a* chor*a* **hesgeech**
Coire Gabhail – kor*a* **gavayl**[y]

Herdgirls and Claimers

Cattle were taken up in summer to the high pastures or shielings in the hills. In the Cuillins of Skye, **Sgurr na Banachdich*** is from Gaelic, *bànanaich*, or *banaraich*, a milkmaid, for it was the custom in the Highlands for young people to take the cattle to the shielings and stay with them. The Gaelic word for these spots is *àirigh*, which can be found in names like Letterewe's **Beinn Àirigh Chàrr*** (the bogland shieling hill). On this peak is a crag named **Martha's Peak**, or Spidean Moirich, and tradition has it that a herdgirl of that name fell down the north-east cliffs to her death while trying to retrieve the spindle for her thread. Skye's **Sgùrr Mhàiri*** (Mary's Peak) on Glamaig, was also named after a herdgirl who died here while on pastoral duty, seeking a lost beast. In Angus, the hill **Boustie Ley** is probably from *buailteach* (the summer sheilings) of (Glen) Lee, where the cattle were pastured by herdgirls.

In the east too there are herdgirl names on the hill. Seton Gordon, collector of the lore of the Cairngorms, relates that one of these shieling milkmaids spent her time, while wandering the heights with her herds, searching for the semi-precious Cairngorm stones, and by repute her collection is buried in **Ciste Mhairearaid*** or Margaret's Chest, one of the clefts on the ski side of Cairn Gorm. However another tradition, related in the SMC guidebook, is of a maiden jilted by her lover MacKintosh of Moy who wandered deranged through the range until she died at this *ciste*, or coffin. Fortunately there is a second Ciste Mhairearaid, nearby in Glen Feshie, so both legends can keep their credibility with a *ciste* each.

Arable farming, the people's mainstay, gets scant mention, although **Shilling Hill** near Muthil was where the corn was husked, or 'shilled' (in Scots); formerly it was Tom Chàtha, knoll of the husk. The hills **Sgùrr nan Ceathreamhan*** (hill of the quarters) and **Meall an Tagraidh** (hill of the pleading or claiming) refer to a concern with land shares. Meall an Tagraidh was disputed by the laird of Locheil although it stood in Glengarry's land. Locheil argued that since a burn rising to the west but running north almost circumnavigates the hill before flowing south, thus the hill was inside his watershed. That such boundaries were important is indicated by the existence of two hills, in different parts of the Highlands, called **Càrn na Crìche**, boundary hill. In the Borders **Threep Hill** near Langholm is from the Scots threap, a quarrel, suggesting a boundary dispute. **Càrn nan Trì-tighearnan**, hill of the 3 landlords, between Spey and Findhorn, suggests a more amicable arrangement!

Sgùrr na Banachdich – skoor na banachteech
Beinn Àirigh Chàrr – bYn aaree chaar
Sgùrr Mhàiri – skoor va:ree   Ciste Mhairearaid – keeshtya vYrarat
Sgùrr nan Ceathreamhnan – skoor nan kayravan
Meall an Tagraidh – myowl an tagree   Càrn na Crìche – kaarn na kree:cha

Warriors and Watchers

Like the Arthurian rock holding fast the sword Excalibur, weapons are embedded in hill-names like **Slioch** (spear), **Sgùrr nan Saighead** (arrows) and **Beinn a'Chlaidheimh** (sword). Weapon-wielders are found in Cairntoul's **Stob Coire an t-Saighdeir** (soldier) and, a few miles away, **Càrn an Fhir Bhogha,** archer's cairn. One particularly nasty warrior, Sigurd the powerful, who plundered the Strathoykel area, met a deserved end that is celebrated in a hill-name. Riding home with the head of a victim dangling from his horse, its tooth pierced his skin and he soon died of septicaemia (the medical term for sweet revenge), and was buried on **Cnoc Skardi**. Few tears were shed over him, unlike at **Creag a'Choinneachan** nearby, the crag of lamentation, where Montrose lost a battle in 1650 and a slaughter followed.

Lookouts were vital to military success and **Càrn an Fhreiceadain,** cairn of the watch, is in a key position looking down the military 'trade route' of the Spey valley, and there's also a **Cnoc an Fhreiceadain** overlooking the Pentland Firth. In this, the far north, the name of **Ward Hill** or **Warth Hill** means a watch or guard hill (from *vardhe* in Old Norse) and there are many of them in the Orkneys, Shetlands, and on this north coast. Far to the south the threat came from the English, and this is the reason for the several **Watch Knowes** and **Hills,** and **Watchman Hill,** all in the Borders. Almost on the Border near Dumfries is **Beacon Hill,** where warning fires could be lit, while just south of the line in Norse-speaking Lakeland is Wardlaw Hay hill, whilst near Dunbar **Knockenhair** is *cnoc na h-aire*, knoll of the watch. The Gaelic *fair* means watching, and indeed the word on its own can simply mean a watch-hill – premodern radar stations! **Hill of Fare** on Deeside, and **Farrmheall** in the north, are examples. In the much fought-over country near Oban, full of forts, crannogs and *dùns*, lie hills like **Cnoc na Faire** (knoll of watching) at the mouth of Loch Feochan, and **Deadh Choimhead**, literally good watching (hill), prominent enough to have a later trig point built on it. Offshore on the island of Luing is **Binnein Fhurachail**, attentive or watchful hill.

A low hill beside Bo'ness on the Firth of Forth is known as **Tidings Hill**. In the autumn, when the local whaling boats were due back from a summer in the dangerous waters of the North Atlantic, their families used to walk up it in the evening to get the first glimpse of their returning menfolk, and to be first to run with the glad tidings to the town.

Slioch – **shlee**ach   Sgùrr nan Saighead – skoor nan **s**Yat
Beinn a'Chlaidheimh – bYn a **chl**Yav
Stob Coire an t-Saighdeir – stob kora an tYdyar^y
Càrn an Fhir Bhogha – kaarn an yeer **voa-**a
Càrn an Fhreiceadain – kaarn a ray**k**atyan
Cnoc na Faire – krochk na fara   Deadh Choimhead – dyay **choo**-at
Binnein Fhurachail – beenyan **foo**rochal

Church and Clerics

The Christian religion played an important part in clansmens' lives, and there are two hills called **Beinn na h-Eaglaise** in the north-west, mountain of the church. One stands above Arnisdale and its little chapel, the other on the shores of Loch Torridon rises above the lochside hamlet of Annat – throughout Scotland the name Annat signifies an ancient parent church cell from which missionary work was done. By Loch Linnhe is **Beinn na Cille**, mountain of the cell or chapel, above Cille-Mhaodain, the cell of early Irish missionary Mhaodain. Throughout Scotland's Lowlands are hills with names like **Mounthooly, Mounthoolie** or **Huly Hill** . . . but they are gentle hills in Scots, *not* holy hills!

Càrn an t-Sagairt Mòr (sometimes spelt as it is pronounced Cairn Taggart), big hill of the priest, was named after Pàdruig, a Braemar priest, who led his flock out to Loch Callater to pray for an end to a severe frost that gripped the land well into May. As they prayed, the ice at the Priest's Well melted along with nature's iron heart, clouds gathered over the hill, and the thaw set in. The locals named that hill after him in gratitude. Elsewhere, **Beinn Mhanach** (hill of the monks) at the lonely head of Loch Lyon was named after those monks who set up a community at the foot of the hill in the distant past. **Mannoch Hill** near Nethan was formerly *cnoc nan manach*, monks' hill, and nearby is a translation, **Priest Hill.**

In the Cairngorms there's a **Cnap a'Chlèirich** (cleric), poised pulpit-like above the huge eastern corrie of Beinn a' Bhùird and its Clach (stone) na Clèirich. There's a 'pulpit' of a less conventional kind in the far north on the shores of the Pentland Firth. Here, just offshore, is Neave Island (from the Gaelic *naomh*, holy) where a community of missionaries had their base. Sallies to the shore had met with assault and murder, so on the Sabbath they *shouted* their services across the 200 metres of sea to the faithful gathered on a knoll, known as **Cnoc a'Phobuill**, knoll of the congregation.

Many Scottish places have saints' names, from St. Andrews to East Kilbride. But the only mountain that seems to have this honour is **Farragon Hill** above Loch Tummel, after St. Fergan, fourth Abbot of Iona, who worked the Pitlochry area. Above Arrochar the hill **A'Chrois** (the cross) has no known religious significance, and its name may come from the way the deep gully on its face is intersected by a broad ledge. The mountain was originally known as Feorlan or An Fheòirling, literally a farthing's worth of land. Perhaps the portion was doled out by the begetter of the high peak in

---

Beinn na h-Eaglaise – bYn na **hyuk**leesha
Càrn an t-Sagairt Mòr – kaarn an tagarsht **moa:r**a
Beinn Mhanach – bYn **van**och
Cnap a'Chlèirich – krahp a **chlay:**reech
Cnoc a'Phobuill – krochk a fobeel^y   A'Chrois – a **chrosh**

the north named **Sgùrr nan Ceannaichean***, peak of the merchants or shopkeepers.

Family Names

Beinn Chaluim* near Tyndrum is the Scots first name Calum (or Malcolm), while **Sgòrr Dhònuill*** (properly Dhòmhnuill) above Ballachulish is from Donald, the descendants of whom as the MacDonald clan were massacred in nearby Glen Coe one black night. There are also two peaks called **Sgùrr Dhòmhnuill** in the west – one of them the most striking peak in Ardgour, for miles around – reflecting the importance of Clan Donald who ruled the isles and the west for centuries after the death of Somerled in 1164. As "Lords of the Isles" (and much of the south-west), many of whose lands were no-go areas for the Scottish crown, they could afford to name two or three peaks after the clan family name. Their mortal enemy the Campbells also have a hill 'plaque' in **Càrn Chailein*** above the moors of their Argyll lands, at the site of inter-clan slaughter where one Colin, a clan chieftain, died. Another much humbler Campbell is named in the Argyllshire hill **Stùchdan Dughaill***, after Duncan Campbell, shepherd, who died in a blizzard here in 1881. The name of a clan as such appears in **Bidein Clann Raonaild** in the north, but it is neither very high nor distinctive. Other sons (*mac* in Gaelic) immortalised in hill-names include the MacDuff clan who owned the Mar estate, including Scotland's second highest mountain **Ben MacDhui*** (for long thought to be the country's highest, hence the prestige of naming it after the family), and **Mullach Coire Mhic Fhearchair,*** peak of the corrie of Farquhar's son, a top as geographically remote as its origin is obscure.

Many of the origins of personal names on mountains are lost to us, swept away in the ebb of time. **Creag Macranaich*** for instance above Killin was named after a robber, now long forgotten. But who do hills like **Creag Pitridh*** (Petrie's crag) commemorate? Is **Leum Uilleim***, William's Leap, above Corrour Station on Rannoch, a record of the passage of William Caulfield, roadmaker extraordinary under General Wade, and builder of the nearby Devil's Staircase over to Kinlochleven? In the north-west, who *was* Farquhar's son whose Mullach and Coire lie five or six miles apart? And who were the Elizabeths in **Càrn Ealasaid*** or **Creag Ealasaid**? Hardly any hill-names are feminine, either in personal names or in occupations. There are

---

Sgùrr nan Ceannaichean – skoor n*a*n **kyaneech**an
Beinn Chaluim – bYn **chal**am   Ben MacDhui – ben m*a*k**doo**ee
Sgòrr Dhonuill – skor **ghaw**-il^y (properly Sgòrr Dhòmhnuill)
Càrn Chailein – kaarn **chal**an^y Stuchdan Dùghaill – stoochkan **doo:gh**Yl^y
Mullach Coire Mhic Fhearchair – moolach **kor**a veechk e**rach**ar^y
Creag Macranaich – krayk **mahk**raneech   Creag Pitridh – krayk **fee**tree
Leum Uilleim – lyaym **ool**yam   Carn Ealasaid – kaarn **yal**asat^y

some, such as **Ceann na Baintighearna**[*] above Balquhidder (the lady or proprietor's wife). **Jean,** the Cobbler's Wife, is of course a later English name, a fancy rather than a factual figure.) **Sgùrr na Bana-mhorair** near Loch Torridon, the peak of the lady, commemorates a poor soul whose cruel lord punished her for some trespass by making her stay on the bleak summit, fed only by shellfish brought to her.

Beinn Fhionnlaidh[*] – there are two – is Finlay's hill: one, in the north, is supposed to bear the name of a gamekeeper on the Kintail estate, a man with an awful temper. Since the hill is one of the most inaccessible Munros, requiring a long walk out to it from the main ridge, perhaps he was despatched along it to let him cool down!

Climbers

Sgùrr Mhic Choinnich[*], named in honour of the great Skye mountain guide John MacKenzie, is one of several Cuillin peaks named after their first recorded climbers, North American style. This is a relatively recent phenomenon, since most of the world's mountains (and Scotland's) were named long before the age of climbing. And indeed most of Skye's "climber-peaks" which follow are minor pinnacles on the ridge, in between older-named and bigger summits that had been picked out and named long ago by the local people. Near Sgurr Mhic Coinnich, **Sgùrr Alasdair**[*] (originally Sgùrr an Lagain, peak of the little hollow) now bears the name of Sheriff Alexander Nicolson of the island, another early explorer who made its first recorded ascent in 1873. Also on this roll of honour of early Cuillin climbers are the **Knight's Peak** after Professor Knight of St. Andrew's University, **Sgùrr Thormaid**[*] after Professor Norman Collie, and **Sgùrr Theàrlaich**[*] after the Lakeland climber Charles Pilkington, surely one of the few Sassenachs to be named on a Scots hill. It's interesting that while the local guide, and the professor, have their surnames used in the hill-names, the other three were apparently on 'first-name terms'!

Once again women were pushed into anonymity: a minor point on the ridge not far from the Inaccessible Pinnacle was named **Sgùrr na Cailleag**[*] (peak of the old woman – or possibly from *caileag*, a (mere) girl), apparently after a lady with whom John MacKenzie was climbing. Whoever the lady was, he was surely no gentleman in so naming it!

Fairies and Fingalians

There are other hill-names relating to groups rather than individuals.

Ceann na Baintighearna – kyown n*a* **ban**tyee*arna*
Beinn Fhionnlaidh – bYn **yoon**lY
Sgùrr Mhic Choinnich – skoor veechk **kun**yeech
Sgùrr Alasdair – skoor al*a*stayr   Sgùrr Thormaid – skoor **horom**it[y]
Sgùrr Theàrlaich – skoor **hyaar**leech   Sgùrr na Cailleag – skoor n*a* **kalik**

Schiehallion* (probably from *sìthean Chailleann*) translates as the fairy hill of the Caledonians, the long-lost Scottish tribe. At over 3,500 feet (1080m) it's rather a large fairyhill. *Sithein* are normally more delicate knolls, such as Handa Island's **Sìthean Mòr*** (406 feet, 124m) or the knolls that give Glenshee its name, but it is the shape that counts (see "Sgurrs and Beinns" chapter, section on *sìthean*). Near Aberfoyle, **Fairy Knowe** and **Doon Hill** are two hillocks where the fairies are reputed to have seized and imprisoned the Reverend Robert Kirk, a 17th-century Gaelic scholar, as punishment for his book investigating them, *The Secret Commonwealth*. His spirit, it is whispered, is locked in a pine tree on the summit.

The Fingalians, the followers of Finn MacCool, recur in Gaelic legend and in peaks from the far north (**Fèinne-bheinn*** above Loch Hope) to **Sgòrr nam Fiannaidh*** above Glen Coe, the peak of the Fian warriors, and **Stob an Fhainne*** at Inversnaid. Across Glen Coe is the black dripping gash of Ossian's Cave, named after Fingal's son who was a famous bard of the Celts. Not far away is **Beinn Lora,** a mountain reputedly one of the portals of Bealach Banruinn Fhionnghail, the pass of Fingal's Queen, the other portal being the sea. We move more concretely into history with **Stob Coir' an Albannaich*** a few miles away across Glen Etive, peak of the corrie of the Scotsman – the Scots were of course 'Irish immigrants' at an early stage! Over to the east the legendary Fionns surface in **Beinn Bhrotain***, named after a large mastiff with which they hunted. **Torinturk** near Loch Etive, **Tòrr an Tuirc***, and **Càrn an Tuirc** are all boar's hills where they hunted, and **Tom Dhiarmaid*** by Glenshee is after Diarmaid o'Duibhe, a Celtic hunter. A Skye tradition says that Diarmaid is buried together with Grainne and two of his hounds, on top of **Beinn Tianavaig***, which was supposedly called **Guilbheinn** in the days before the Norse invasions. The name **Ben Gulbin,** occurring in several places in the Highlands, is a Fingalian hallmark. For instance, a 16th-century poem set in Glenshee, runs;

> "In the glen, below Ben Gulbin green,
> Whose tulachs gleam in the sun,
> The river's flow was stained with red
> When deer fell to Fionn of the fairies"

and goes on to tell ". . . hear my lay . . . of Ben Gulbin, of generous Fionn, and Diarmid O'Doon . . . a tale of grief." Other legends tell of Diarmid slaying the great boar of Ben Gulbin, before being poisoned by its bristles.

Schiehallion – sheehaly*a*n   Sìthean Mòr – shee:han **moa:r**

Fèinne-bheinn – **fayn**y*a* vYn   Sgòr nam Fiannaidh – skor n*a*m **fee***a*nee

Stob an Fhainne – stop *a*n any*a*

Stob Coir' an Albannaich – stob kor*a* *a*n al*a*paneech

Beinn Bhrotain – bYn **vroht**Yn^y   Torr an Tuirc – tor *a*n **toohrk**

Tom Dhiarmaid – tom **ghee***a*rmit^y   Beinn Tianavaig – bYn **tyee***a*navYk

Over in Argyll **Sliabh Ghaoil*** is literally the darling hill, locally translated as the Mount of Love. On its slopes, according to legend, the Fionn warriors caught up with the eloping lovers Diarmaid and the beautiful Grainne. Unfortunately for him, she was still the legally-wedded wife of Fionn MacCumhaill, a chief, who then devised a trap for his wife's lover in which he perished poisoned by a boar's bristles. The same way that he died, in the other legend, in Glenshee!

Spaniards and Sassenachs

From Glen Shiel rises **Sgùrr nan Spàinnteach*†**. Spaniards' Peak, which commemorates the two hundred Iberians captured here in 1719 during a Jacobite rising against the British goverment. Catholic allies in Spain had ventured this force as a token of their support, landing them at the head of Loch Duich to join a Jacobite force. However these brave white-coated soldiers stood their ground at the first challenge from the English redcoat armies, retreating in orderly fashion up the hill to surrender the next day in the Coire nan Spàinnteach†. It may be that those Spaniards who fell in battle are buried on the hill.

Further up the same Glen is **Aonach Shasuinn***: *Sasunn* means England, and the adjective *Sasunnach* has passed into Scots with little alteration. Could this hill be 'a corner of a foreign fell that is forever England', where some of the redcoats lie buried?

Sliabh Ghaoil – shleeav **ghoe-eel**ʸ
Sgùrr nan Spàinnteach – skoor n*a*n **spaan**tyoch
Aonach Shasuinn – oenach **has**Ynʸ

Gaelic Glossary

This list of some Gaelic words commonly-used in placenames is confined to words not examined in the text of the book. For example, all the colour words (*gorm, glas,* etc) will be found instead in the chapter on colours, as well as in the main index.

For a fuller list, the Ordnance Survey publish a booklet called *Place-names on maps of Scotland and Wales* containing a fuller list of Gaelic, Scandinavian and Welsh name elements.

Please bear in mind that the spellings on maps, etc may not always be exactly the same as those in this glossary due to the corruption of names over time (eg – baile often becomes bal), or to the inaccuracies of the O.S. surveyors. The letter 'h' may well appear as a second letter (eg – bhaile is the same in meaning as baile). I have included anglicisations after Gaelic words in brackets (eg – *ach* is an anglicisation of *achadh*).

abhainn	river
achadh (ach, auch)	field
ail	rock
àiridh	high pasture, shieling
allt	stream
àth	ford
bac	bank
bad	place, copse
baile (bal)	farm, township
bàthach	byre
beag (beg)	wee, small
bealach (balloch)	pass (in hills)
beàrn	pass, gap
blàr, blair	plain
bò, bà	cow, cattle
both	cottage
cadha	steep slope, pass
cam	bent, crooked
camas (camus, cambus)	bay, river bend
caol (kyle)	narrows

caora	sheep
cas	steep
cath	battle
clach	stone
clais	narrow valley, gap, ditch
coille (coyle)	wood
coire	corrie, cwm, cirque, hollow
corran	point shaped like a hook
craobh	tree
croit	croft, small farm
crom	curved
cù, coin	dog, dogs
cùil	nook
dà	two
dail (dal)	field
damh	deer
deas	south
dìollaid	saddle, pass
dobhar	water
doire	copse, wood
drochaid	bridge
each	horse
eadar	between
eag	cleft, notch
eaglais	church
ear	east
eas	waterfall
eilean	island
eun, eòin	bird, birds
fada	long
feadan	small valley
fear	man
feàrna	alder
fèith	bog, moss
fraoch	heather
fuar	cold
fuaran	spring, well
gabhar	goat
gaineamh	sand
gall (gaill)	stranger, foreigners
gaoth	wind
garbh (garve)	rough, stony
geàrr	short

gil	gully
giuthas	Scots pine, fir-tree
gleann (glen)	valley
gobhal (gavel)	fork, prong
greigh	herd
iar	west
inbhir (inver)	river-mouth
innis, innse	isle, meadow
iochdar	lower part
iolair	eagle
lag (lagg, laggan)	hollow
làirig	pass
leac (leck)	stone, slab
learg	slope, hillside
leitir (letter)	steep slope
linne	pool
loch; lochan	lake; small lake/tarn
lòn	marsh, pool, meadow
loisgte	burnt, charred
lùb, lùib	bend
machair	seaside meadow
magh (moy)	plain
meadhon	middle, central
meanbh	small
mòine	moss, bog
mòr (more)	big
muilinn	mill
pait	hump, knoll
poll	pool, pit
preas	wood
raineach	ferny
ràth	fort
reamhar	fat
ros	headland
rubha (rhu)	sea headland
saighead	arrow
saobhaidh	beast's den
sgoilte	split
sgriogalach	bare mountain top
sleamhuinn	smooth
sloc, slochd	hollow
srath (strath)	valley
tairbert (tarbert)	isthmus, narrow neck of land

tigh	house
tìr	land
tobar (tibber)	well
toll	hollow
torc	boar
tràigh	beach
tuath	north
uachdar	upper part
uamh	cave
uan	lamb
uisge	water

Bibliography

BENNET, Donald – *The Munros*, 1985. (The Scottish Mountaineering Club's District guides, in the same series, also have list of some meanings in their appendices)

BROWN, Hamish – *Climbing the Corbetts*, London 1988

CURRIE, Ronald – *The Place-names of Arran*, Glasgow 1908

DILWORTH, Anthony – 'Strathavon in Banffshire,' in *Scottish Gaelic Studies* 9 (1962)

ELLICE, Edward – *Place-Names of Glengarry and Glenquoich*, London 1931

FRASER, Ian – 'The place-names of Argyll – an Historical Perspective' in *TGSI (Transactions of the Gaelic Society of Inverness)*, 54 (1984-6)

FORBES, Alexander – *Place Names of Skye and adjacent islands*, Paisley 1923

GAMBLES, Robert – *Lake District Place-Names*, Lancaster 1975

GILLIES, H. – *The Place-names of Argyll*, London 1906

IRVING, I. *Place Names of Dumbartonshire*, Dumbarton, 1928.

JOHNSTON, J.B. – *Place-Names of Scotland*, Edinburgh 1934 (reprint 1976)

JULYAN, Robert – *Mountain Names*, Seattle 1984. (American and world mountain names)

LIDDALL, W.J. – *Place-Names of Fife and Kinross*, 1896

LIVINGSTONE, Colin – 'The Place-names of Lochaber' in *TGSI* 13 (1886-7)

MACAOIDH, G. – 'Gàidhlig Ghallghallaibh agus Alba-a-Deas' (The Gaelic of Galloway and Southern Scotland) in *Gairm* 101 (1977-8)

MACBAIN, Alexander – 'The Norse Element in the Topography of the Highlands and Islands' in *TGSI* 19 (1893-4)

MACBAIN, Alexander – 'The Place-names of Inverness-shire' in *TGSI* 25 (1901-3)

MACBAIN, Alexander – 'The Place-names of Badenoch' in *TGSI* 26 (1904-7)

MACBAIN, Alexander – *Place-Names, Highlands and Islands of Scotland*, Stirling 1922

MACIVER, Duncan – *The Place-names of Lewis and Harris*, Stornoway 1934

MACKAY, John – 'The Place-names of Assynt' in *TGSI* 15 (1888-9)

MACKENZIE, W.C. – *Scottish Place-Names*, London 1931

MACQUARRIE – *The Place-names of Mull*, Inverness 1982

NICOLAISEN, W.F.H. – 'Distribution of Certain Gaelic Mountain Names' – in *TGSI* 45 (1967-8)

NICOLAISEN, W.F.H. – *Scottish Place-names*, London 1976
ORDNANCE SURVEY – *Place-Names on Maps of Scotland and Wales*, 1981.
(A booklet listing common Gaelic, Norse and Welsh place-name elements.)
PURVES, A. – 'Àit-ainmean Gàidhlig ann an Roinn nan Crìoch' (Gaelic place-names in the Borders Region) in *Gairm* 144 (1988)
STEWART, T.F. – *Gaelic-English Hill-Names of Perthshire*, 1974
WATSON, Adam and ALLAN, Elizabeth – *The Place-Names of Upper Deeside*, Aberdeen 1986
WATSON, W.J. – *The Place-names of Ross and Cromarty*, Inverness 1904 (reprinted 1976)
WATSON, W.J. – *The History of the Celtic Place-Names of Scotland*, Edinburgh 1926
WATSON, W.J. – 'The Place-names of Breadalbane' in *TGSI* 34 (1927-8)
WATSON, W.J. – 'The Place-names of Perthshire: the Lyon Basin' in *TGSI* 35 (1929-30)
WILL, C.P. – *Place-Names of North-East Angus*, Arbroath 1963
YEAMAN, W.J. – *Handbook of the Scottish Hills*, Arbroath 1989

Dictionaries
For Gaelic, I used Edward Dwelly's *The Illustrated Gaelic-English Dictionary* (reprinted by Gairm Publications, Glasgow 1988) and Malcolm MacLennan's *Gaelic Dictionary*, 1925, (reprinted by Acair/AUP). For Scots, I used *The Concise Scots Dictionary* (AUP, 1985), which draws on the ten-volume *Scottish National Dictionary*.

198

Index

214